How to Make
Money in
Stocks
Getting Started

How to Make Money in Stocks

Getting Started

A GUIDE TO PUTTING *CAN SLIM*® CONCEPTS INTO ACTION

MATTHEW GALGANI

New York   Chicago   San Francisco
Lisbon   London   Madrid   Mexico City   Milan
New Delhi   San Juan   Seoul   Singapore
Sydney   Toronto

1 2 3 4 5 6 7 8 9 0   DOC/DOC   1 9 8 7 6 5 4 3

ISBN: 978-0-07-181011-1
MHID: 0-07-181011-0

e-ISBN: 978-0-07-181012-8
e-MHID: 0-07-181012-9

This publication is designed to provide accurate and authoritative information in regard to the subject matter covered. It is sold with the understanding that neither the author nor the publisher is engaged in rendering legal, accounting, or other professional service. If legal advice or other expert assistance is required, the services of a competent professional person should be sought.

—From a Declaration of Principles jointly adopted
by a Committee of the American Bar
Association and a Committee of Publishers and Associations

Library of Congress Cataloging-in-Publication Data
Galgani, Matthew.
   How to make money in stocks, getting started : a guide to putting CAN SLIM concepts into action / Matthew Galgani.
      pages cm.
   ISBN 978-0-07-181011-1 (alk. paper) — ISBN 0-07-181011-0 (alk. paper)
1. Investments.   2. Stocks.   I. Title.
   HG4521.G1833 2013
   332.63'22—dc23

                                                                    2013008260

McGraw-Hill Education books are available at special quantity discounts to use as premiums and sales promotions or for use in corporate training programs. To contact a representative, please visit the Contact Us pages at www.mhprofessional.com.

This text contains the following, which are trademarks, service marks, or registered trademarks of Investor's Business Daily, Inc., William O'Neil + Co., Inc., or their affiliated entities in the United States and/or other countries: *Investor's Business Daily*®, IBD®, CAN SLIM®, Stock Checkup®, and *e*IBD™.

This book is printed on acid-free paper.

· CONTENTS ·

How to Make Money in Stocks—Getting Started is an important book for all investors.

If you're new to the stock market and unsure—perhaps nervous—about how to begin investing, Matt's book may be the missing link you've been looking for. You'll find a step-by-step game plan with checklists and routines to make sure you start out right. More experienced investors can reference these same strategies and tools to streamline their routines and further improve their returns.

From the time I founded Investor's Business Daily in 1984, we've focused on education, knowing that anyone with a desire to learn can become a successful investor. Since then, countless people from all walks of life have used IBD® and the CAN SLIM® Investment System to achieve significant results.

I first met Matthew Galgani a decade ago when he came to us to help market IBD to more investors. He also had a strong desire to master the CAN SLIM System to build his own financial future. Matt began attending dozens of IBD workshops around the country, then went on to help establish and expand the IBD Meetup® program in its early stages.

Since then, he has been involved in several pivotal educational products, including co-hosting IBD's weekly radio show, editing the *IBD®extra* Newsletter, and creating *IBD TV®* videos. Matt also helped me develop the *IBD Meetup Investor Education Series*, a 13-part course created specifically for Meetup members. Each month, those interactive lessons are used by local groups all over the nation and are one of the best ways we've found to help investors establish a clear plan for making money in the market.

Getting Started is a natural complement to my earlier work, *How to Make Money in Stocks*. Matt's book helps you take those crucial first steps while creating proper investing habits that help you build wealth over time. No one becomes a successful investor overnight. Like all skills, investing takes time and effort to learn. But anyone with patience and perseverance can do it. The key is to follow a sound plan and never give up.

I've read this book carefully and can tell you that in the pages ahead, you'll discover an investing plan that works. The rest is up to you. I have no doubt that if you study and stick to the rules outlined in *Getting Started*, you can benefit greatly.

Understand that you do not need to do this on your own. IBD is here to help you every step of the way with free educational resources, including the IBD Meetup program, product training, *IBD TV* videos, and more. If you ever have any questions, call our toll-free educational hotline (800-831-2525) to get the help you need.

We're wishing you the very best in your investing journey.

Sincerely,

William J. O'Neil
Chairman and Founder
Investor's Business Daily

• INTRODUCTION •

This is a book about taking action. About taking specific steps to get started on *your* path to making more money in the stock market.

Let me start with a little story about my own journey...

Before I began investing in the mid-1990s, I read several books about the market. They were definitely helpful in terms of deciding what to buy.

It wasn't until later I realized something was missing.

They didn't address the other—equally important—pieces of the puzzle: *When to buy* and *when to sell*.

But at the time, I was making money. And when you're making money, who needs sell rules?!

The rise of personal computers, the Internet and cell phones had launched an explosive bull market, and I was making 35% one year, 40% another. Like millions of other investors, my "strategy" was basically to buy and just hold on for the glorious ride.

But in reality, I was blissfully unaware of my own ignorance.

I didn't know that in a bull market, the vast majority of *all* stocks go up. So while I may have *thought* my gains were due to my newfound investing genius, I was actually just getting lucky. It was pure coincidence that I happened to buy at the right time. In fact, I had no idea there even was a "right" and "wrong" time to invest.

And that led to my next rather painful epiphany: I had no sell rules. When the dot-com bubble burst in 2000, I had no clue what to do because I didn't understand how market cycles work. I didn't realize my primary goal should be to make money when the market is up and protect those profits when the market heads south. So I just sat there and watched a frustratingly large portion of my gains disappear.

A Better Way

It was after that episode that I joined Investor's Business Daily (IBD) and discovered I did *not* have to be at the mercy of the market:

- I *could* see the right—and wrong—time to invest.
- I *could* have a game plan for locking in profits.
- I *could* use simple sell rules to avoid any serious losses.

That was a game-changing epiphany for me—one that has proved invaluable in the decade since. Now, whether I'm making *Daily Stock Analysis* and *2-Minute Tip* videos, editing the *IBD®extra* Newsletter, or co-hosting IBD's weekly radio show with Amy Smith, that crucial revelation is never far from my mind.

So when I got the opportunity to write this book, I started with a simple question: What kind of book do I wish I had when *I* was starting out?

It quickly boiled down to 3 things:

1. **Keep it simple:** Focus on the basics so even new investors can see how to get started while staying profitable and protected.

2. **Make it interactive and actionable:** Include hands-on action steps and videos that make the key points sink in, helping you quickly put what you learn into action.

3. **Use easy-to-follow routines and checklists:** Lay out a *specific* step-by-step game plan anyone can use to make—and keep—solid gains.

Having the checklists and Action Steps you'll find in this book would have helped me *tremendously* when I was starting out. And if you stick to these time-tested rules as *you* get started, you'll be following a proven roadmap for growing—and protecting—*your* money.

History, Not Hunches

As you'll see, everything IBD does is based on a simple concept: To find tomorrow's winning stocks, you need to understand what past winners looked like just *before* they made their big gains. And you need to know what sell signals they flashed as they eventually topped and began to decline.

In other words, if you want to significantly improve your investing results, start by studying the best stocks—and the best investors.

One legendary investor you definitely should learn from—and one I've been very fortunate to work with for a decade—is William J. O'Neil, chairman and founder of Investor's Business Daily.

And that leads us to a question you may be asking . . .

What's the Difference Between *Getting Started* and Bill O'Neil's *How to Make Money in Stocks*?

Bill's classic book, which has sold well over 2 million copies, is the definitive explanation of the CAN SLIM® Investment System he developed many decades ago.

If you haven't already, **I *strongly* encourage you to read Bill's book.**

It provides invaluable insight into over 130 years of market history, a detailed look at what big winning stocks look like before—and after—they make a big run, and a clear set of buy and sell rules to guide you.

This book, *How to Make Money in Stocks—Getting Started*, is meant to supplement, not replace, Bill's classic work.

Think of it this way: Bill's book gives you the grand strategy. *Getting Started* shows you how to begin *applying* the basics of that strategy right now.

Investing is a skill. And like any skill, it's best learned in stages. But where do you begin?

That's where *Getting Started* comes in. Together, we'll go through specific steps you can take right now to improve how you pick stocks and, just as importantly, how you handle them *after* you buy.

Whether you're a new or experienced investor, the routines and checklists we'll go over provide a solid foundation for making substantial profits. With that foundation in place, you'll be able to invest with confidence from the start and add to your skills over time.

What You'll Learn in *Getting Started*

Again, this book is about taking action. You'll find a **Simple Weekend Routine** that helps you zero in on today's top stocks and **Buying and Selling Checklists** that show you the right time to get into—and out of—the market.

Plus, by taking the **Action Steps** you'll find throughout the book, you'll get the hands-on experience you need to apply these rules in the real world. If you follow these steps and stick to the checklists, you will see a *major* difference in your ability to buy and sell stocks profitably.

After reading the book and practicing the Action Steps, you'll know how to:

- Protect your money
- Quickly identify stocks with the greatest potential
- Use simple routines and checklists to buy—and sell—those stocks at the right time

How to Get the Most Out of This Book

A few years ago, I spent several months working with Bill O'Neil to create the *IBD Meetup Investor Education Series*, a 13-part course designed specifically for members of the free IBD Meetup program, a nationwide network of local investing groups.

That course was made to be highly interactive: Each IBD Meetup group can go through a lesson at their monthly get-together, then members can apply what they learned on their own at home.

This book is also meant to be highly interactive. As an old IBD slogan used to say, "Don't just read it. Use it!"

Nothing would make me happier than to see your copy of *Getting Started* marked up with highlighters and notes and dog-eared with coffee stains. (You should see my copies of *How to Make Money in Stocks*.)

Don't Try to Do It All in One Go!

I suggest you take this book in bite-sized pieces.

First, check out Chapter 1, "Start Here." That'll give you a "big picture" look at the basic game plan for making money in the market.

Then go through the subsequent chapters one at a time . . . take the Action Steps . . . then take a little time to digest and practice what you've learned using the simple routines (Chapter 4).

In other words, don't force it. You're not going to read and remember all this in one sitting! Take it step by step, and you'll start to see how all the pieces fit together. Then the light bulb will turn on, and you'll be ready to start right—and begin making money in stocks.

Start Right with 3 Must-Do Steps

To see how to check each of these items off your "To Do" list, visit www.investors.com/GettingStartedBook.

1. Get Started with Action Steps

Be sure to do the Action Steps you'll find throughout the book.

Everyone learns differently, but I like to *do* as I learn. So I suggest you complete the Action Steps in one chapter before moving on. It'll help the concepts sink in faster.

See How to Apply the Strategy with Free Videos

On the web page we created specifically for this book, you'll find several videos that give you an "in-action" look at the key rules and routines we'll cover in the pages ahead. Be sure to watch them! It's an easy way to enhance and expand on what you learn in the book.

You'll find some overlap in the Action Steps from chapter to chapter. That's intentional. As legendary UCLA basketball coach John Wooden said, "Repetition is the key to learning." Going through each step in each chapter will help you start investing *correctly* right out of the gate.

2. Activate Your Free Trial of IBD

Because this book is about *applying* the strategy you'll learn, many Action Steps are based on seeing what's going on in the market *right now*:

- What stocks are in today's *IBD 50* or *Stock Spotlight*?
- Is now a time to buy stocks—or take defensive action?
- Do the stocks you're looking at get pass—or fail—ratings in *Stock Checkup*®?

If you don't already have a subscription to IBD, you'll need to activate your trial to access some of the tools and features as you go through the Action Steps.

3. Take Advantage of IBD's Free Investor Training

We can all use some help when learning a new skill, and investing is no different. So don't think you need to go it alone. Here are two *free* ways you can jump-start the process and get answers to any investing questions you may have.

Join Your Local IBD Meetup Group

I used to run the IBD Meetup program, so I can tell you from personal experience it's a great way to put into action all the rules and concepts you'll learn in this book.

We have over 250 local groups all around the country (and overseas) where people just like you get together monthly to discuss the market, build a watch list, and help improve each other's skills.

We actively support these independently-run groups with the *IBD Meetup Investor Education Series* I developed with Bill O'Neil, and by sending IBD speakers to give free workshops.

Visit the website below to find the group near you.

Sign Up for a Free IBD Training Session

In these phone or online sessions, an IBD trainer will show you how to use IBD and Investors.com to apply the investing strategy we'll cover in this book. On your computer, you can follow along as the trainer walks you through the tools and features—and feel free to jump in anytime with whatever questions you may have.

You can see how to take the Action Steps, start your free trial, sign up for a free training session, and find your local IBD Meetup group at: www.investors.com/GettingStartedBook.

Now let's jump right in.

Let Me Know How You're Doing!

I'm always curious to hear from investors, so I hope you'll let me know how *your* getting started process is coming along. You can send me any questions and feedback at GettingStartedBook@investors.com.

I look forward to hearing from you—and wish you much investing success!

How to Make
Money in
Stocks
Getting Started

• CHAPTER •
1

Start Here

Before we get into the details in later chapters, I want to make sure you see the primary goals—the big picture—here.

So let's start with a quick look at the investing *forest*, then we'll start examining the *trees*.

If you ever start to feel a little overwhelmed as we go through the checklists and charts later in the book, take a breather and come back here. You may even want to put in a bookmark or dog-ear this page as a reminder.

That will help you stay grounded and focused on what matters most: Using basic rules and routines to both grow—and protect—your money.

1

How to Protect Your Money

Talking about how to *protect* your money—how to *avoid big losses*—is not the most exciting way to kick off a discussion about building wealth. But it's absolutely critical.

Job #1 in making money in stocks is to protect the money you already have.

And you can do that just by following two basic rules. They will protect you even when—in fact, *especially* when—the market becomes volatile and slips into a downtrend.

When we go through the **Selling Checklist** later in the book, you'll see several common signals that tell you it's time to lock in your gains or cut any losses. Over time, you'll become better and better at spotting those signs, but for now—at a minimum—be sure to stick to these two rules. They'll help you safeguard your money as you learn new ways to grow it.

1. If a Stock Drops 7% to 8% Below What You Paid for It, Sell. No Questions Asked.

This one simple rule puts a cap on potential losses—like having insurance to protect you against whatever the market does. Simple and sensible.

You'll find it's much easier to *grow* your money if you follow this rule. Instead of trying to make up for larger *losses*, you'll be adding to and compounding your *gains*.

I can't emphasize enough how important this rule is.

Every investor—including legendary traders like Bill O'Neil—makes mistakes. But *successful* investors quickly acknowledge those mistakes—and cut their losses short. Always. You should do the same, and you can do it by following this one simple rule.

*See the **Selling Checklist** section for more on this rule—and how I learned it the hard way.*

2. Only Buy Stocks When the Overall Market Is in a "Confirmed Uptrend"

IBD's study of every market cycle since 1880 shows 3 out of 4 stocks move in the same direction as the overall market, either up or down.

The "overall" or "general" market refers to the major indexes, primarily the Nasdaq Composite, S&P 500, and Dow Jones Industrial Average.

When the market is trending down, about 75% of all stocks will eventually decline with it.

Does that sound like a good time to *buy* stocks? To keep the odds in your favor and make it *much* easier to grow your money, be sure to only make new purchases when the market is in an uptrend.

As you'll see in the next section, "The Basic Game Plan for Making Money in Stocks," you'll know if the market is in an uptrend or downtrend simply by checking the *Market Pulse* inside IBD's *The Big Picture* column.

Only make new buys when the current outlook is "Confirmed uptrend."

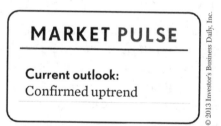

MARKET PULSE

Current outlook:
Confirmed uptrend

© 2013 Investor's Business Daily, Inc.

See the **Buying Checklist** section for more on this key rule and how to apply it.

Protect and Prosper

Most people start out focusing on what stocks to *buy* and ignore the other absolutely critical part of the puzzle—when to *sell*.

All too often, a new investor won't realize he or she needs some sell rules until *after* suffering a large loss. Don't let that happen to you!

Start off right by sticking to these two basic rules. They'll help protect your money as you learn to pick winning stocks and prosper.

The Basic Game Plan for Making Money in Stocks

We'll go through the CAN SLIM® Investment System in the next chapter, but for now just understand that by using this approach, you can:

- **See when the market trend is changing** so you'll always know if it's time to buy stocks or take defensive action.

- **Identify stocks with the most potential** by looking for 7 traits the biggest winners typically display just *before* they launch a major price move.

Then, using the routines and checklists in this book, you'll see the specific steps you can take to make money in:

- Individual stocks
- Exchange-traded funds (ETFs) that cover the Nasdaq and S&P 500
- Or a mix of both stocks and ETFs

The focus of this book is on individual stocks. The biggest winners in a strong bull market can go up 100%, 300%, even 1,000% or more. In the bull cycle that started in March 2009, Apple, Priceline, Lululemon Athletica, Ulta Beauty, Green Mountain Coffee Roasters, Chipotle Mexican Grill, Rackspace Hosting, 3D Systems, Michael Kors, and many others did just that. In other words, the huge, life-changing gains are made by zeroing in on the true market leaders—and you'll see how to do that using the Simple Weekend Routine and Buying Checklist.

That said, you *can* generate solid gains following the ETF approach we'll go over in a minute, and it takes less time.

Should You Invest in Stocks, ETFs, or Both?

The choice is up to you. There is no right or wrong answer, and you can always do both: Put a certain percentage of your money into individual stocks and another portion into an index-based ETF.

Many CAN SLIM investors follow a mixed approach, and I think it's an excellent way—especially for new investors—to get started.

Basic Game Plan for Making Money in Exchange-Traded Funds (ETFs)

As we'll see again and again throughout this book, staying in sync with the general market trend is the first crucial step to making money—whether you're trading stocks or ETFs. The reason for that will become crystal clear in a minute.

What is an Exchange-Traded Fund?

An ETF is essentially a "basket" of stocks compiled into one "fund" that you can buy and sell just like an individual stock. It could be a sector-based ETF focused on a particular industry, such as energy or real estate. Or it could be an index-based ETF that tracks the S&P 500 or another index as a whole.

For this game plan, we'll focus on index-based ETFs that give a broader representation of the general market.

3 Easy Steps

IBD has a simple approach to tracking the general market trend. (We'll get into the details in the Buying Checklist section.)

Each day, you can check the *Market Pulse* in IBD's *The Big Picture* column to see which of 3 possible stages the market is in right now:

• THE 3 MARKET STAGES •

MARKET PULSE	MARKET PULSE	MARKET PULSE
Current outlook: Confirmed uptrend	Current outlook: Uptrend under pressure	Current outlook: Market in correction
Best time to buy: General market is trending higher.	Proceed with caution: Market trend may be changing.	Take defensive action: Major indexes now in downtrend.

© 2013 Investor's Business Daily, Inc.

Based on that, you can see if it's time to buy, sell, or hold an index-based ETF. Here's how it works.

• BASIC GAME PLAN FOR MAKING MONEY IN INDEX-BASED ETFs •

Step 1: Buy an index-based ETF when the outlook changes from "Market in correction" to "Confirmed uptrend."

Step 2: Sell 50% when the outlook changes from "Confirmed uptrend" to "Uptrend under pressure."

Step 3: Sell the remaining 50% when the outlook changes from "Uptrend under pressure" to "Market in correction."

Note: In particularly volatile markets, the outlook may change immediately from "Confirmed uptrend" to "Market in correction," without going through the "Uptrend under pressure" stage. In that case, reduce your index-based ETF holdings to zero when the outlook is "Market in correction."

Protect Your Money with Stop-Loss Rules

To protect yourself from a sharp market downturn, you can set stop-loss orders ahead of time with your broker (Chapter 4). Here are some simple guidelines you can also follow as part of this ETF trading plan, in conjunction with the 3 steps outlined above:

- Sell 50% of your index-based ETF position if the index closes 0.5% or more below the follow-through day closing price. (A "follow-through day"—see Big Rock #1, Chapter 3— is what triggers a new market uptrend and causes the *Market Pulse* outlook to change from "Market in correction" to "Confirmed uptrend.")

- Sell 100% of your remaining index-based ETF position if the index drops 2.5% (intraday) below the follow-through day closing price.

Learn More

For more details on using this approach, see the ETF section of IBD.

The following chart shows how this simple approach can help generate significant profits. Think back to the severe bear market that started in late 2007, then look at how the *Market Pulse* alerted readers to that change in trend—and later noted the start of a new bull cycle in March 2009.

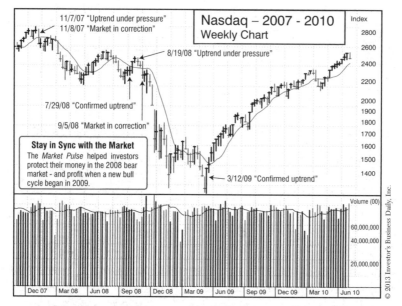

How the *Market Pulse* helped investors stay protected in the 2008 bear market, and get back in for the 2009 bull rebound.

How IBD's Approach Nearly Doubled the Nasdaq Performance

Following the 3-step approach listed above, from August 15, 2006 (start of new uptrend) to March 28, 2013 (last trading day of first quarter), IBD's *Market Pulse* strategy gained 97% compared to a 54% gain for the Nasdaq and a 55% gain for the S&P 500. While that does not guarantee you'll get those kinds of gains in every market cycle, it does show how this approach has the potential to generate significant profits.

Keep in mind: *Those gains were generated even with the severe 2008 bear market caused by the housing and financial crisis.*

How many people do you know made—and held on to—a 97% gain from 2006–2012? If you had invested $10,000 the day after the *Market Pulse* changed to "Confirmed uptrend" on August 15, 2006, it would have grown to over $19,000 *just by following this simple strategy.*

So whatever your goal is—building a college fund for your kids, paying off your mortgage, having a worry-free retirement—you can see how this approach may help you achieve it over time.

Tips on How to Generate ETF Profits

 Check out a short video that shows how you can use stop-loss orders and other simple steps to help generate substantial returns at www.investors.com/GettingStartedBook.

Basic Game Plan for Making Money in Individual Stocks

Now that we've seen how you may make substantial profits investing in index-based ETFs, let's see how to potentially capture even larger gains by buying and selling individual stocks.

Keep in mind: In a strong uptrend, the top-rated CAN SLIM stocks typically go up *much* more than the Nasdaq or S&P 500.

For example, from the start of a new bull market on March 12, 2009, through May 4, 2010, when the market slipped into a downtrend, the Nasdaq gained 70%. During that same period, the market leaders of the time shot up even more: Lululemon Athletica (522%), Ulta Beauty (322%), Baidu (309%), Priceline (231%).

Of course, let's manage expectations and be realistic.

Not even the best investors capture every last dollar of a big winner's move. (In fact, *trying* to do that will just get you into trouble as we'll see later.) But you *can* lock in a good-sized portion of those huge gains—and a little piece of a 300% move means a nice boost for your portfolio.

Yes, it takes more effort and elbow grease to tap into those potentially "monster" gains in individual stocks, but that's why you're reading this book, right? And once you get familiar with the routines and checklists, I think you'll be pleasantly surprised at how you can do this by sticking to a step-by-step approach. (To see what I mean, check out the Simple Weekend Routine in Chapter 4).

And I'll show you how to *get started*, one step at a time, using easy-to-follow checklists. We'll start right now with a quick overview of the basic 3-step game plan.

• BASIC GAME PLAN FOR MAKING MONEY IN STOCKS •

Step 1: Only buy when the overall market is in an uptrend.

Step 2: Buy stocks with CAN SLIM traits as they break out from a telltale chart pattern.

Step 3: Take most profits at 20% to 25%. Cut all losses at no more than 7% to 8%.

We'll cover the details of each step as we go through the buying and selling checklists. But for now, let's take a peek at these 3 steps in action.

Step 1: Only Buy When the Overall Market Is in an Uptrend

You can always see if the market is in an uptrend or downtrend just by checking the *Market Pulse* in *The Big Picture* column. In the following chart, you can see how the *Market Pulse* outlook helped investors buy and sell at the right time in 2010.

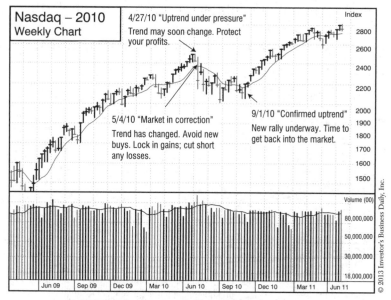

The *Market Pulse*'s 3-stage approach helps you see
when to buy and when to take defensive action.

Step 2: Buy Stocks with CAN SLIM Traits as They Break Out of a Telltale Chart Pattern

Even if you're not yet familiar with charts, you'll find highlights of top-rated stocks—and alerts to potential buy points—in the *IBD® 50*, *Your Weekly Review*, *Sector Leaders*, and other features.

Chipotle Mexican Grill increased 186% from September 2010 to April 2012.

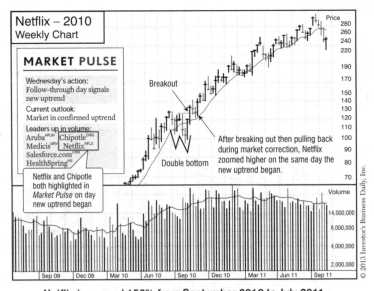

Netflix increased 150% from September 2010 to July 2011.

Step 3: Take Most Profits at 20% to 25%.
Cut All Losses at No More Than 7% to 8%.

Start with this simple selling plan to make sure you lock in some good gains and avoid any serious damage.

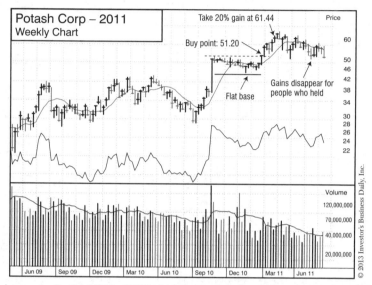

Take most gains at 20% to 25% to lock in good profits and grow your portfolio.

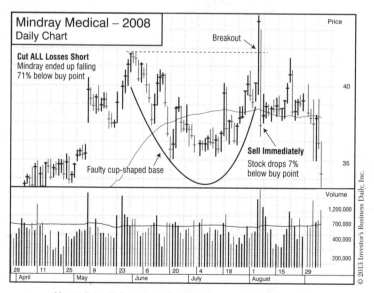

Never let a little loss become a big one: Always sell if
a stock drops 7% to 8% below your purchase price.

"Life is really simple, but we insist on making it complicated."

—CONFUCIUS

To a large degree, the same can be said of investing.

In the chapters ahead, we'll go through checklists that outline the traits of winning stocks, and see what buy and sell signals to look for in a chart. Those are all important details that you'll need to learn to be a successful investor.

But never lose sight of the big picture—and the basic game plans we just went through. With all the news and noise that surrounds the market, it's easy to overthink investing and become the proverbial deer in the headlights.

So especially if you're just getting started, stick with the simple game plans and routines we'll cover in this book. They'll keep you focused on the big-ticket items that ultimately determine if a stock heads up—or down.

And in the next chapter, we'll find out what those key factors are.

• ACTION STEPS •

Here are some quick *To Dos* to reinforce and start using what we've learned so far. To see how to take these steps, visit www.investors.com/GettingStartedBook.

1. Watch two short videos on:
   - *Simple Weekend Routine*
   - *How to Make Money Trading Index ETFs*
2. Check *The Big Picture* column in IBD or Investors.com.
   - Is the market in a confirmed uptrend—or correction—right now?

• CHAPTER •

The CAN SLIM®
Investment System

The 3 "Big Rocks" of CAN SLIM Investing

The buying and selling checklists in this book—and all the stock screens and tools you'll find in IBD®—are based on the **CAN SLIM® Investment System**, developed in the 1960s by IBD founder and chairman William J. O'Neil.

For years now, I've had the privilege of helping people get started with CAN SLIM investing—at workshops, in videos, at IBD Meetup groups, in a monthly newsletter, and on our radio show.

There's one piece of advice I give to anyone just starting out: **Don't over-complicate it! Keep it simple.**

Yes, there are important details and some things that take a little time and effort to learn, like how to read a stock chart. But all of them can be broken down into a few simple concepts you can learn step by step, using checklists to guide you. And that's what we'll do together throughout this book.

I love the saying, "Put the big rocks in first." You can always add the tiny pebbles—the details—later, but when you're getting started, make sure you stay focused on what matters most.

When it comes to understanding why the CAN SLIM Investment System works so well and how you can use it to make money in the market, it comes down to 3 "big rocks" you *always* want to put in first:

- **Big Rock #1:** Only buy stocks in a market uptrend. Take defensive action as a downtrend begins.

- **Big Rock #2:** Focus on companies with big earnings growth and a new, innovative product or service.

- **Big Rock #3:** Buy stocks being heavily bought by institutional investors. Avoid those they're heavily selling.

As you go through this book—and, most importantly, as you start using the checklists and Simple Weekend Routine to invest—always keep those 3 "big rocks" in mind.

They may not make sense to you just yet (they will very soon)—or maybe they seem overly simplistic at first. But IBD's study of every top stock since 1880 shows that always starting with these 3 core tenets is the key to making money in the market.

The CAN SLIM Concept

CAN SLIM investing is based on two simple ideas:

- To find tomorrow's big winners, look for stocks with the same traits *past* winners had just *before* they launched their big runs.

- To know when it's time to sell, look for the same warning signs these past winners flashed when they eventually topped and began to decline.

What Does a Winning Stock Look Like
Before—and After—It Makes Its Big Move?

In the late 1950s, Bill O'Neil was a young broker who asked a simple question: What common traits do the best stocks have *before* they make their big price moves?

To find out, he began studying the biggest winners of all time. These were stocks that went up 100%, 300% or much more very quickly, often in just 1 or 2 years.

These were the days before personal computers and the Internet, so Bill covered his office walls and cabinets with charts and reams of data. He studied every available performance metric to see which ones truly mattered— to see what characteristics and telltale signs these top-performing stocks displayed just before they rocketed higher. He found:

The best stocks display seven common traits just *before* they make their biggest gains.

Each letter in CAN SLIM stands for one of those traits, and they form the basis of the rules you'll find in the **Buying Checklist**.

Bill also studied what happens to leading stocks *after* they've had a big run. Just as they share certain traits before they surge, they also flash similar warning signs as they top and begin to decline. Those signals form the basis of the sell rules you'll find in the **Selling Checklist**.

Over 130 Years of Market History

The study O'Neil launched in the 1960s continues to this day and now covers every market cycle and top-performing stock from 1880 to the present.

Whether it's Bethlehem Steel in 1914, Xerox in 1963, Google and Apple in 2004, Priceline.com in 2010, SolarWinds in 2011, or 3D Systems in 2012, year after year, decade after decade, the biggest winners display these same 7 CAN SLIM traits just *before* they launch their massive runs.

The company names will change, new technology and industries will emerge, but *the basic profile and attributes of an emerging big winner always look the same*. So once you understand what to look for, your search for the next game-changing stock won't be based on hunches or hype. It'll be based on history and a targeted checklist of specific, telltale signs.

Only about 1% to 2% of all stocks will have these CAN SLIM character-istics. But as the results of an independent study by the American Association of Individual Investors (AAII) show, it pays to be picky: *If you stay disciplined and look for stocks with CAN SLIM traits, you will spot today's most promising stocks in the early stages of their big moves.*

#1 Growth Strategy from 1998–2012

Since 1998, the American Association of Individual Investors has been con-ducting an ongoing, real-time study of over 50 leading investing strategies. From 1998–2012, AAII found the CAN SLIM Investment System was the #1 growth strategy, generating an annualized return of 24.7%.

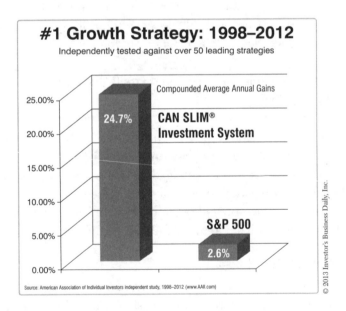

Think about all of the roller-coaster rides we had in the market during those 15 years: The dot-com boom and bust, the 2003 bull market, the housing and financial crisis in 2008, and the bull market rebound in 2009.

The CAN SLIM Investment System's independently tested performance through all those cycles shows that **if you stick to the Buying and Selling Checklists we'll cover together in this book, you can make—and** *keep*—**significant gains in any type of market.**

The 7 Traits of Winning Stocks

In *How to Make Money in Stocks: A Winning System in Good Times or Bad*, Bill O'Neil gives a detailed description of each of the 7 CAN SLIM traits and countless historical examples of winning stocks that shared those characteristics. It's the definitive guide to CAN SLIM investing by the man who developed it, so I strongly encourage you to read that book.

Since the purpose of *this* book is to show you how to quickly *get started* with the CAN SLIM Investment System, we'll take a slightly different approach.

Again, let's keep it simple and stay focused on what really matters most. Here's how we'll do that.

First, I'll give a brief overview of the 7 CAN SLIM traits and show how they relate to the 3 "big rocks" I noted earlier. We'll also go through some CAN SLIM case studies so you can see how top stocks in the 2009–2012 bull market had these same traits *before* they surged.

Then in the next chapters, we'll go step by step through routines and checklists that will help you systematically spot *today's* CAN SLIM stocks and pinpoint the best time to buy—and sell—them.

The 7 Traits and the 3 Big Rocks

See the **Buying Checklist** for the specific numbers and ratings needed to meet the benchmarks for the 7 CAN SLIM traits.

Big Rock #1: Only Buy Stocks in a Market Uptrend. Take Defensive Action as a Downtrend Begins.

The "M" in CAN SLIM—market direction—may be the last letter, but in many ways it's the most important. To a very large degree, the difference between making or losing money comes down to simply staying in sync with the direction of the overall market (i.e., the major indexes like the S&P 500 and Nasdaq).

Market direction
History shows 3 of 4 stocks simply follow the direction of the general market, either up or down. So you must learn to follow, not fight, the current trend.

We'll get into what steps you can take to handle changes in market direction later, but understand up front that:

You do *not* need to be fully invested in the stock market at all times. Make money when the market is trending up—and protect your profits when the market starts trending down.

Sounds obvious, right?

But the reality is, many people pay *no* attention to the overall market direction and just blindly "buy and hold." That's because they don't understand how market cycles work. They don't realize that when the overall market trends down for an extended period, about 75% of all stocks go down with it.

Investors with a "buy and hold" strategy may make money when the market is going up, but they often end up giving it all back (and then some) when it goes down.

It's time to step off that roller coaster and start using buy and sell rules based on how market cycles actually work.

You'll learn how to do that in this book:

- The Buying Checklist pinpoints the best time to get into the market.

- The Selling Checklist shows you when it's time to lock in your gains and move to the sidelines.

Big Rock #2: Focus on Companies with Big Earnings Growth and a New, Innovative Product or Service.

Big, accelerating earnings growth is the #1 factor to look for in a stock. And it's innovative companies with game-changing new products that generate that type of explosive profitability.

That's why the first three CAN SLIM traits are so important:

C **Current quarterly earnings per share (EPS)**
Earnings should be strong and accelerating in recent quarters. Plus, to prove the company has the ingredients to sustain that growth, look for solid sales growth, a high return on equity, and industry-leading profit margins.

A **Annual earnings per share**
To help make sure the current quarterly growth is not a fluke, also look for strong *annual* earnings growth over the last 3 years.

N **New company, product/service, industry trend, or management**
Focus on companies with something "new": An innovative product or service in high demand, a new CEO, or a game-changing industry trend.

Think about it: If a stock's share price goes up 100%, 200% or more, there has to be a reason. There has to be *something* that is making mutual fund managers and other big investors continue to push the stock higher.

History shows the main cause is earnings growth. And that was proven again in the 2009–2012 bull market. The biggest winners—stocks like Baidu, F5 Networks, Apple, Priceline.com, SolarWinds, Rackspace Hosting, Alexion Pharmaceuticals, Lululemon Athletica, Chipotle Mexican Grill, and Michael Kors—tended to be highly profitable companies whose earnings growth was not only strong but accelerating as their share prices rose higher. And they all had new, innovative products or services that made them leaders in their industries.

Big Rock #3: Buy Stocks Being Heavily Bought by Institutional Investors. Avoid Those They're Heavily Selling.

"Institutional investors"—primarily mutual funds but also hedge funds, banks, pension funds, insurance companies, and other large "institutions"—account for the bulk of all trading. They provide the buying power or fuel a stock needs to make a big, sustained upward move. And when they sell, it's their heavy dumping of shares that drives a stock down.

That's why it's absolutely critical to watch what they're doing—and you'll see how to do that using IBD *SmartSelect*® Ratings and charts when we get to the Buying Checklist.

For now, just understand you essentially want to ride their coattails. You want to buy stocks fund managers and other big investors are heavily buying, since those are the stocks most likely to make a big gain. And just as importantly, you want to sell and get out of the way when you see fund managers start to unload their shares, since those stocks will likely drop sharply.

The next 3 CAN SLIM letters outline the kind of institutional buying you want to see in a stock *before* you invest:

S Supply and demand

At key buy points, the best stocks will have *above-average* increases in volume (i.e., a sharp rise in the number of shares traded). That shows fund managers and other professional investors are heavily buying that stock.

L Leader or laggard

Focus on the top-rated stocks in the top-ranked industry groups. A stock becomes a true leader by showing strong earnings and innovation ("C," "A" and "N" in CAN SLIM) *and* by being the clear leader in a top-ranked group—where institutions are putting their money.

I Institutional sponsorship

"Institutional sponsorship" refers to ownership of a stock by large institutions, primarily mutual funds. Look for an *increasing* number of funds owning a stock in recent quarters, plus ownership by a few top fund managers that have out-performed the market over the last one or two years. It's good confirmation to see these top investors buying a stock you're considering.

Follow the Funds!

> *"It's key to buy the better stocks mutual funds buy and avoid ones they may be selling on a heavy basis.* **Trying to go against this monumental amount of trading will only hurt your results.**"

—WILLIAM J. O'NEIL, IBD CHAIRMAN AND FOUNDER

Bottom line: Make sure some mutual fund managers are moving heavily into a stock before you buy. And when they start to sell aggressively, move to the sidelines and get out of the way.

• WHAT ABOUT P/E RATIOS? •

You may have noticed there was no mention of price/earnings (P/E) ratios among the 7 traits of winning stocks. The reason is simple: Our studies show P/E ratios (share price divided by earnings-per-share) are not an important factor in a stock's price movement and have very little to do with whether a stock should be bought or sold.

That may come as a shock since most investors are told to focus on stocks with a low P/E ratio and avoid those with a high one. But the fact is, 130+ years of market history show that **investors who fixate on low P/E ratios miss out on virtually *every* big winner**.

Here's why.

A low P/E ratio is usually a sign of weakness, not strength. The strongest stocks—those with big earnings growth and other CAN SLIM traits—will typically have a higher P/E ratio. Why? Because institutional investors are willing to pay more for quality, fast-growing stocks. A baseball team has to pay more to sign a .300 hitter averaging 40 home runs a year than to sign a benchmarker with a .200 batting average. As the table below shows, it's the same in the stock market: You get what you pay for.

P/E Ratios of Leaders in 2009–2012 Bull Market

Company	Year Run Started	P/E at Start of Run	Subsequent % Gain
Baidu	2009	69	322%
Green Mountain Coffee Roasters	2009	36	1104%
Priceline.com	2010	29	183%
Lululemon Athletica	2010	33	196%
SolarWinds	2011	28	137%

If you focus only on low P/Es, you're essentially taking the best merchandise off the shelf and restricting yourself to the clearance bin. So instead, focus on stocks with big and accelerating earnings growth. That's the true mark of a potential big winner.

CAN SLIM® Case Studies

A new crop of leading stocks emerges in every bull market cycle, giving you new opportunities to make money.

Some will be household names, but many will be companies you've likely never heard of. You may not be familiar with their products or services, but now that you know the 7 CAN SLIM traits to look for, you'll know how to spot them—and you'll see where to find them using the Simple Weekend Routine (Chapter 4).

Below are profiles of 3 CAN SLIM winners.

One is a company we all know—Apple. But back in 2004 when it launched a massive run that would turn it into the world's most valuable company by 2012, was it on your radar screen?

You'd probably heard of the iPod and iTunes, maybe even used them. But as an investor, did you make the connection that with a revolutionary, extremely popular new product (the "N" in CAN SLIM), Apple could become a big stock market winner?

The iPod generated explosive earnings growth, and that was followed by even more profits with the release of the iPhone. Those two game-changing innovations revolutionized the music and mobile phone industries, leading to a 1,418% rise in Apple's share price in less than 4 years.

But even if you missed that *entire* move, Apple still offered new opportunities to get in during the 2009–2012 bull market. (As you'll see later in the book, it's rare for a stock that leads in one bull market cycle to come back and lead in the next one too. That's why it's so important to always hunt for the *new* crop of leaders. More on that later.)

Like most stocks, Apple got hammered during the 2007–2008 financial crisis, but when the market turned around in 2009, Apple came roaring back. What gave it that kind of power? As you can see in the case study below, it still had the CAN SLIM traits, including big earnings and sales, hot new products, and growing demand from fund managers. And that was *before* it released yet another new innovation—the iPad.

Unlike Apple, the other two case studies, Green Mountain Coffee Roasters and Ulta Beauty, were not household names when they launched their big price moves. I had never heard of them before they started showing up in IBD's stock lists—and until my teenage daughter tipped me off to the popularity of Ulta Beauty, which sells brand-name cosmetics at discount prices.

That brings up an important side note: Pay attention to where your children shop. They might steer you to a new leader in the retail industry, which has been a good source of CAN SLIM stocks over the years.

But back to the case studies. While you might not have tasted Green Mountain's K-Cup gourmet coffee or visited an Ulta store, as a CAN SLIM investor, their superior earnings performance would have put them on your radar screen. Both companies had the traits we look for, and that's why they started appearing in stock lists like the *IBD 50* (known as the *IBD 100* at the time) and *Your Weekly Review*.

As you look through these profiles, note how the 3 "big rocks" were all in place when these stocks launched their big moves:

- The overall market was in an uptrend.
- Each company had explosive earnings growth and innovative products.
- Mutual funds were aggressively buying shares.

These types of money-making opportunities appear in every bull market cycle. And by studying these examples and by using the checklists and routines we'll go over throughout this book, you'll see exactly what steps you can take to profit from them.

How to Find & Own America's Greatest Opportunities by Bill O'Neil

 Each week, Bill O'Neil personally writes a short column that walks you through the full "life cycle" of a winning stock. You'll see what CAN SLIM traits it had before it made its big price move—and what sell signals it eventually flashed. Reading Bill's insights each week will help you spot tomorrow's big winners—and handle them profitably when you do. See a sample column at www.investors.com/GettingStartedBook.

CAN SLIM Case Study: Apple (AAPL)

381% gain from July 2009–September 2012

All 3 "big rocks" and key CAN SLIM® traits in place *before* breakout.

Only buy stocks when the overall market is in an uptrend.

Market Direction: New bull cycle had just begun in March, following the 2008 housing and financial crisis.

Focus on companies with big earnings growth and a new, innovative product or service.

Current Earnings: EPS growth in 3 quarters prior to big move: 37% → 47% → 61%.

Annual Earnings: Average 3-year annual EPS growth: 48%.

New Product/Service: Apple's iPods, iPhones, iTunes, and apps market made it the innovative leader in the music and smartphone industries and also sparked new interest and market share for its line of Mac computers.

Buy stocks being heavily bought by institutional investors.

Supply and Demand: Apple's Accumulation/Distribution Rating of B+ (see Buying Checklist) showed institutional investors had been scooping up shares over the prior 3 months.

Leader or Laggard: 98 Composite Rating showed Apple was outperforming 98% of *all* stocks in terms of key CAN SLIM traits.

Institutional Sponsorship: Number of funds owning Apple rose in 3 quarters before it launched its new run: 286 → 316 → 321.

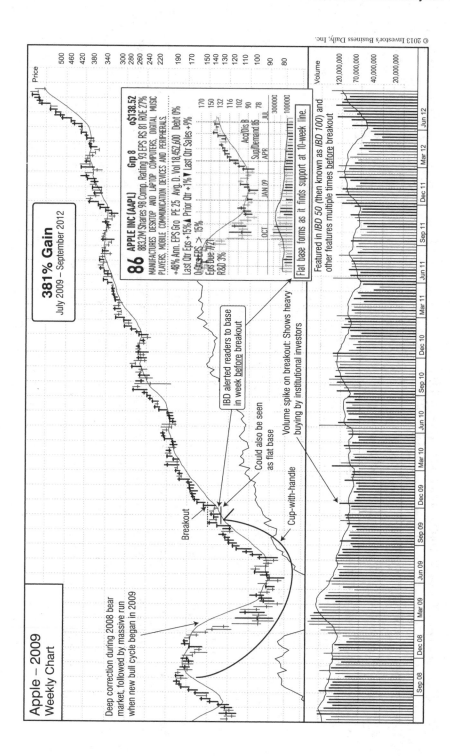

Apple – 2009
Weekly Chart

381% Gain
July 2009 – September 2012

Deep correction during 2008 bear market, followed by massive run when new bull cycle began in 2009

Breakout

Could also be seen as flat base

Cup-with-handle

IBD alerted readers to base in week before breakout

Volume spike on breakout: Shows heavy buying by institutional investors

Flat base forms as it finds support at 10-week line.

Featured in *IBD 50* (then known as *IBD 100*) and other features multiple times before breakout

86 APPLE INC (AAPL)   Grp 8   o$138.52
883.2M Shares 98 EPS Rating 93 Comp. Rating 93 EPS RS 81 ROE 27%
MANUFACTURES DESKTOP AND LAPTOP COMPUTERS, DIGITAL MUSIC
PLAYERS, MOBILE COMMUNICATION DEVICES AND PERIPHERALS.
+49% Ann. EPS Gro PE 25 Avg. D. Vol 18,452,600 Debt 0%
Last Qtr Eps +15%▲ Prior Qtr +1%▼ Last Qtr Sales +9%
Qtrs+EPS > 15%
Eps Due 7/21
R&D 3%

CAN SLIM Case Study: Green Mountain Coffee Roasters (GMCR)

1,104% gain from March 2009–September 2011

All 3 "big rocks" and key CAN SLIM® traits in place *before* breakout.

Only buy stocks when the overall market is in an uptrend.

Market Direction: Green Mountain launched its new run just days after a new bull cycle began on March 12, 2009. Bullish sign: Stocks that go on to big gains often start their runs right when a new market uptrend begins.

Focus on companies with big earnings growth and a new, innovative product or service.

Current Earnings: Green Mountain's 93 EPS Rating (see Buying Checklist) showed it was outperforming 93% of all stocks for both current and annual earnings growth. Sales jumped 56% in the prior quarter.

Annual Earnings: Average 3-year annual EPS growth: 43%.

New Product/Service: Green Mountain was stirring up the coffee industry with its Keurig K-Cup single-serving gourmet coffees.

Buy stocks being heavily bought by institutional investors.

Supply and Demand: Green Mountain's 97 Relative Strength Rating (see Buying Checklist) told you its price performance was out-pacing 97% of all stocks.

Leader or Laggard: Highest-possible 99 Composite Rating showed GMCR was in top 1% of *all* stocks for key CAN SLIM traits.

Institutional Sponsorship: Number of funds owning GMCR rose sharply in 3 quarters prior to breakout: 183 → 197 → 219.

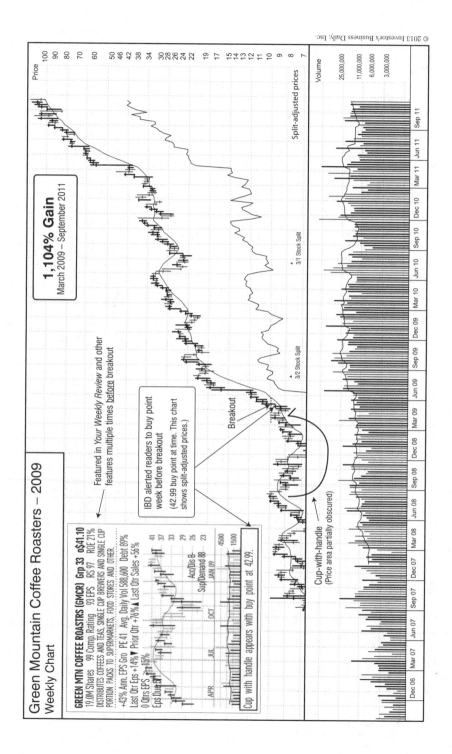

Green Mountain Coffee Roasters – 2009
Weekly Chart

1,104% Gain
March 2009 – September 2011

Featured in *Your Weekly Review* and other features multiple times before breakout

IBD alerted readers to buy point week before breakout
(42.99 buy point at time. This chart shows split-adjusted prices.)

Breakout

Cup-with-handle
(Price area partially obscured)

3/2 Stock Split

3/1 Stock Split

Split-adjusted prices

Price

100
90
80
70
60
50
46
42
38
34
30
28
26
24
22
19
17
15
14
13
12
11
10
9
8
7

GREEN MTN COFFEE ROASTRS (GMCR) Grp 33 o$41.10
19.0M Shares 99 Comp. Rating 93 EPS RS 97 ROE 21%
DISTRIBUTES COFFEES AND TEAS, SINGLE CUP BREWERS AND SINGLE CUP
PORTION PACKS TO SUPERMARKETS, FOOD STORES AND OTHER.
+43% Ann. EPS Gro PE 41 Avg. Daily Vol 588,600 Debt 89%
Last Qtr Eps +14%▼ Prior Qtr +76%▲ Last Qtr Sales +56%
0 Qtrs EPS ▼ 15%
Eps Due

41
37
33
29
26
23

Acc/Dis B–
Sup/Demand 88

4500
1500

APR JUL OCT JAN 09

Cup with handle appears with buy point at 42.99.

Volume
25,000,000
11,000,000
6,000,000
3,000,000

Dec 06 Mar 07 Jun 07 Sep 07 Dec 07 Mar 08 Jun 08 Sep 08 Dec 08 Mar 09 Jun 09 Sep 09 Dec 09 Mar 10 Jun 10 Sep 10 Dec 10 Mar 11 Jun 11 Sep 11

CAN SLIM Case Study: Ulta Beauty (ULTA)

165% gain from September 2010–July 2011

All 3 "big rocks" and key CAN SLIM® traits in place *before* breakout.

Only buy stocks when the overall market is in an uptrend.

Market Direction: New uptrend had begun just 2 weeks earlier.

Focus on companies with big earnings growth and a new, innovative product or service.

Current Earnings: EPS growth in 3 quarters prior to big move: 56% → 62% → 188%.

Annual Earnings: Average 3-year annual EPS growth: 31%.

New Product/Service: Ulta was revolutionizing the cosmetics retail business with a Home Depot–style, big-store format featuring a wide range of popular brand items at discount prices.

Buy stocks being heavily bought by institutional investors.

Supply and Demand: Weekly trading volume was 207% *above* average the week ULTA started its run, showing fund managers were aggressively buying shares.

Leader or Laggard: 96 Composite Rating told you Ulta was outperforming 96% of *all* stocks in terms of key CAN SLIM traits.

Institutional Sponsorship: Number of funds owning ULTA rose sharply in 4 quarters *prior* to breakout: 197 → 223 → 231 → 315.

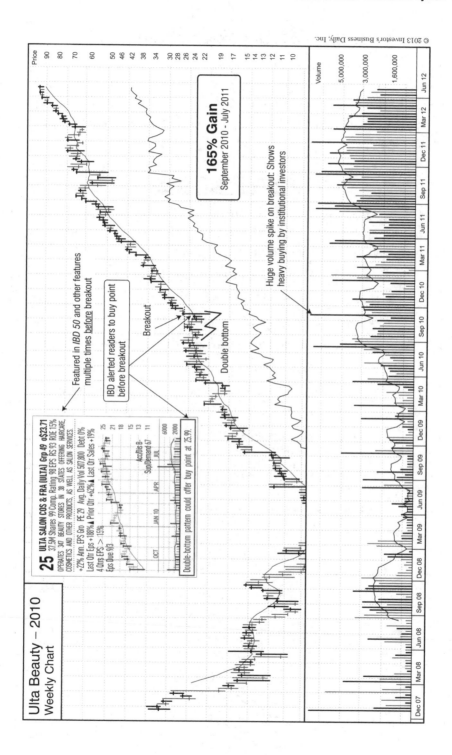

© 2013 Investor's Business Daily, Inc.

Ulta Beauty – 2010
Weekly Chart

25 **ULTA SALON COS & FRA (ULTA) Grp 49 o$23.71**
37.5M Shares 99 Comp. Rating 98 EPS RS 93 ROE 15%
OPERATES 347 BEAUTY STORES IN 38 STATES OFFERING HAIRCARE,
COSMETICS AND OTHER PRODUCTS, AS WELL AS SALON SERVICES
+22% Ann. EPS Gro PE 29 Avg. Daily Vol 507,800 Debt 0%
Last Qtr Eps +180% ▲ Prior Qtr +62% ▲ Last Qtr Sales +19%
4 Qtrs EPS > 15%
Eps Due 9/3

Acc/Dis B-
Sup/Demand 67

Double-bottom pattern could offer buy point at 25.99.

165% Gain
September 2010 - July 2011

Featured in *IBD 50* and other features
multiple times <u>before</u> breakout

IBD alerted readers to buy point
<u>before</u> breakout

Breakout

Double bottom

Huge volume spike on breakout: Shows
heavy buying by institutional investors

Price
90
80
70
60
50
46
42
38
34
30
28
26
24
22
19
17
15
14
13
12
11
10

Volume
5,000,000
3,000,000
1,600,000

Dec 07 Mar 08 Jun 08 Sep 08 Dec 08 Mar 09 Jun 09 Sep 09 Dec 09 Mar 10 Jun 10 Sep 10 Dec 10 Mar 11 Jun 11 Sep 11 Dec 11 Mar 12 Jun 12

Next Up: How to Find *Today's* CAN SLIM Stocks

Now that you know what to look for, let's see how to find stocks that have these same CAN SLIM traits *right now*. We'll do that using a Buying Checklist that shows you what specific traits to look for before you invest.

But first, take the Action Steps below to help reinforce what we covered in this chapter.

• ACTION STEPS •

Here are some quick *To Dos* to help you get more familiar with and start using the CAN SLIM Investment System. To take these steps, visit www.investors.com/GettingStartedBook.

1. See CAN SLIM investing in action with these short videos:

- *How to Spot Great Story Stocks*
- *When to Get Into—and Out of—the Market*

2. See what's "new" with today's top-rated CAN SLIM stocks.

- Check the top 5–10 stocks in the current *IBD 50* list.
  - You can also use stocks from the *CAN SLIM Select* list in the *IBD Screen Center* on Investors.com.
- Check their websites and read about them on Investors.com to find out what new products or services they offer and what industry trends are driving their growth.

· CHAPTER ·

Buying Checklist

Buying Checklist

Does Your Stock Pass or Fail?

Make sure the 3 "Big Rocks" of CAN SLIM® are always in place before you invest.

Use this checklist to see if your stock has the CAN SLIM traits big winners typically display just *before* they launch a major price move.

Big Rock #1: Only buy stocks in a market uptrend. Take defensive action as a downtrend begins.

❏ Market in confirmed uptrend

Big Rock #2: Focus on companies with big earnings growth and a new, innovative product or service.

❏ Composite Rating of 90 or higher

❏ EPS Rating of 80 or higher

❏ EPS growth 25% or higher in recent quarters

❏ Accelerating earnings growth

❏ Average Annual EPS growth 25% or more over last 3 years

❏ Sales growth 25% or higher in most recent quarter

❏ Return on equity (ROE) of 17% or higher

❏ SMR® Rating (Sales + Margins + Return on Equity) of A or B

❏ New products, service, or management

❏ Among the top-rated stocks in its industry group

❏ Ranked in top 40–50 of IBD's 197 industry groups

Big Rock #3: Buy stocks being heavily bought by institutional investors. Avoid those they're heavily selling.

❏ Increase in number of funds that own the stock in recent quarters

❏ Accumulation/Distribution Rating of A or B

❏ Relative Strength Rating of 80 or higher

❏ Share price above $15

❏ Average daily volume of 400,000 shares or more

Chart Analysis: Buy stocks as they break out of the common patterns that launch big moves.

❏ Breaking out of sound base or alternative buy point

❏ Volume at least 40% to 50% above average on breakout

❏ Relative strength line in new high ground

❏ Within 5% of ideal buy point

You can download and print this checklist at www.investors.com/GettingStartedBook.

Does Your Stock Pass or Fail?

Find Out with *IBD Stock Checkup*®

Before we go over each item on the Buying Checklist, note that you can *quickly* see if your stock passes or fails using *Stock Checkup* on Investors.com. You'll find Pass (green), Neutral (yellow) or Fail (red) grades for most items.

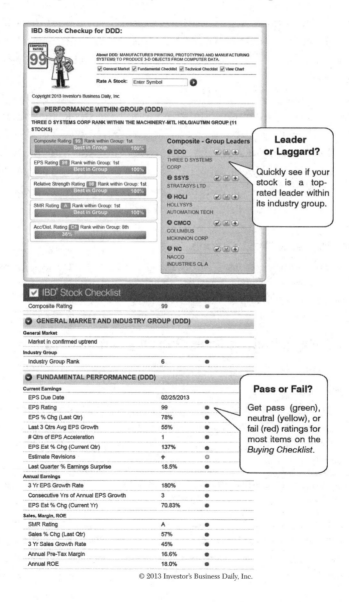

© 2013 Investor's Business Daily, Inc.

See the Checklist and *Stock Checkup* in Action

 Watch a short video on how to quickly run your stock ideas through the Buying Checklist at www.investors.com/GettingStartedBook.

It Pays to Be Picky

As we go through each item, keep in mind the concept behind this checklist.

We just saw how the CAN SLIM Investment System outlines what traits the best-performing stocks typically have just *before* they launch a major price move. The Buying Checklist helps you see which stocks have those same traits *right now*.

Stocks that pass this test are the ones most likely to go up 50%, 100%, 200% or even more. You'll see countless examples of stocks that did just that as we check off each item.

Using the Buying Checklist will become second nature very quickly. Once you've done it a few times, you'll be surprised at how fast you can evaluate *multiple* stocks. And since you'll know exactly what characteristics to look for, it won't be difficult to separate the leaders from the laggards.

Practice Now with *Stock Checkup*

 If you're near a computer, I suggest you pull up *Stock Checkup* as we go through each item on the checklist. It'll help you get used to the process even quicker. See how at www.investors.com/GettingStartedBook.

Forget All the Hype, Hunches and Hearsay

All too many investors choose stocks based on little more than tips, opinions and rumors. You might hear a pundit say a stock that just fell 30% is now "undervalued." Or an investing newsletter might promote a company with no sales and profits but a "promising" product in the pipeline. Going on nothing more than a hunch or interesting story, many folks will just jump right in.

But that kind of wishful-thinking, impulsive speculation rarely ends well. Fortunately, it's also totally unnecessary.

You'll find that having rules and checklists—and sticking to them—will be the real "secret" to increasing the amount of money you make.

So instead of picking stocks based on hype and hunches, focus on the *facts*. **Use the Buying Checklist to make each stock prove itself before you buy.**

Think of using this checklist like building the foundation of your home. If you want to create a solid portfolio, don't start by cutting corners and using cheap, inferior materials. Take the time up front to do it right. If you focus on stocks that have these CAN SLIM traits, you'll be creating a solid foundation for success rather than a shoddy structure that more closely resembles a house of cards.

Stay disciplined and picky. Only about 1% to 2% of stocks will make the grade, but that's the point: You're not looking for unproven or run-of-the-mill companies. You only want the best-of-the-best A players on your team. The Buying Checklist will help you build that winning lineup.

• CHECK THE CHART BEFORE YOU BUY •

Make sure your stock also passes the "Chart Analysis" section of the checklist before you invest. We'll get into how to do that in Chapter 6, "Don't Invest *Blindly*: Use Charts to *See* the Best Time to Buy and Sell."

You'll find chart-reading is the most important investing skill you'll ever learn. And once you know what to look for, it's not that hard to do. You'll also find features like the *IBD 50* and *Your Weekly Review* do a lot of the checklist legwork for you. They highlight stocks near a potential buy point and note what kind of chart pattern they're forming.

So even as you're still getting familiar with charts, you can use IBD stock lists and the **Simple Weekend Routine** (Chapter 4) to catch winning stocks *before* they launch their big moves.

Big Rock #1: Only Buy Stocks in a Market Uptrend. Take Defensive Action as a Downtrend Begins.

It's no coincidence that the very first item on the Buying Checklist deals with general market direction.

The reason is simple: **A stock may earn stellar grades for the first six CAN SLIM® traits, but if the "M" (Market Direction) fails, look out!**

We touched on this earlier, but we'll come back to it again and again because it's critical that you understand this *fact* and take it to heart:

---

3 of 4 stocks simply move in the same direction as the general market, either up or down.

How does that impact *you*?

- If you buy during a market *uptrend*, you have a 75% chance of being *right*.
- If you buy during a market *downtrend*, you have a 75% chance of being *wrong*.

I think you'll agree: That's a *very* compelling reason to stick with the checklist and only buy stocks when the market is in an *uptrend*.

Of course, the question is: How can you tell which way the market is trending right now?

Let's find out using the checklist . . .

Buying Checklist

Big Rock #1: **Only buy stocks in a market uptrend.** Take defensive action as a downtrend begins.

❏ **Market in confirmed uptrend**

 Market in confirmed uptrend

As we saw earlier, the general market is always in 1 of 3 stages: "Confirmed uptrend," "Uptrend under pressure," or "Market in correction."

You can see which stage we're currently in just by checking the *Market Pulse* inside *The Big Picture* column found in IBD every day. (In Chapter 5, "Selling Checklist," we'll cover what to do when the market stage is "Uptrend under pressure" or "Market in correction.")

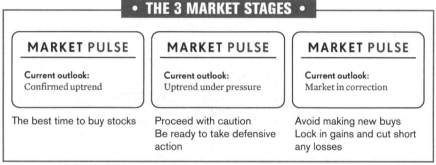

• THE 3 MARKET STAGES •

MARKET PULSE	MARKET PULSE	MARKET PULSE
Current outlook: Confirmed uptrend	Current outlook: Uptrend under pressure	Current outlook: Market in correction
The best time to buy stocks	Proceed with caution Be ready to take defensive action	Avoid making new buys Lock in gains and cut short any losses

© 2013 Investor's Business Daily, Inc.

Can You Really Time the Market?

Conventional wisdom says no. Actual market *history* says yes.

The *Current Outlook* in the *Market Pulse* changes based on certain signals that appear *every time* a major shift in trend occurs.

Now keep in mind: Saying you can time the market does *not* mean you'll sell at the very top and buy at the very bottom. And it does *not* mean you can predict where the market will be six months from now.

But it *does* mean you can spot when a potential new uptrend has begun. And you can see when the market is starting to weaken and roll over into a downtrend.

This isn't about predicting the future. It's simply about understanding what is going on in the major indexes *right now*: Are institutional investors pushing the indexes higher by continuing to buy, or are they driving the market down by selling more aggressively?

No crystal ball required here: Simply understanding the *current* direction is enough to build yourself a financially secure *future*. As you can see in the next two figures, following the 3 stages in the *Market Pulse* will help you make money when the market is up—and protect those profits when selling pressure mounts and a downtrend begins. (Also go back and look at the two examples we covered in Chapter 1, "Start Here.")

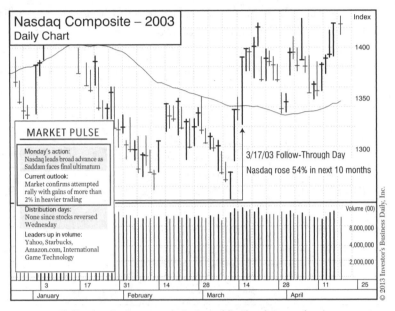

Following the bear market caused by the dot-com bust,
the *Market Pulse* alerted readers to the start of a new uptrend.

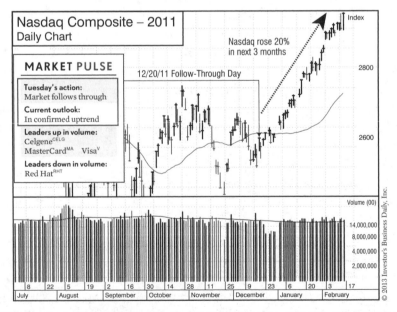

After several months of volatility, the *Market Pulse* noted the start of a new uptrend in
December 2011, giving investors a chance to profit as leading stocks launched new runs.

"See" How to Time the Market

 Learn more about how to spot changes in market trends with short videos at www.investors.com/GettingStartedBook.

Two Signs of a Change in Market Trend

Below is a brief explanation of the two main signals that indicate a shift in market direction: "Follow-through days" that note the start of a new uptrend, and "distribution days" that alert you to a weakening market.

Since this book is focused on helping you *get started*, I'll just cover the basics here. You can dig deeper by taking the Action Steps at the end of this chapter and by doing the "Must-Do Steps" we discussed in the Introduction.

You *Don't* Have to Track These Changes on Your Own

If the market shifts from a correction to an uptrend or vice versa, you'll know it just by looking at the *Market Pulse*. So while it's definitely helpful to understand the mechanics behind follow-through days and distribution days, don't worry if it doesn't sink in on the first go. Remember, investing is a skill best learned in stages. You can dig into more details and advanced topics later.

"Follow-Through Days" Mark Start of New Uptrend

When the market is in a correction, how can you tell if the direction has changed and a new uptrend has begun?

Look for a "follow-through day."

IBD's ongoing study of *every* market cycle since 1880 has found that **no sustained uptrend has ever begun without a follow-through day**.

So when you're in a down market and wondering when it'll be time to get back in, don't guess. Wait for this time-tested signal to appear and the *Market Pulse* outlook to shift from "Market in correction" to "Confirmed uptrend."

How Does a Follow-Through Day Work?

Let's answer that by seeing how the March 12, 2009 follow-through day marked the end of the severe 2008 bear market and the start of a robust new bull cycle.

Think back to what the mood in the country was at that time. In 2007–2008, the housing market had tanked, and the entire financial system had been shaken to the point of near collapse. The Nasdaq had lost over half its value since the start of the bear market in November 2007, and countless investors had suffered similar losses. (Of course, anyone who followed the Selling Checklist in this book would have avoided any serious damage. Hint, hint . . .)

So by March 2009, a lot of folks had taken a beating and were in no mood to jump back into the stock market anytime soon. The doom and gloom headlines only seemed to confirm those fears.

But for investors who understood how market cycles work, the signs of a potential new uptrend were there—as were the tremendous money-making opportunities that emerge at the beginning of every new bull market.

That brings up another important fact: **New market uptrends tend to begin when the economic and other news is *bad*.**

That's why the follow-through day is such a valuable tool: Instead of wringing your hands at the latest headlines and trying to guess when the market might turn around, just wait for a follow-through day, knowing that new uptrends *never* begin without one.

We'll get into how to read charts later in Chapter 6, "Don't Invest *Blindly*," but for now let's just walk through the "story" the Nasdaq chart was telling you as the market began to rebound.

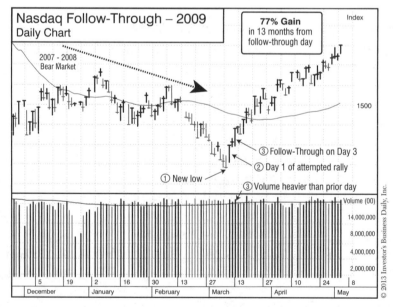

See below for an explanation of points 1 through 3 and how follow-through days alert you to new market uptrends.

1. **New Low:** When the market is in a downtrend, look for at least one of the major indexes (S&P 500, Nasdaq, or Dow) to hit a new price low. The Nasdaq did that on March 9, 2009 (Point 1 in the previous chart).

2. **Attempted Rally:** After hitting that new low, look for a day when the index closes higher. That *might* mean the index has stopped its decline, established a new "bottom," and is on its way to a rebound.

   The Nasdaq did that on March 10, when it made a nice gain on higher-than-normal volume (Point 2). What does that above-average volume tell you? That institutional investors are buying—a bullish sign. But one up day isn't enough to tell if the market trend has truly changed. So we count that as Day 1 of an *attempted* rally.

3. **Follow-Through Day:** Once the attempted rally is under way, we start looking for a follow-through day to confirm that a new uptrend has begun. Here are the basic requirements:

   - Typically occurs sometime after Day 3 of the attempted rally. Many occur between Days 4–7, but they can come later. The March 12, 2009, follow-through actually occurred on Day 3, which is fairly rare (Point 3).

   - The index should make a big one-day price gain, typically 1.5% or higher, on volume *heavier* than the prior day.

Get Back in *Gradually* After a Follow-Through Day

Not every follow-through day leads to a big, sustained uptrend. About one-third will fail, and the market will quickly fall back into a correction. That's why you want to get back into the market *gradually* when a follow-through day occurs and the *Market Pulse* shifts from "Market in correction" to "Confirmed uptrend."

If the uptrend takes hold and the leading CAN SLIM stocks start to move higher on heavy buying by institutional investors, you can start to get in more aggressively. If the uptrend fails, use the Selling Checklist and move safely back to the sidelines.

What to Do When a New Uptrend Begins

 See my *2-Minute Tip* video on "What to Do After a Follow-Through Day" at www.investors.com/GettingStartedBook.

"Distribution Days" Alert You to a Weakening Market

When the market is in an uptrend, you know at some point the tide will turn and a new downtrend will begin. You can see when that shift may be occurring by looking for what we call "distribution days"—days of heavy selling in the major indexes. ("Distribution" is just another word for selling.)

A distribution day is when one of the major indexes closes down at least 0.2% on volume heavier than the day before. (Stalling action—when the trading volume increases, but the closing price barely budges—can also count as distribution.)

We'll get into how to handle a weakening market when we go through the Selling Checklist, but here's the key point: **A rising number of distribution days shows that *institutional investors* are beginning to sell more aggressively.** And we've already seen, it's the enormous buying (and selling) power of mutual funds and other big investors that ultimately drives the market—and individual stocks—either up or down.

Of course, fund managers try not to sell so aggressively that it becomes obvious to everyone what they're doing. Yet their size and trading volume make it difficult to hide. That's why tracking distribution days is so important: It helps you gauge how serious the selling is and see if a true change in trend is emerging.

When the number of distribution days begins to mount, the *Market Pulse* outlook shifts from "Confirmed uptrend" to "Uptrend under pressure." That's a warning sign that more trouble may be on the way.

That selling may ease and fade away, allowing the market to continue its climb. But if that downward pressure picks up steam, look out!

If you get 6 distribution days within any 4- or 5-week period, the uptrend will typically roll over into a downtrend. You can see the current number of distribution days in the *Market Pulse*, and if you get enough days, the *Current Outlook* will shift to "Market in correction."

See the following S&P 500 chart for an example of how distribution days mount, and the *Market Pulse* changes from "Confirmed uptrend" to "Uptrend under pressure" and finally to "Market in correction."

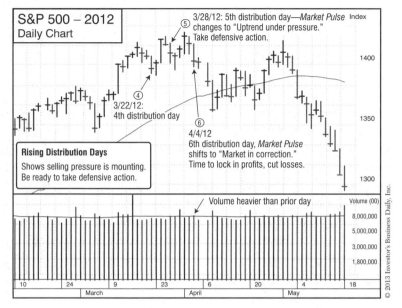

S&P 500 – 2012
Daily Chart

③ 3/28/12: 5th distribution day—*Market Pulse* Index
changes to "Uptrend under pressure."
Take defensive action.

④ 3/22/12:
4th distribution day

⑥ 4/4/12
6th distribution day, *Market Pulse*
shifts to "Market in correction."
Time to lock in profits, cut losses.

Rising Distribution Days
Shows selling pressure is mounting.
Be ready to take defensive action.

Volume heavier than prior day

Volume (00)
8,000,000
5,000,000
3,000,000
1,800,000

1400
1350
1300

10 24 9 23 6 20 4 18
March April May

© 2013 Investor's Business Daily, Inc.

Protect your money: Take defensive action when distribution days start to mount.

We'll see how to handle that type of weakening market in Chapter 5, "Selling Checklist."

Feeling a Little Overwhelmed?

I don't blame you—it's a lot to take in! But don't forget: You don't have to track all of this on your own. Just check the *Market Pulse* to instantly see which way the market is currently headed.

5 Things You Need to Know About Market Cycles

1. Your Goal is to Make Money When the Market is in an Uptrend—and Protect Those Profits as a Downtrend Begins

I mentioned earlier how I learned this lesson the hard way. Like millions of other investors, I made a lot of money in the bull market of the mid- to late-1990s, but gave back much of those gains when the dot-com boom ended in 2000.

Even back then, I *knew* the stock market was "cyclical," but I didn't understand what impact those cycles have on *my* portfolio. I didn't know:

- How to tell when the market trend is changing?
- What action to take when that change occurs?

Most folks don't. And that's not surprising since we're constantly told that (a) you can't time the market, and (b) "buy and hold" is the "safe" approach. *Those market myths have cost a lot of people a lot of money.*

But now you see how the market *actually* works. "Buy and hold" investors may make money in a strong market uptrend, but they'll likely give it all back (and then some!) when a sharp downturn hits.

By using the buying and selling checklists in this book, you can unstrap yourself from that market roller coaster. Sticking to basic rules will help you generate solid profits when the market is up and lock in the bulk of those gains when the trend changes.

2. Know Where You're at in the Market Cycle

We all know a "bull market" is when the market is moving higher, and a "bear market" means it's trending down.

But it's important to understand that even within a bull market, you will have what we call "interim corrections." The major indexes will take a rest and pull back for a few weeks or a couple of months, then resume their climb. The depth of these interim corrections varies, but the Nasdaq or S&P 500 might pull back somewhere around 10% to 15%. That's a fairly mild decline—not enough to change the underlying bull market uptrend.

As a general rule, a decline of *under 20%* indicates an interim correction. A drop of *20% or more* constitutes a bear market.

The following figure shows an example of how that works.

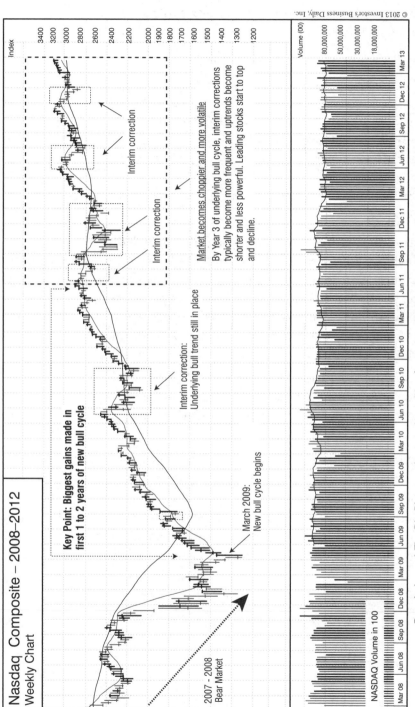

Nasdaq Composite – 2008–2012
Weekly Chart

Key Point: Biggest gains made in
first 1 to 2 years of new bull cycle

Index

3400
3200
3000
2800
2600
2400
2200
2000
1900
1800
1700
1600
1500
1400
1300
1200

Interim correction

Interim correction

Interim correction

Market becomes choppier and more volatile

By Year 3 of underlying bull cycle, interim corrections
typically become more frequent and uptrends become
shorter and less powerful. Leading stocks start to top
and decline.

Interim correction:
Underlying bull trend still in place

March 2009:
New bull cycle begins

2007 - 2008
Bear Market

Volume (00)

80,000,000
50,000,000
30,000,000
18,000,000

NASDAQ Volume in 100

Mar 08 Jun 08 Sep 08 Dec 08 Mar 09 Jun 09 Sep 09 Dec 09 Mar 10 Jun 10 Sep 10 Dec 10 Mar 11 Jun 11 Sep 11 Dec 11 Mar 12 Jun 12 Sep 12 Dec 12 Mar 13

Regularly read *The Big Picture* column to know if we're in the early or later stages of the current market cycle.

How Long Do Bull and Bear Markets Typically Last?

The length varies, but here are some *general* guidelines:

- Bull markets typically last 2 to 4 years.
- Bear markets typically last 8 to 9 months.

Why Should You Pay Attention to What "Stage" the Bull Market Cycle Is In?

Because the really big gains typically happen within the first two years of a bull market.

By the time you get into the third year of a bull cycle, two things tend to happen:

- **The market becomes more choppy and volatile.** That's a sign the bull is getting tired, and the enthusiasm found at the beginning of the cycle is starting to fade. Interim corrections may become more frequent and deep. But as long as the bull market uptrend remains in place, you may still find plenty of money-making opportunities. Just stay on your toes and stick to the buying and selling checklists since you know a bear market *will* emerge at some point.

- **Leading stocks start to peak and roll over.** As they say, nothing goes up forever. In the later stages of a bull market, institutional investors will start to cash out of the big leaders—and when they start to sell, those stocks start to drop.

When that happens, it doesn't matter how great the company's earnings growth and products may be, it's time for *you* to protect your hard-earned profits. Whether it's Apple, Google, Netflix, Chipotle Mexican Grill, or any other leading stock in any bull market, at some point you'll need to lock in your gains—and that becomes particularly important when a bear market begins to take hold. (More on that in Chapter 5, "Selling Checklist.")

Find Out What Stage the Market is in with *The Big Picture*

 If you regularly read *The Big Picture* column, you'll always have a good sense of where we're at in the current market cycle—and what steps you should take to handle it.

3. Always Stay Engaged—Even in a Down Market

One of the biggest mistakes you can make is to stop doing your routine and ignore the market just because it's currently in a correction.

Even in a severe market downtrend, we're never more than four days away from the start of a potential new rally. That's all it takes for a follow-through day to occur and switch the *Market Pulse* outlook from "Market in correction" to "Confirmed uptrend."

And as you'll see in #5 below, if you don't keep your watch list up to date while the market is down, there's a good chance you'll miss the biggest money-making opportunities in the next uptrend.

Think of a downtrend like the off-season in baseball. You're not buying stocks right now, but if you want to have stellar results when a new "season" begins, you need to stick to your training regimen in the off-season. You never want to be out of shape on "Opening Day" when that new uptrend begins.

4. Look for *New* Leaders in a New Bull Market

In every bull market cycle, a new group of top-rated CAN SLIM stocks emerges to lead the market higher. They'll often double or triple in price in just 1 to 2 years. Some will go up even more.

They'll be the innovative leaders in whatever new inventions or industries are driving that particular bull market. In the 1990s, it was the Internet revolution and the rise of cell phones and personal computers that propelled the market higher. No surprise, then, that it was the companies driving those innovations—AOL, Qualcomm, Yahoo!, Amazon, Cisco, and others—that became the big market winners.

But here are two *other* things you need to know about leading stocks:

- When leaders eventually peak and begin to decline, they drop 72% on average.

- Only about 1 in 8 stocks that led in the prior bull market go on to lead again in the next one.

We'll get into that in more detail in Chapter 5, "Selling Checklist," but here's the point: **When a new bull market begins, don't stay focused on *past* winners. Look for *new* leaders**.

That's how you capture big gains—and you can find the *next* crop of winning stocks by regularly doing the Simple Weekend Routine, *especially* when the market is still in a correction.

5. The Big Money is Made in the *Early* Stages of a New Uptrend

Think of a market correction like a forest fire. It ain't pretty, but it's a necessary part of the cycle.

The forest fire burns down the old trees to make room for new growth. And the heat of the fire pops open the seeds so new trees can take root.

Same with the market. During a correction, most of the past leaders fall and a new crop of CAN SLIM innovators—the new growth—emerges.

But just as a new tree can't grow while the fire is still burning, a new leading stock can't shoot higher while the market is still in a correction.

However, as soon as that market "fire" dies down and a new uptrend begins, the next crop of leaders take off. In fact, you'll find that:

Winning stocks often launch their big moves *right* on or immediately after a follow-through day.

This happens at the start of every strong new uptrend. Below are examples of how the top stocks took off right when follow-through days occurred in 2003, 2010 and 2011. As you look at the charts, note how these new leaders started their runs within days or just a couple of weeks after the *Market Pulse* shifted from "Market in correction" to "Confirmed uptrend."

Also keep this in mind: You'll typically find such stocks highlighted in the *IBD 50* and/or *Your Weekly Review* before they launch these big moves. By using the Simple Weekend Routine, you can have such stocks on your watch list as they start those big price runs.

How Top Stocks Launch New Runs Right
When a New Market Uptrend Begins

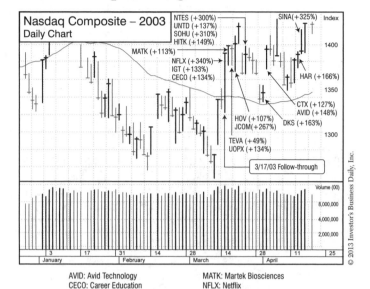

AVID: Avid Technology
CECO: Career Education
CTX: Centex
DKS: Dick's Sporting Goods
HAR: Harmon Int'l Industries
HITK: Hi-Tech Pharmacal
HOV: Hovnanian Enterprises
IGT: International Game Technology
JCOM: J2 Global

MATK: Martek Biosciences
NFLX: Netflix
NTES: Netease
SINA: Sina
SOHU: Sohu.com
TEVA: Teva Pharmaceutical
UNTD: United Online
UOPX: University of Phoenix

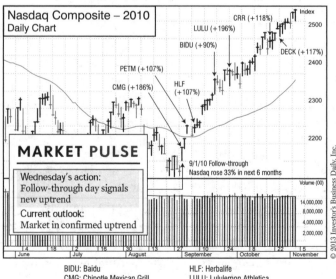

BIDU: Baidu
CMG: Chipotle Mexican Grill
CRR: Carbo Ceramics
DECK: Deckers Outdoor

HLF: Herbalife
LULU: Lululemon Athletica
PETM: Petsmart

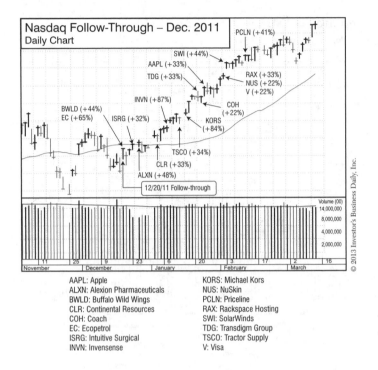

Nasdaq Follow-Through – Dec. 2011
Daily Chart

PCLN (+41%)
SWI (+44%)
AAPL (+33%)
TDG (+33%)
RAX (+33%)
NUS (+22%)
V (+22%)
INVN (+87%)
COH (+22%)
BWLD (+44%)
EC (+65%)
ISRG (+32%)
KORS (+84%)
TSCO (+34%)
CLR (+33%)
ALXN (+48%)
12/20/11 Follow-through

Volume (00)
14,000,000
8,000,000
4,000,000
2,000,000

11 25 9 23 6 20 3 17 2 16
November December January February March

© 2013 Investor's Business Daily, Inc.

AAPL: Apple
ALXN: Alexion Pharmaceuticals
BWLD: Buffalo Wild Wings
CLR: Continental Resources
COH: Coach
EC: Ecopetrol
ISRG: Intuitive Surgical
INVN: Invensense

KORS: Michael Kors
NUS: NuSkin
PCLN: Priceline
RAX: Rackspace Hosting
SWI: SolarWinds
TDG: Transdigm Group
TSCO: Tractor Supply
V: Visa

See how all the market cycle pieces fit together?

- Make money in an uptrend—and protect your profits as a downtrend begins.

- Focus on "new growth"—not *past* leaders.

- Keep doing your routine and building your watch list *during* the downtrend.

- If you *don't* stay engaged while the market is down, you'll likely miss the *next* crop of big winners that shoot higher right when a new uptrend begins.

I hope this makes clear why you definitely need to understand how market cycles work—and how easy it is to stay in sync with those trends. Just check the *Market Pulse* and read *The Big Picture* regularly.

And as you'll see when we get into the Simple Weekend Routine, you can also spot the next group of potential winners by regularly checking the *IBD 50, Your Weekly Review*, and other lists that highlight today's CAN SLIM stocks.

The Trend Is Your Friend

It's an old cliché, but it's stuck around all these years for a reason: It's true!

You *will* build a solid foundation for making money in stocks if you simply buy when the market is trending up, and protect yourself when it starts trending down.

Everything flows from understanding market cycles and the current market direction.

In a strong uptrend, the top-rated CAN SLIM stocks will give you multiple opportunities to make significant profits. By following the rest of the Buying Checklist and the Simple Weekend Routine, you can have them on your watch list, ready to act when those opportunities arise.

Next up: Let's see what specific traits to look for as you search for the next big winners.

• ACTION STEPS •

Here are some quick *To Do*s to learn more about how market cycles work—and see which way the market is trending right now. To take these steps, visit www.investors.com/GettingStartedBook.

1. Read *The Big Picture* column in IBD or on Investors.com.

- Is the market currently in an uptrend—or correction?
- What else does it say about current market conditions and the action of leading stocks?

2. Watch the latest *Market Wrap* video under the *IBD TV* tab on Investors.com.

Big Rock #2: Focus on Companies with Big Earnings Growth and a New, Innovative Product or Service

Big, Accelerating Earnings Growth is the #1 Factor in Choosing a Stock

It's the primary trait that attracts fund managers and other institutional investors—the big players that provide the needed fuel for a stock's big run.

And what drives that explosive earnings growth? It's usually a game-changing product or service, new management, a major new industry trend—or some combination of all of the above.

Just think back to some of the biggest winners over the last 100+ years.

IBM: In the 1920s, IBM's high-tech punch card machines were revolutionizing how large organizations kept records. Starting in 1926, IBM soared 1,992% in 168 weeks.

Brunswick: Bowling was extremely popular in the 1950s, and Brunswick came out with a game-changing product: Automatic pin-spotters for bowling alleys. Earnings soared and the stock shot up 1,500% in 162 weeks.

Home Depot: The new "big-box store" would forever change the hardware and do-it-yourself industries. In 1982, the stock bolted 892% in 64 weeks.

AOL: In the early 1990s, cyberspace was the realm of tech-savvy geeks. Then AOL created a fun and easy way for *everyone* to go online. Starting in 1994, the stock rose 570% in just 75 weeks.

Crocs: In 2006, what caused this shoemaker's stock to soar 431% in only 59 weeks? The unmistakable "Crocs craze" created by its unique—and seemingly ubiquitous—new line of casual footwear made of a proprietary resin.

And that doesn't even mention major moves by Google, Apple, Priceline, Netflix, Baidu, F5 Networks, Intuitive Surgical, cloud computing leaders Rackspace Hosting and SolarWinds, or 3D printing innovators 3D Systems and Stratasys, just to name a few.

What did they all have in common as they made their big moves? Big earnings growth driven by a hot new product or industry trend.

Not every stock you buy will be one of these big winners, but a new crop of innovators does emerge in every new bull market cycle. They're the true market leaders that have the potential to go up 100%, 300%, 500%, or more. And since they share the same CAN SLIM® traits, you'll find them highlighted in features like the *IBD 50*, *Sector Leaders*, and *Your Weekly Review*.

Think what catching just one or two of these stocks in the *next* big uptrend could do for your portfolio.

Let's see how you can make that happen using the Buying Checklist.

Buying Checklist

Big Rock #2: Focus on companies with big earnings growth and a new, innovative product or service.

❏ Composite Rating of 90 or higher

❏ EPS Rating of 80 or higher

❏ EPS growth 25% or higher in recent quarters

❏ Accelerating earnings growth

❏ Average Annual EPS growth 25% or more over last 3 years

❏ Sales growth 25% or higher in most recent quarter

❏ Return on equity (ROE) of 17% or higher

❏ SMR® Rating (Sales + Margins + Return on Equity) of A or B

❏ New products, service, or management

❏ Among the top-rated stocks in its industry group

❏ Ranked in top 40–50 of IBD's 197 industry groups

IBD *SmartSelect*® Ratings

A big part of the Buying Checklist is making sure your stock gets passing grades for IBD *SmartSelect* Ratings, which show how strongly a company fits the CAN SLIM profile. You'll find these unique ratings in *Stock Checkup* on Investors.com and in the *IBD Smart NYSE + NASDAQ Tables* (Chapter 7) in the *Making Money* section of Investor's Business Daily.

It's All Relative

With the exception of the Accumulation/Distribution Rating, each rating is *relative*. In other words, they show how your stock compares to *all other* stocks on the market.

That's a huge advantage, instantly separating the leaders from the laggards.

For example, the Earnings-Per-Share (EPS) Rating goes from 1 (worst) to 99 (best). A 95 rating instantly tells you the company is outperforming 95% of all other stocks in terms of *both* current and annual earnings growth. A 99 Composite Rating means the company's overall strength puts it in the top 1% of *all* stocks.

Think how easy that is—and how much time it saves.

For example, we saw that big earnings growth is the #1 factor to look for in a stock. With one glance at the EPS Rating, you know how your stock's earnings growth stacks up against every other company on the market.

As we go through the checklist, you'll see what each rating measures and the minimum grades to look for. While you never want to buy a stock just because it has a high rating, these grades save you a tremendous amount of time by identifying stocks that do—and don't—have the CAN SLIM traits.

Unless otherwise noted below, ratings range from 1 (worst) to 99 (best).

Overall Strength

 *Composite Rating of 90 or higher*

The Composite Rating combines all the IBD *SmartSelect* Ratings into one, with more weight on the EPS and Relative Strength (RS) Ratings.

A rating of 90 or higher tells you that, in terms of overall fundamental and technical strength, the stock is outperforming 90% of all other stocks.

A rating of 90 is the minimum. You'll find the true market leaders have a Composite Rating north of 95 and often have the highest-possible score of 99.

Earnings Growth

☑ *EPS Rating of 80 or higher*

We saw earlier that you need to look at *Current* quarterly earnings growth (the "C" in CAN SLIM) and *Annual* earnings growth (the "A"). The EPS Rating measures *both*.

An EPS Rating of 80 tells you the company's earnings-per-share growth is in the top 20% of all stocks. You'll find the biggest winners often have a 95 or higher EPS Rating *prior* to launching a major move.

☑ *EPS growth 25% or more in recent quarters*

As a *minimum*, you want to see earnings-per-share growth of 25% or higher in recent quarters. But you'll often find top performers have even more impressive numbers prior to launching their big moves.

For example, in the two quarters *before* Google shot up 558% in just over three years starting in 2004, it posted EPS growth of 155% and 143%. And in 2006, shoe maker Crocs also showed two quarters of explosive earnings growth—122% and 330%—*before* its share price skyrocketed 431% in just over a year.

☑ *Accelerating earnings growth*

Ideally, EPS growth should be big *and* accelerating (i.e., increasing quarter over quarter). That shows the company is continuing to grow its profits.

It's a warning sign if a stock's EPS growth rate starts to *decelerate* and move in the wrong direction. The stock market is forward looking, and institutional investors are looking for increasing—not declining—growth.

Case in point: As we saw in the earlier CAN SLIM case study, in the three quarters *before* Ulta Beauty surged 165% from September 2010 to July 2011, its EPS growth accelerated from 56% to 62% to 188%.

☑ *Average Annual EPS growth of 25% or more over last 3 years*

A company can cut costs or take other measures to drive up its earnings per share for a quarter or two. That can mask more serious underlying problems the company may be facing in terms of demand for its products, declining profit margins, or negative industry trends.

That's why you also want to make sure the company is delivering solid *annual* EPS growth.

Here again, 25% annual growth over the last three years is the minimum. The top stocks often post numbers that dwarf that. Going back to Google in 2004, its three-year annual EPS growth rate was 293% *before* it launched its five-fold gain.

Sales Growth and Return on Equity
Does your stock have the key ingredients that drive earnings growth?

Since big, accelerating earnings growth is the #1 factor to look for, make sure the company has the basic ingredients that *generate* that type of earnings performance: **Superior sales, a high return on equity, and industry-leading profit margins.**

Sales growth shows how much demand there is for the company's products or services. Profit margins and return on equity gauge how efficiently the company is generating that sales revenue. All three factors ultimately impact a company's earnings growth.

   SMR Rating of A or B
   *SMR Rating: **S**ales, Profit **M**argins and **R**eturn on Equity*

The quickest way to see if a stock has the ingredients that drive earnings is to check the SMR Rating. It measures a company's **S**ales growth, profit **M**argins (both pre-tax and after-tax) and **R**eturn on equity. Then it compares that to the performance of all other stocks and assigns a rating from A (best) to E (worst).

An A rating means that, in terms of sales, margins and return on equity, the company is in the top 20% of all stocks.

Keep in mind, too, that the SMR Rating is a more accurate gauge than if you looked at these three factors in isolation. For example, a company could have rising sales growth but shrinking profit margins—which could have a negative impact on EPS growth down the road. By looking at the more comprehensive SMR Rating, you get the full picture.

If a stock has good earnings growth but weak sales, profit margins, and ROE, beware! That EPS growth may be less impressive—and less sustainable—than it appears.

In general, you want to buy stocks with an A or B SMR Rating and avoid those with a D or E. The next table shows why that's important.

SMR Ratings of Leaders in Q1 2012 Uptrend

These stocks broke out during a 4-month uptrend that began December 20, 2011.
Ratings are from the day of each stock's breakout.

Company	SMR Rating at *Start* of Run	Subsequent % Gain
InvenSense	A	87% in 11 weeks
Michael Kors	A	84% in 8 weeks
Monster Beverage	A	60% in 22 weeks
Sturm Ruger	A	58% in 18 weeks
Tractor Supply	A	34% in 15 weeks

☑ *Sales growth 25% or higher in most recent quarter*

If sales growth is less than 25%, it should at least be *accelerating* over the last three quarters.

For example, look at Netflix's sales growth just before it rocketed 683% from March 2009 to July 2011. It was under the 25% growth you prefer but was *accelerating*.

Netflix's Accelerating Sales Growth *Before* Launching 683% Run

Quarter	Sales Growth
Jun-08	11%
Sep-08	16%
Dec-08	19%

Ideally, you'd see three quarters of acceleration in both sales *and* earnings.

☑ *Return on equity (ROE) of 17% or higher*

Return on Equity separates the best-run companies from the also-rans.

I have to say, in my countless conversations with investors over the years, return on equity is one of the most overlooked factors. (IBD calculates ROE by dividing net income by average shareholder equity over the last two years.) But it's a critical clue to look for when picking a stock: *A strong return on equity identifies the best-run companies making the most efficient use of their capital.* Ultimately, that leads to higher profitability and earnings growth.

A 17% return on equity is the minimum benchmark, but stocks that go on to make monster moves often sport an ROE of 25%, 35% or more. The bigger, the better. The following table shows why that's true.

ROE of Leaders in 2009–2012 Bull Cycle

Company Name	ROE at Start of Big Run	Year Run Started	Subsequent % Gain
Green Mountain Coffee Roasters	21%	2009	1,104% in 30 months
Apple	27%	2009	381% in 38 months
Lululemon Athletica	30%	2010	196% in 10 months
Priceline.com	42%	2010	182% in 21 months
Herbalife	69%	2010	173% in 21 months
Chipotle Mexican Grill	19%	2010	186% in 20 months
SolarWinds	43%	2011	137% in 11 months

 New products, service or management

"Out with the old, in with the new." That could be the official mantra for the stock market, which is always looking ahead in search of companies with new, paradigm-shifting products and services.

Such leaders emerge in every bull market cycle, and here are some quick ways to see if your stock has the "N" in CAN SLIM:

- Check the company's website and press releases.

- Read IBD stories about the stock on Investors.com. Pay special attention to *The New America* section (Chapter 7), which profiles innovative companies every day.

- Learn what companies featured in IBD lists actually do. Pay particular attention to stocks highlighted in the *IBD 50* and *Sector Leaders* lists.

As we saw in the earlier CAN SLIM case study, Apple is an example of an established company that rejuvenated itself—and its stock—with new, innovative products.

More often, you'll find groundbreaking innovations in younger, entrepreneurial companies—often those that had their initial public offering (IPO) within the last 15 years, many within the last 7 to 8 years.

In every major uptrend, these game-changers emerge to lead the market's advance, driven by some product or service that's revolutionizing how we work or live.

You may have never even heard of these companies at that point. But as you search for stocks with CAN SLIM traits, they'll naturally start to appear on your radar screen.

I had never heard of Alexion Pharmaceuticals, F5 Networks, Stratasys, Lululemon Athletica, SolarWinds, Mellanox Technologies, Transdigm, or Tractor Supply until they started showing up in IBD's stock lists. But they all had something new, and that was driving exceptional earnings and sales growth. That's why they showed up early on our screens—and that's why they all made impressive price gains during the bull market that began in 2009.

Don't Ignore a Stock Just Because You've Never Heard of the Company

If it has the "N" and other CAN SLIM traits, get to know more about it: Go to their website, and read articles and profiles in IBD and other sources. You might be looking at a stock that could double or triple in price.

In 2009, not many Americans had heard of Baidu. I'm sure many still haven't.

Called the "Chinese Google," Baidu emerged as the dominant search engine in China as millions of new Internet users came online. It was a strong new leader in a new and rapidly growing industry and rose 322% from September 2009 to April 2011. (Using the Simple Weekend Routine, you could have seen Baidu highlighted in the *IBD 50*, *Your Weekly Review* and other IBD features *multiple* times as it made that big move.)

New Industry Trend

The "N" in CAN SLIM can also refer to a new industry trend, which can be a boon for companies in that field, especially for the innovators driving that change.

The emergence of cloud computing is a good example. There's been a major shift away from running applications and storing data on a local computer, and instead pushing that functionality to the online "cloud." That's meant big business—and nice share price gains—for leaders in that industry, such as Rackspace Hosting, SolarWinds, and Amazon.

That's just one example. The company names and industry trends are always changing. So regardless of what the latest technology or innovations are when you're reading this, here's the key question to ask: *Is the stock you're reviewing benefiting from a significant new industry trend, and is it one of the companies leading that change?*

New Price High

Here's another "new" thing you should know about the best stocks: They usually start their big moves as they hit or close in on a new price high (i.e., the highest share price the stock has hit over the last 52 weeks).

We'll talk more about that when we get into charts in Chapter 6, "Don't Invest *Blindly*," but just keep this in mind: **Stocks hitting new *lows* tend to go *lower*. Stocks hitting new *highs* tend to go *higher*.**

Translation: Don't go "bargain" hunting for beaten down stocks—chances are they'll go even lower. Instead, focus on stocks showing *strength* as they move *upward* to new price highs.

New Does Not Mean Unproven

You're not looking for companies making *promises* of a revolutionary new product or service. Those may pan out, they may not.

You're looking for companies with new products *already* on the market showing strong demand. That demand is reflected in the company's fundamentals we noted earlier: Rising sales revenue, high profit margins, and accelerating earnings growth.

Whether it's a young company making its initial public offering (IPO) or an established outfit with a new product, make it prove itself by showing CAN SLIM traits *before* you buy.

The Facebook Fiasco

Look at what happened to Facebook when it debuted in 2012. It was a new IPO in a new and growing industry—social media. And it was the dominant player in that space. So it got high marks for "new" but did not pass the rest of the Buying Checklist.

Remember how we saw that big, accelerating earnings growth is the #1 factor to look for—and that you want to see particularly strong EPS growth over the last three quarters?

Facebook showed the exact *opposite*. Just prior to its IPO, it posted three consecutive quarters of *decelerating* earnings, dropping from 83% to 17% to 9%. Sales growth was also trending down.

Facebook's Earnings and Sales Growth at Time of 2012 IPO

Quarter	Earnings	Sales
Sep-11	100%	104%
Dec-11	25%	55%
Mar-12	9%	45%

So despite all the buzz and pre-IPO hype, you could have looked objectively at Facebook and seen the bottom-line facts: Sales and earnings were *both* heading in the wrong direction. And what happened next? From its May debut through August, the stock dropped 50%.

Down the road, Facebook may have all the pieces of the puzzle in place, but if you had used this Buying Checklist, you would have clearly seen that—even prior to the IPO—the stock did not earn a passing grade. And in the company's first two reports after going public, Facebook reported 0% earnings growth.

Remember: Never buy a stock just because someone recommends it or because with all the buzz, you're "sure" it will go up. Instead, pick stocks based on *rules*: Make every stock prove itself by passing the Buying Checklist.

 Among the top-rated stocks in its industry group

Here's a simple rule of thumb for successful investing: **Focus on the top-rated stocks in the top-ranked industry groups.** This part of the checklist shows if your stock fits that bill.

Stock Checkup shows the Top 5 stocks in each industry group based on IBD *SmartSelect* Ratings. In general, you want to focus on the #1 or #2 stock in the group in terms of Composite Rating.

Keep in mind: "Top-rated" does not necessarily mean "best-known."

Here's an extreme example: Everyone knows mortgage giant Fannie Mae, but its stock completely collapsed during the 2008 housing crisis, and by August 2012, it had already been delisted from the Nasdaq and was trading around 25 cents a share. Yet its industry group was ranked #1 out of the 197 groups IBD tracks.

So what was the "top-rated" stock in Fannie Mae's Finance–Mortgage & Related Services group?

The lesser-known—but much more profitable—Nationstar Mortgage Holdings. It certainly wasn't a household name like Fannie Mae, but it had explosive earnings growth of 600% and 999% in the two quarters since going public in March 2012. And from May to August 2012, Nationstar's stock jumped 88% in just 14 weeks.

Is Your Stock a Leader Within its Industry Group?

Nationstar Mortgage vs. Fannie Mae

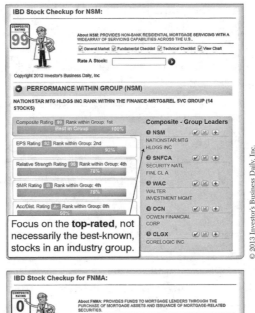

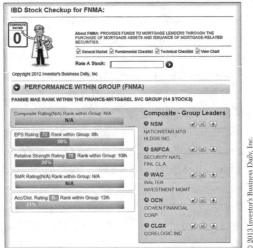

Nationstar Mortgage's "Best in Group" ranking and 99 Composite Rating showed it was the true industry group leader.

☑ *Ranked in top 40–50 of IBD's 197 industry groups*

As IBD founder Bill O'Neil has said, "You cannot overstate the importance of being aware of new group movements."

Almost half of a stock's price move depends on the strength of its industry group and sector:

Sector	=	12%
Industry group	=	37%
Total	=	49%

That means your stock has a better chance of moving up if its *industry* shows strength. Here's why.

As we'll see in detail later, it's the buying and selling power of institutional investors that ultimately pushes the general market and individual stocks up or down.

So when they shift their money into a certain sector or industry group, that sector or group will move up in the rankings. You want to follow their lead and put your money into the same industries. (And on the flip side, when a sector or industry group starts to *sink* in the rankings, beware! Get ready to take defensive action since the stocks within that industry will likely decline as big investors sell their shares and move that money somewhere else.)

How to Track Sectors → Industry Groups → Group Leaders

You can see where institutional investors are putting their money by regularly checking IBD's rankings for 33 sectors and 197 industry groups. Then, as we saw earlier, you can see which particular companies are the leaders within each group by checking the five top-rated stocks in *Stock Checkup*. The following graph outlines how that works.

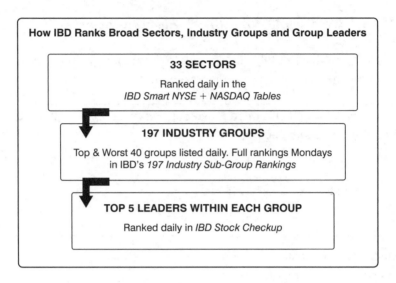

How IBD Ranks Broad Sectors, Industry Groups and Group Leaders

33 SECTORS

Ranked daily in the
IBD Smart NYSE + NASDAQ Tables

197 INDUSTRY GROUPS

Top & Worst 40 groups listed daily. Full rankings Mondays
in IBD's *197 Industry Sub-Group Rankings*

TOP 5 LEADERS WITHIN EACH GROUP

Ranked daily in *IBD Stock Checkup*

We start with sectors, dividing all stocks into broad categories like Retail, Building, Computers, Energy and Medical. Those 33 sectors are then ranked daily based on the price performance of the stocks within each sector.

That's an important first step, but it doesn't tell you the whole story. To more clearly pinpoint where institutional investors are putting their money, check the industry group rankings.

IBD's 197 industry groups break down the broad sectors into smaller factions made up of stocks that are closely aligned in terms of the specific business they're in.

This is crucial because, for example, Retail may be the #1 sector, but which specific groups are leading that growth? Which groups are lagging?

There are 18 different industry groups within the Retail sector, including Consumer Electronics, Discount & Variety, Internet, Leisure Products, and Restaurants. You want to know which ones are showing the most strength and moving up in the rankings—because you want to see where institutional investors are putting their money.

Rise of the Discounters

Here's just one example of why checking industry group rankings is an important part of your stock-picking process . . .

In February and March 2010, the Retail sector was consistently among the top five sectors. Within that sector, the Retail–Discount & Variety industry group was moving sharply higher in the rankings: In mid-March, the group was ranked #25 out of the 197 groups, up from #176 seven months earlier.

Remember: At that time, the economy was struggling. People on tight budgets do more shopping at discount stores, and that's why institutional investors began shifting their money into stocks in the Discount & Variety industry group.

So it's no coincidence that around the same time, top-rated stocks within that group started impressive runs: Those moves were being fueled by the institutional money moving into that industry.

Dollar General   124% gain in 29 months

Dollar Tree   225% gain in 30 months

By checking the rankings, you would have seen that another group in the Retail sector, Retail–Apparel/Shoes/Accessories, had also been moving up rapidly. As of February 24, 2010, the group had jumped from #117 to #19 over the last seven months.

Two leaders in that group also happened to be discount retailers: Ross Stores and TJX Companies, which owns T. J. Maxx and Marshalls. That further confirmed the big institutional money was flowing into operators of bargain stores. Both TJX and Ross broke out within a week and generated solid gains for investors over the next two years:

Ross Stores   176% gain in 29 months

TJX Companies   125% gain in 30 months

Coincidence? Not at all. Year after year, countless examples reinforce this simple strategy: **Focus on the top-rated stocks in the top-ranked industry groups.**

Why put yourself at a disadvantage by buying low-rated stocks in a low-ranked group?

Where to Find Industry Group Rankings

You can see the current ranking for your stock's group in *Stock Checkup*.

Pay particular attention to stocks in the top 40 groups, and avoid those in the bottom 40.

You'll find the top 40 and worst 40 groups each day in the print and digital editions of IBD. The full list of *IBD's 197 Industry Sub-Group Rankings* is published every Monday. (Note: "Sub-group" and "group" are used interchangeably.)

Rank				Group		Days	Rank				Group		Days
	3	6				%		3	6				%
This Wk	Wks Ago	Wks Ago	Industry Name	Composite Rating	YTD % Chg.	Chg	This Wk	Wks Ago	Wks Ago	Industry Name	Composite Rating	YTD % Chg.	Chg
			Top 40 Groups (6 mos.)							**Worst 40 Groups (6 mos.)**			
			Day's best bolded, worst underlined. Full Group List in Monday's issue.										
1	1	88	Energy Solar	..	+4.1	–2.8	158	159	51	CmpSftwr–Spc–Entr	66	+2.9	–5.3
2	8	18	Media–Radio/Tv	..	+31.6	+0.5	159	151		Cosmetics/PersnlCre	64	+7.1	+0.4
3	28	48	Medcal–Hospitals	90	+15.5	–1.7	160						–0.3
4	2	2	Mchnry–MtlHdlg	89	+7.9	+1.1	161			**Is the group moving up or down?**			+0.7
5	67	65	Leisure–Mvies&Rel	90	+19.3	+0.8	162			See where the group ranked 3 and			–0.5
6	3	1	Fin–Mrtg&RelSvc	90	+4.2	–0.1	163			6 weeks ago.			+1.9
7	4	3	**Bldg–Cment/Cncrt**	87	+9.8	+2.0	164						–0.9
8	19	9	Bldg–Rsidnt/Comml	90	+12.4	+1.3	165	161	142	Utility–WaterSupply	67	+4.1	+1.1
9	10	4	Bldg–CnstrPrds/Msc	86	+8.7	+0.9	166	185	163	Retail–Spr/MiniMkts	61	+6.3	+0.4
10	9	15	CommlSvcs–Stffng	90	+7.7	–0.2	167	166	161	Banks–Midwest	51	+4.5	+0.5
11	17	17	**MetalPrds–Distribtr**	..	+7.6	+1.8	168	181	193	ComptrSftwr–Mdcl	78	+11.5	+0.1
12	5	16	Mchinry–Cnstr/Mng	78	+7.9	+0.3	169	167	166	Financ–PblInvFdeqt	..	+6.9	+0.2
13	54	37	RtailWhlsleOffcSup	..	+12.5	+0.4	170	160	168	Leisre–TrvlBking	..	+11.9	–0.5
14	12	8	CommlSvcs–Leasing	91	+9.5	+0.1	171	158	115	Retail–DprtmntStrs	..	+2.2	+1.3
15	7	5	Chemicals–Plastics	88	+6.7	–0.9	172	176	160	Soap&ClngPreparat	..	+4.7	+0.7
16	27	14	**Oil&Gas–Rfing/Mkt**	78	+12.7	+2.3	173	168	134	EnergyCoal	36	+5.2	+0.7
17	6	6	Auto/Trck–RplcPrts	..	+4.9	–1.1	174	193	179	Retail/Wsl–AutoPrt	..	+3.8	–1.2
18	21	30	Fin–InvestBnk/Bkrs	87	+10.5	+0.8	175	179	152	Food–Confectionary	..	+8.0	+0.3
19	24	87	Trnsprttin–Airlne	91	+8.2	0.0	176	172	158	Medical–GenercDrgs	61	+0.6	–0.1
20	11	26	Banks–MoneyCntr	83	+6.2	+0.8	177	186	175	Retail–Specialty	73	+2.6	–0.4

© 2013 Investor's Business Daily, Inc.

You can also see if the group's ranking has been moving up or down. The list shows current ranking and where the group stood 3 and 6 weeks ago.

3 Key Points

We've gone through a lot of details, so let's take step back for a minute and look at the 3 main takeaways from this chapter:

- Focus on companies with big earnings growth and a game-changing new product or service.

- Fish where the fish are: Look for the top-rated stocks in the top-ranked industry groups.

- Use *Stock Checkup* to quickly see if your stock passes or fails this part of the checklist.

Check out the Action Steps below to start using the Buying Checklist and make sure these key points really sink in.

And remember: You can find today's top-rated CAN SLIM stocks by doing the Simple Weekend Routine (Chapter 4).

Next up: Let's see if institutional investors are heavily buying—or selling—your stock.

• ACTION STEPS •

Here are some quick *To Dos* to reinforce the stock-picking skills we've learned so far. To take these steps and start using the Buying Checklist, visit www.investors.com/GettingStartedBook.

1. See how to go through the checklist with a short video: *Does Your Stock Pass or Fail? Find Out with Stock Checkup.*

2. Check IBD's industry group rankings to see which groups are in the Top 40 right now.

   • Rankings are found in the *Making Money* section of Investor's Business Daily each day.

3. Find out what's "new" and innovative about today's *Sector Leaders*.

   • See which stocks are on the *Sector Leaders* list (Chapter 7) in the *Making Money* section of IBD, then read IBD articles about them.

   • Read the *Smart Table Review* column, which covers the latest action of the sector leaders. You'll find it on Investors.com and in the *Making Money* section of IBD.

Big Rock #3: Buy Stocks Being Heavily Bought by Institutional Investors. Avoid Those They're Heavily Selling.

For a stock to go up 50%, 100% or more, *someone* has to keep buying shares at a continually higher price to fuel that move. And they have to buy a *lot* of shares—hundreds of thousands, even millions. Only *institutional* investors— primarily mutual fund managers—have that kind of buying power.

So if you want to find stocks with the potential to double or triple in price, focus on those being bought heavily by these professional investors. It's not a guarantee of success, but *without* that fuel, a stock won't be able to make a sustained upward move.

And when those same institutional investors start to sell, look out! That high-volume selling pressure will likely push the share price sharply lower. Fighting that deluge is like trying to swim up a waterfall. You're essentially guaranteed to get pummeled. So move to the sidelines and wait for big investors to start buying the stock again. You'll find it's much easier to swim *with* the current than *against* it. (More on that in Chapter 5, "Selling Checklist," and Chapter 6, "Don't Invest *Blindly*.")

Yes, You *Can* See What Big Investors Are Up To

In some ways, the massive buying power of institutional investors gives them an advantage. But there is a downside for them—and an upside for you and me: *They're too big to hide what they're doing.*

The best way to literally *see* what they're up to is to use stock charts. If you've never used charts before, I think you'll be amazed at the "behind-the-scenes stories" they reveal—how they lift the curtain to show you if fund managers are heavily buying or selling a stock, or if they're just sitting tight and quietly scooping up a few more shares.

I personally find it fascinating that a few simple lines on a graph can tell you so much about what's really going on. But they can—and you'll find that once you know what to look for, it's really not that hard to do. In fact, in many cases, you'll find the story is actually hard to *miss*. You'll see telltale patterns stocks form just before they launch a big move and early warning signs that tell you it may be time to lock in your gains.

We'll get into charts and what they reveal about the trading of institutional investors in Chapter 6, "Don't Invest *Blindly*." (Feel free to jump ahead to that if you're curious.)

For now, let's focus on some other quick ways you can see what the all-important fund managers and other institutions are up to.

Buying Checklist

Big Rock #3: **Buy stocks being heavily bought by institutional investors.** Avoid those they're heavily selling.

❑ **Increase in number of funds that own the stock in recent quarters**

❑ **Accumulation/Distribution Rating of A or B**

❑ **Relative Strength Rating of 80 or higher**

❑ **Share price above $15**

❑ **Average daily volume of 400,000 shares or more**

Get Pass or Fail Ratings for Each Item

You can instantly see if your stock gets a pass, neutral or fail rating for each item in this section of the checklist using *Stock Checkup* on Investors.com. If you're near a computer, take a look at the ratings in *Stock Checkup* as we go through the descriptions below.

 Increase in number of funds that own the stock in recent quarters

To confirm that your stock is in demand by institutional investors, make sure the number of funds that own the stock rose in the most recent quarter. Ideally, the number of funds should be rising over the last 3 or 4 quarters.

Also, look for a *material increase* in the number of funds in the most recent quarter.

If that number is *not* increasing—or worse, if it's *decreasing*—what does that tell you?

It could indicate a lack of enthusiasm for the stock among fund managers. Until they start getting in, that stock will probably not go up in any meaningful way.

How Do You Know if Fund Ownership Is Rising or Dropping?

In *Stock Checkup*, you'll find a pass, neutral or fail grade for your stock's institutional sponsorship. You'll also see how many quarters of rising fund ownership the stock has.

✔ IBD® Stock Checklist		
Supply and Demand		
Market Capitalization	3.70 B	●
Acc/Dis Rating	C+	●
Up/Down Volume	1.3	●
% Change in Funds Owning Stock	18%	●
Qtrs of Increasing Fund Ownership	3	● Pass

© 2013 Investor's Business Daily, Inc.

Don't Be the First to Arrive at the Party!

There are many misconceptions about how the stock market actually works. One is that you have to get into a stock before the big investors do. In fact, the *opposite* is true: The best stocks have *rising* institutional sponsorship *before* they soar.

The mutual fund managers at Fidelity, Vanguard, Janus, Dreyfus, CGM, and elsewhere all have teams of researchers who dig into the current performance and future prospects of thousands of publicly traded companies.

If a stock is *not* owned by a significant number of funds (say, 50 or more), it means that at least some of the 10,000 institutional investors out there have studied the stock and decided to take a pass.

That's *not* a cause for celebration, thinking you've somehow stumbled upon a hidden gem. It's a cause for *concern*.

To see why you won't be late if you wait for funds to start getting in, you need to understand that it can take these big institutions weeks, even months, to establish their positions in a stock.

For example, if the manager of a $2 billion fund decides he or she wants to put 1% of the fund's capital into a certain stock, that manager has to buy a $20 million position. If the stock trades around $20 a share, that fund manager has to buy 1 million shares.

If the manager tried to buy all those shares in one go, it would quickly drive up the price of the stock beyond the price he or she wanted to pay. So instead, over a few weeks or months, the fund's traders will quietly buy shares in smaller increments until they've established the desired $20 million position around the average cost-per-share they were targeting.

And that's just *one* fund. If dozens, hundreds, or even thousands of funds are moving in to the same stock, do the math! By the time Apple topped in 2012, it was owned by over *4,300* funds.

That doesn't happen overnight. It can take many months of continued buying before all these professional investors establish their positions.

That gives you time to get in and ride their coattails.

Good Gains Come to Those Who *Wait* for Confirmation

The table below shows how it pays to be patient and make sure the number of funds with a position in the stock is rising before you jump in.

Examples of Rising Fund Ownership *Before* a Big Run

Company	Starting Year of Run	# of Funds Owning Stock in 4 Quarters *Prior* to Price Move	Subsequent % Gain
Green Mountain Coffee Roasters	2009	148 → 187 → 201 → 227	1104% in 30 months
Watson Pharmaceuticals	2009	606 → 586 → 619 → 669	154% in 26 months
Netflix	2009	300 → 375 → 395 → 436	683% in 28 months
Ulta Beauty	2010	149 → 149 → 152 → 169	165% in 11 months
Chipotle Mexican Grill	2010	327 → 360 → 436 → 463	186% in 19 months

In the table above, look at the four quarters of fund ownership for Watson Pharmaceuticals and Ulta Beauty. In the first two quarters, the number of funds that owned Watson Pharmaceuticals actually dropped, and for Ulta Beauty that number stayed flat. But in the most recent quarter just *before* both stocks launched their big runs, note how the number of funds jumped significantly higher. That's the kind of "material increase" you want to see. It shows institutional investors are moving in and picking up shares.

☑ *Accumulation/Distribution Rating of A or B*

Here's another way to see if institutional investors are buying or selling your stock: Check the Accumulation/Distribution Rating (ACC/DIS RTG®).

Accumulation is a fancy word for buying. Distribution refers to selling. The Acc/Dis Rating, which ranges from A (best) to E (worst), tracks *institutional* trading in a stock over the last 13 weeks (roughly three months). It does that by focusing exclusively on the large-volume trades only professional investors make.

The table below shows what the A to E ratings mean. In general, only buy stocks with an A or B Accumulation/Distribution Rating, and avoid those rated D or E.

Accumulation/Distribution Rating

Measures the level of buying and selling by *institutional investors* in a stock over the last 13 weeks

A = Heavy buying
B = Moderate buying
C = Equal amount of buying and selling
D = Moderate selling
E = Heavy selling

The info below for Netflix shows the kinds of gains that are possible when a stock passes the institutional sponsorship criteria and other areas of the Buying Checklist.

Netflix's Institutional Sponsorship Just *Before* Rising 683%

March 2009–July 2011
Accumulation/Distribution Rating at time of breakout: A−
Fund ownership in 4 quarters *prior* to big move: 300 → 375 → 395 → 436

☑ *Relative Strength Rating of 80 or higher*

You're not looking for just *good* stocks. You're looking for the *best* ones—those that are clearly outperforming the rest of the pack. The Relative Strength (RS) Rating is yet one more way to separate the cream from the rest of the crop.

The RS Rating tracks a stock's share price performance over the last 52 weeks and compares it to that of the S&P 500, which is often used as a bellwether for the general market. To see how that compares to every other stock, a rating from 1 (worst) to 99 (best) is given.

An RS Rating of 80 means the stock's share price performance is outpacing 80% of all other stocks.

Look for a Strong Relative Strength *and* EPS Rating

The RS Rating focuses on the strength of the *stock* as valued by the market (i.e., the "technicals"). The EPS Rating gauges the strength of the *company* (i.e., the "fundamentals").

Think of it as the yin and yang of investing: By insisting that your stock has strong ratings for *both*, you're looking at the whole picture, not just half of it.

As Bill O'Neil has said, if you look at the stocks that have made enormous runs over the last several decades, **"The vast majority of superior stocks will rank 80 or higher on both the EPS and the RS ratings *before* their major moves."** And 80 is the *minimum*. The top stocks often rate much higher for both EPS and RS.

85-85: A Profitable Combination

The *IBD*® *85-85 Index* tracks the performance of stocks that score 85 or higher for both the EPS and RS Ratings. These are the stocks included in IBD's *Your Weekly Review*.

While hindsight is 20-20, you could say *foresight* is 85-85: From inception on November 13, 2000, through February 5, 2013, the *IBD 85-85 Index* rose 275% compared to the S&P 500's 12% gain. While that does not mean every stock with 85 or higher EPS and RS ratings will make a big run, it does show how this powerful combination of solid earnings growth and relative price strength can lead to substantial profits—and why you want to focus your research on stocks with similar ratings.

☑ *Share price above $15*

We're all human. It can be tempting to chase low-priced stocks, thinking they offer the most potential for a big gain. But they're usually cheap for a reason: Weak (or nonexistent) earnings growth, lackluster sales, or a lack of new and exciting products. Because of that, they have a hard time attracting institutional investors, and we've already seen how important it is to have rising institutional sponsorship.

So the two takeaways here are:

1. Avoid cheap, low-priced stocks.

2. Don't be afraid to buy seemingly "high-priced" stocks with a share price of $50, $100 or more.

Focus on the CAN SLIM traits, not the "high" share price.

When Priceline *started* a 182% run in 2010, it was already trading around $270 per share. And Apple may have *seemed* expensive when its share price hit $150 in July 2009. But less than three years later, it had climbed to $644.

Not all CAN SLIM stocks have triple-digit share prices. SolarWinds launched its 137% move in 2011 from a share price around $25. The prices for these three stocks were different, but their winning profiles were the same: They had the CAN SLIM characteristics.

By definition, CAN SLIM stocks are the fastest-growing, most profitable companies on the market. Just as you can't buy a Mercedes for the price of a Chevy, CAN SLIM leaders tend to command a higher share price and a higher P/E ratio than inferior stocks (Chapter 2).

So focus on the CAN SLIM traits . . . don't chase cheap stocks . . . and if all the other checklist items are in place, don't worry if the share price *seems* high.

☑ *Average daily volume of 400,000 shares or more*

"Volume" refers to the amount of shares a stock trades in a given period (e.g., in a day or week). Stocks that have a *low* average daily volume are said to be "thinly" traded.

You want to avoid thinly traded stocks for the same reason you want to steer clear of low-priced ones: Institutional investors tend to avoid them, so you should too. Plus they tend to be more volatile.

The average daily volume varies widely and can change over time for the same stock. At the time of this writing, Google, for example, is trading around 2.5 million shares on average every day, while Fleetcor Technologies is trading much less, around 670,000.

Mutual fund managers tend to establish large positions, buying tens of thousands or even millions of shares. That's hard to do in a stock that only trades 50,000 shares a day. It's easier to establish a meaningful position—without driving up the price too quickly—in a stock that trades a few *million* shares on average.

Also, when it comes time to sell, it's easier for institutional investors to unload their shares in a "liquid" stock—one that has a big pool of buyers and sellers and trades in large volume. It's much harder for fund managers to quickly get out of thinly traded stocks: Their own high-volume selling can quickly drive down the price, which either reduces their profits or increases their losses.

Keep in mind that while any stock can be subject to a sudden price swing, thinly traded stocks tend to be more volatile. It takes much less volume to significantly impact the price of a stock that trades 50,000 shares a day than one that trades 3 *million*.

So focus on stocks that trade *at least* 400,000 shares per day. A more conservative investor trying to reduce the risk of volatility might look for stocks trading 1 million shares or more each day. One place to find such stocks is the *IBD Big Cap 20* (Chapter 7).

Funds Will Determine the Fate of *Your* Stocks

By now you understand that mutual funds and other institutional investors account for the bulk of all trading, and therefore they ultimately determine the fate of a stock. If they're heavily buying, the stock will go up. If they're heavily selling, the stock will go down.

It's the same for the overall market. New uptrends begin when these big investors start buying aggressively and end when they start to sell.

People can talk about all kinds of fancy technical indicators and throw around exotic Wall Street lingo, but that's the bottom line. And that's why it's critical you make sure (a) the market is in an uptrend, and (b) your stock passes this section—and the "Chart Analysis" segment—of the Buying Checklist before you invest.

It's not that hard to do, and that little extra effort will go a long way to generating superior profits.

Next up: Let's compare two potential CAN SLIM stocks using the criteria on the Buying Checklist.

• ACTION STEPS •

Here are some quick *To Dos* to start using the Buying Checklist and reinforce what we've covered so far. To take these steps, visit www.investors.com/GettingStartedBook.

1. Run 2 to 3 stocks through the Buying Checklist. As practice, you can skip the "Chart Analysis" section for now, but *don't buy a stock without first checking the chart.* We'll cover chart-reading in Chapter 6, "Don't Invest *Blindly.*"

   • **Check market direction:** Use the *Market Pulse* in *The Big Picture* column to see if we're currently in an uptrend or correction.

   • **Review potential CAN SLIM® stocks:** If you don't have a stock in mind, choose one from the *IBD 50, Your Weekly Review, Sector Leaders,* or *Stock Spotlight* (Chapter 7).

2. See how to go through the checklist with a short video: *Does Your Stock Pass or Fail? Find Out with Stock Checkup.*

A Tale of 2 Stocks: Priceline.com vs. Expedia

In July 2009, we were just a few months into a new bull market that began in March. As you were searching for stocks to buy, you might have come across two big players in the online travel booking business, Priceline.com and Expedia.

As we saw in the checklist, you want to pay particular attention to the top-rated stocks in the top-ranked industry groups. In July, the Leisure–Travel Booking group (known as Leisure–Services at the time) was ranked #11.

With that in mind, let's look at the key *facts* known about Priceline and Expedia at the time.

As you go through this, consider what you now know about what to look for in a stock *before* you buy, and ask yourself:

- Which company looks stronger?
- Which stock has a higher likelihood of making a big price gain?
- Which one would you choose to invest your hard-earned money in?

Think about how each company stacks up against the "big rocks" we've been discussing.

All data as of July 2009

Does the Company Have Big Earnings Growth?

Earnings-Per-Share (EPS) Growth in Prior 3 Quarters

Quarter	Priceline.com EPS Growth	Expedia EPS Growth
Sep-08	51%	−31%
Dec-08	34%	−13%
Mar-09	43%	−5%

While Expedia has shown *negative* earnings growth the last 3 quarters, Priceline's EPS growth has been above the 25% minimum and accelerated in the most recent quarter.

Avg. Annual Earnings Growth over Last 3 Years

Priceline.com	Expedia
74%	8%

Priceline's *annual* earnings growth is over 9 times better than Expedia's, which gets a failing grade because it's well below the 25% benchmark.

EPS Rating

Priceline.com	Expedia
99	63

The highest-possible 99 EPS Rating shows Priceline is outperforming 99% of *all* stocks in terms of recent quarterly and annual earnings growth. Expedia scores a mediocre 63, which is under the minimum 80 rating we look for in the Buying Checklist.

SMR Rating

Priceline.com	Expedia
A	B

Return on Equity

Priceline.com	Expedia
44%	10%

While Expedia's SMR Rating of B earns a passing grade, Priceline's score is even better. That shows Priceline has superior performance in the 3 main ingredients that drive EPS growth: **S**ales, Profit **M**argins and **R**eturn on Equity. And Priceline's ROE is over 4 times stronger than Expedia's 10%, which again fails to meet the 17% minimum.

Always keep in mind: Big earnings growth is the #1 factor to look for in a stock. And at this point in time, Priceline's growth was clearly outpacing that of Expedia.

Does the Company Have a New, Innovative Product or Service?
Priceline's innovative and exclusive "Name Your Own Price" system had already been in place for years, but was still a major—and unique—draw for consumers. They also had several "new" things driving growth, including kitschy commercials featuring William Shatner.

To increase sales, Priceline had earlier dropped its booking fees. Competitors—including Expedia—didn't take similar action until 2 years later.

Priceline was also rapidly expanding in a new market—Europe—with its recent acquisition of Booking.com. That marked a new and growing opportunity, since European travelers were still just starting to go online to book their hotels and airfare.

Expedia's main "new" change was to its service policies and fees—done primarily in reaction to steps Priceline had taken earlier. It hoped to attract more travelers by eliminating cancellation fees for hotels, car rentals, cruises and most airline tickets.

Are Mutual Funds Heavily Buying the Stock?

Accumulation/Distribution Rating

Priceline.com	Expedia
A	B

No. of Funds Owning Stock in Prior 4 Quarters

Quarter	Priceline.com	Expedia
Sep-08	654	761
Dec-08	632	727
Mar-09	716	740
Jun-09	773	795

With an Accumulation/Distribution Rating of B and rising fund ownership, Expedia clears the institutional sponsorship criteria in the Buying Checklist. But here again, Priceline's institutional demand is even stronger: It is actually being *more* heavily bought by fund managers.

What Is the Stock's Overall Strength?

Composite Rating

Priceline.com	Expedia
99	95

Expedia's 95 Composite Rating was strong, showing it was in the top 5% of all stocks. But you're looking for the best of the best, the true market leaders. And Priceline's 99 Composite Rating meant it was in the top 1%.

What About the P/E Ratio?

Price/Earnings (P/E) Ratio

Priceline.com	Expedia
21	18

In Chapter 2, we already discussed why P/E ratios are *not* an important factor when it comes to deciding what stocks to buy. In fact, investors who only buy stocks with low P/E ratios and never buy ones with so-called "high" P/Es will miss out on virtually *every* big winner.

So ask yourself: After seeing everything else we just covered about these two companies, would you buy Expedia just because it had a lower P/E ratio?

What Happened Next?

Do you see how it quickly becomes obvious which stock is stronger as you go through the checklist? No guesswork—just the *facts*. And the more you do it, the quicker and easier it gets.

The difference in the gains that followed proves the payoff for using the Buying Checklist can be life-changing.

Subsequent Gains for Priceline.com and Expedia

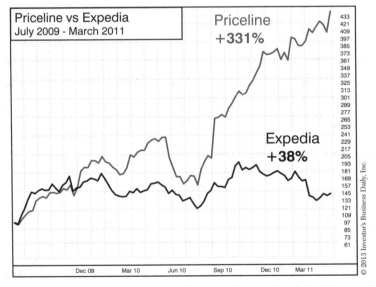

Next up: Now it's your turn to review 2 stocks and decide which one has more potential.

You Make the Call:
Which Stock Looks Stronger?

Now it's *your* turn to choose.

Below are the actual earnings, ratings, institutional sponsorship and other vital facts about two companies in the same industry group. Based on what we've covered so far, compare the two and ask yourself: *Which stock looks stronger?*

At the end, I'll reveal the names of the two companies and what happened next to their stocks.

Does the Company Have Big Earnings Growth?

Earnings-Per-Share (EPS) Growth in Prior 3 Quarters

Quarter	Company A EPS Growth	Company B EPS Growth
Dec	47%	−38%
Mar	86%	−3%
Jun	75%	20%

Avg. Annual Earnings Growth over Last 3 Years

Company A	Company B
48%	1%

EPS Rating

Company A	Company B
93	30

SMR Rating

Company A	Company B
A	C

Does the Company Have a New, Innovative Product or Service?

Company A	Company B
New products have made it a leading player in two industries.	Major player in its industry, but no game-changing innovations in recent years.

Are Mutual Funds Heavily Buying the Stock?

Accumulation/Distribution Rating

Company A	Company B
B+	C

No. of Funds Owning Stock in Prior 4 Quarters

Quarter	Company A	Company B
Sep	2956	1765
Dec	3097	1806
Mar	3247	1776
Jun	3512	1808

Time to choose: Which company looks stronger, A or B?

Apple vs. Dell July 2009

The checklist results clearly show **Apple (Company A)** was demonstrating much more strength than **Dell (Company B)**.

The return of founder Steve Jobs in 1997 spurred a phenomenal period of innovation for Apple. The iPod®, iTunes®, iPhone® and the "app" ecosystem were revolutionizing the music and smartphone industries, leading to the explosive earnings growth you saw above.

Dell had been following a different trajectory. While still a major player in the computer industry, Dell's growth had slowed dramatically compared to the 1990s. Founder Michael Dell's return as CEO in 2005 failed to rejuvenate the company in the way Jobs's return had for Apple.

What Happened Next?

Subsequent Gains for Apple and Dell

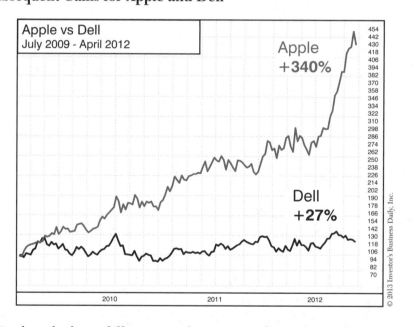

Look at the huge difference in those gains. *That's* why you want to put your money into stocks that have CAN SLIM® traits.

When you're screening stocks, your choices won't always be that clear-cut. But 100+ years of market history make the most essential point *very* clear.

To find the best stocks—the ones most likely to make a huge price gain—look for stocks that:

- Have big earnings growth and new, innovative products
- Are top-rated leaders in a top-ranked industry group
- Are being heavily bought by institutional investors

When you focus on stocks that pass the Buying Checklist by displaying those traits—and make sure the overall market is in a solid uptrend—that's a time-tested recipe for making money in stocks.

Next up: What do you do if your stock gets a mix of pass *and* fail marks on the Buying Checklist?

What if Your Stock Gets
Both Pass *and* Fail Ratings?

This will certainly happen. Investing, after all, is not an exact science. Few stocks—even those that go on to stellar gains—are picture perfect in every single respect.

So here are tips on how to handle stocks that have a few blemishes.

- **If the stock fails in *several* areas, take a pass and move on.**

  You're not looking for mediocre stocks. You're looking for the market's strongest leaders. These top stocks may have one, two or maybe three flaws, but they won't have a lot of serious ones. So if a stock fails on several items on the Buying Checklist, keep your powder dry and keep looking.

  As T. Boone Pickens has said, "If you're going to hunt elephants, don't get off the trail for a rabbit."

- **Focus on the "big rocks"—the most important factors in deciding *what* to buy.**

  - Does the stock have big earnings growth and a new, innovative product or service?

  - Are mutual funds heavily buying the stock?

  Always put those big rocks in first. A stock may come up short on a checklist item or two, but make sure you can answer a definite "yes" to those two key questions above.

Let's look at a few "mixed bag" scenarios you're likely to encounter.

Scenario 1: Strong Stock but Relatively Weak Industry Group

If you find a stock that passes everything on the checklist, *except* its industry group is *not* ranked in the top 40–50 groups, should you toss it by the wayside? Not necessarily.

Yes, you want to focus on the top-rated stocks within the top-ranked industry groups. But there are times when a big winner will emerge from a somewhat lower-ranked group.

One example is Ulta Beauty. As we saw in the case study for Ulta (see Chapter 2), it had explosive earnings growth; it had a popular new retail concept that was revolutionizing how cosmetics were sold; and mutual funds were heavily buying its stock.

But when it launched its 165% run, Ulta Beauty's Retail–Specialty industry group was only ranked #82.

The group ranking is important because a higher ranking means funds and other institutional investors are moving into that industry. So if you do invest in a stock that is *not* in a top 40–50 group, make sure the stock gets flying colors for the other checklist items. You also need to make sure mutual funds are heavily buying the stock to at least partially make up for the *lower* group ranking. That was the case for Ulta: In the 4 quarters before its big move, the number of funds that owned shares jumped from 197 to 315.

Also, if the group ranking is sub-par, make sure there is at least one *other* top-rated stock in the group. That confirms institutions are showing some interest in the industry. You had that for Ulta Beauty: Fellow retailer Sally Beauty Holdings sported a solid 95 Composite Rating and launched a big run around the same time as Ulta.

Scenario 2: Drop in Fund Ownership in Most Recent Quarter but Strong Accumulation/Distribution Rating

Let's say you were running Lululemon Athletica through this checklist in September 2010.

Did it have big earnings growth? Yes, its EPS growth in the prior 3 quarters accelerated from 43% to 100% to 180%. It also had a very strong 30% return on equity.

Did it have a new, innovative product or service? Yes, again. It had found a profitable niche with high-end yoga apparel as the popularity of yoga was rising.

Were mutual funds heavily buying the stock? Yes, but with some caveats.

In the first quarter of 2010, the number of funds that owned Lululemon jumped from 189 to 223. But in Q2, it *dropped* to 206. As we saw in the "Big Rock #3" section of the checklist, you'd prefer to see that number rise in the most recent quarter.

But there were mitigating factors that made up for that flaw. One was that even with that drop, the number of funds that owned shares was up over the last 4 quarters, from 195 to 206.

Also, when Lululemon launched its big move, it had an Accumulation/ Distribution Rating of B+, indicating moderate to heavy buying by institutional investors over the last 13 weeks. And just a few days before it launched its big move, it released its latest earnings report and professional investors poured in, driving a spike in trading volume that was over 600% higher than normal.

So while Lululemon did have a flaw or two, it was strong overall, and it had the three most important elements we look for: Big earnings; a new, innovative product or service; and mutual funds were heavily buying shares.

From that point, it shot up 196% in just 10 months. (By the way, over the next 4 quarters, the number of funds that owned Lululemon jumped from 205 to 359.)

Scenario 3: Strong but Not Accelerating Earnings Growth

In September 2010, Chipotle Mexican Grill was a CAN SLIM® leader, but it had a flaw: Its EPS growth had *decelerated* over the last 3 quarters, from 90% to 53% to 33%. Obviously, you'd prefer to see that going in the opposite direction.

But again, when you ask the most important questions, Chipotle got a "yes" in response to each one.

Did it have a new, innovative product or service? Chipotle's chain of organic gourmet burrito restaurants was extremely popular and well-positioned to serve the growing number of people who wanted a healthier alternative to typical fast food fare.

Were mutual funds heavily buying the stock? Yes. Just before it broke out, Chipotle had a solid Accumulation/Distribution Rating of B, and the number of funds that owned shares had risen sharply over the last 4 quarters.

Did it have big earnings growth? Since Chipotle's EPS growth had decelerated in recent quarters, were there any mitigating factors that could garner a positive answer to this key question?

One was that, while deceleration is certainly not ideal, Chipotle's earnings growth was still above the 25% minimum we look for.

Also, its *annual* earnings growth over the last 3 years was 38%—well above the 25% minimum benchmark.

Chipotle's EPS Rating was 97, meaning in terms of overall current and annual earnings growth, it was outpacing 97% of all stocks. Plus, it had a solid return on equity of 19% and the highest possible Composite Rating of

99, meaning it was in the top 1% of all stocks in terms of overall strength—including current and annual earnings growth.

So while not picture perfect, Chipotle—like Lululemon—showed market-leading power, and it went on to gain 186% over the next 20 months.

Don't Let the "Perfect" Become the Enemy of the "*Very* Good"

If you come across a stock that gets a passing grade for almost all the items on this checklist but misses on one or two, don't automatically write it off. Look at the big picture, and see if it has the most critical things to look for: Big earnings growth, a hot new product or service, and clear demand from fund managers.

What if Your Stock Doesn't Pass?
Check the Group Leaders in IBD Stock Checkup

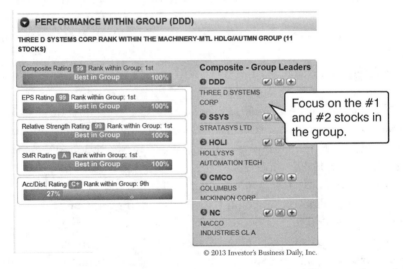

© 2013 Investor's Business Daily, Inc.

If the company you're looking at doesn't pass the checklist, try this: Check the top-rated stocks in the same industry group, found at the top of *Stock Checkup* (see the example above).

Focus primarily on the #1 and #2 stocks, and run them through the same checklist. It's a great way to discover the true industry leaders and build a quality watch list.

Be Cautious—but on the Hunt— During Earnings Season

Four times a year, publicly traded companies report their earnings and sales figures for the prior quarter. The latest numbers can pleasantly surprise—or bitterly disappoint—professional analysts and investors. That's why you often see dramatic swings—up or down—when a company reports.

So during earnings season, you often see a lot of breakouts, but you may also see several *breakdowns*.

Because you don't know which way that pendulum will swing, **don't buy a stock just before it releases its latest earnings report.**

Instead, wait for the stock to announce the numbers, and see how the market reacts. If the stock shoots past a proper buy point on heavy volume, that could offer a chance to get in. If it sells off on massive volume, you'll be glad you didn't try to "guess" and jump in early.

Here are 3 simple tips on how to handle earnings season:

- **Check to see when any stock you own or have on your watch list is scheduled to report.** You can find that information on the company's website or through other services. During earnings season, IBD publishes the *Earnings Calendar*, a list of key stocks scheduled to report the following week. You'll find that in the Monday edition.

- **Have your buying and selling game plans in place *ahead of time*.** If you're considering buying a stock that could potentially break out of a base when it reports earnings, know the exact buy point you're looking for and how many shares you'll purchase. If you own a stock that's about to report, be sure to have a defensive selling plan in place, just in case it suddenly sells off.

- **Consider using automatic trade triggers.** If you can't watch the market during the day, set a trade trigger with your broker ahead of time (see Chapter 4). You can set a conditional buy order for a stock on your watch list to make sure you catch it if it breaks out while you're away from your computer. And you can set a stop-loss order to help protect your profits or cap any losses if a stock you already own declines.

Expect the Unexpected

Earnings season can sometimes leave you scratching your head. A stock may soar higher on a seemingly weak quarterly report, while another may sell off despite posting stellar numbers. Again, that's why your best bet is to wait for the company to report and see how the market reacts.

Below are examples of two very different reactions to two seemingly positive earnings announcements. They're good reminders of how you can keep the odds of success in your favor by keeping your powder dry until you see how the company's earnings story plays out.

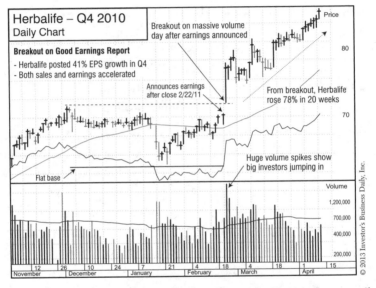

Herbalife soared 78% in 20 weeks after reporting accelerating earnings growth.

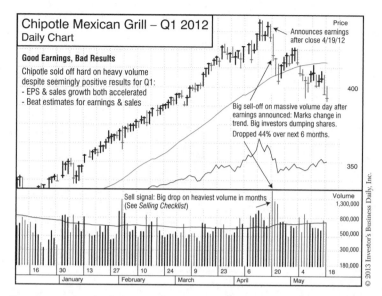

Chipotle Mexican Grill – Q1 2012
Daily Chart

Price

Announces earnings
after close 4/19/12

Good Earnings, Bad Results

Chipotle sold off hard on heavy volume
despite seemingly positive results for Q1:
- EPS & sales growth both accelerated
- Beat estimates for earnings & sales

400

Big sell-off on massive volume day after
earnings announced: Marks change in
trend. Big investors dumping shares.

Dropped 44% over next 6 months.

350

Sell signal: Big drop on heaviest volume in months
(See *Selling Checklist*)

Volume
1,300,000

800,000

500,000

300,000

180,000

| 16 | 30 | 13 | 27 | 10 | 24 | 9 | 23 | 6 | 20 | 4 | 18 |

January | February | March | April | May

© 2013 Investor's Business Daily, Inc.

Despite posting accelerating earnings and sales growth, Chipotle sold off.

Simple Routines for Finding Winning Stocks

Want Good Results?
Stick to a Good Routine!

*"We are what we repeatedly do.
Excellence, therefore, is not an act but a habit."*

—ARISTOTLE

It's impossible for me to overemphasize how important it is to have a routine that:

1. Helps you identify the best stocks *before* they surge.

2. Fits *your* schedule.

Both elements are crucial. You could have the greatest routine known to Wall Street, but if you don't have time to use it *regularly*, what good does it do you?

That's why these routines are designed for busy people with limited time to invest.

Maybe you work during the day. Maybe you're retired. Either way, I'm sure you have family, hobbies and other interests *outside* of the stock market—those things we commonly refer to as "life"!

So here are two routines designed to be quick and easy for *anyone* to use:

- **Simple Weekend Routine:** This uses two of IBD's most powerful screens to identify stocks that have CAN SLIM® traits and are near a potential buy point right now.

- **10-Minute Daily Routine:** Keeps you on top of the market throughout the week and makes sure your watch list and game plan stay up to date.

Think of the Simple Weekend Routine as your core prep time. It's where you update your watch list and make your game plan so you're ready for the week ahead. Once that's in place, use the 10-Minute Daily Routine to refresh and execute your plan as needed.

Understand that these are just two sample routines to get you started. As you become more familiar and comfortable with CAN SLIM investing and Investor's Business Daily, you might come up with your own routine.

More Routines by Successful CAN SLIM Investors

You can learn about the investing routines of other CAN SLIM investors by reading my radio show co-host Amy Smith's book, *How to Make Money in Stocks–Success Stories*. I think you'll agree it's a very inspiring and informative read.

Have a Selling Plan in Place *Before* You Buy

I encourage you to jump right in and start using these routines, but with one important caveat: *Don't buy any stocks until you've gone through the Selling Checklist chapter.* Buying stocks without having a selling game plan is like driving a car with no brakes—very exciting at first, not so pleasant at the end!

So be sure to go through the Selling Checklist and understand basic sell rules before you invest.

Always Stick to Your Routine–Even in a Market Downtrend

I'm repeating this point because it's *extremely* important: One of the biggest mistakes you can make is to walk away and stop doing your routine just because the market is currently in a correction. That's how you *miss* the next big winners.

The best stocks form bases during a market correction then shoot out of the gate right when a new uptrend begins.

If you want to catch the *next* crop of leaders—and cash in on the big profits they deliver—keep doing your routine even when (in fact, especially when) the *Market Pulse* says "Market in correction."

Snooze, You Lose—Stay Awake, You Rake (In the Profits)

To see mini case studies of why it's so important—and profitable—to always stay engaged with the market, see "Finding Winners Using the Simple Weekend Routine" later in this chapter.

Have You Started Your Free Trial of IBD?

To start your free trial and get access to the tools in these routines, visit www.investors.com/GettingStartedBook. You'll also find short videos that walk you through each step of the daily and weekend routines.

Simple Weekend Routine

20–30 Minutes

Step 1: Check overall market direction in *The Big Picture*.

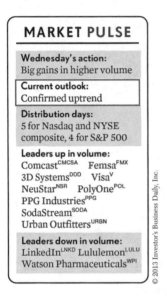

MARKET PULSE

Wednesday's action:
Big gains in higher volume

Current outlook:
Confirmed uptrend

Distribution days:
5 for Nasdaq and NYSE
composite, 4 for S&P 500

Leaders up in volume:
Comcast^CMCSA   Femsa^FMX
3D Systems^DDD   Visa^V
NeuStar^NSR   PolyOne^POL
PPG Industries^PPG
SodaStream^SODA
Urban Outfitters^URBN

Leaders down in volume:
LinkedIn^LNKD Lululemon^LULU
Watson Pharmaceuticals^WPI

© 2013 Investor's Business Daily, Inc.

Don't ignore this step—it's critical. Most stocks move in the same direction as the overall market, either up or down.

So as we noted earlier: **Only buy stocks when the *Current Outlook* says "Confirmed uptrend."**

I *strongly* encourage you to read *The Big Picture* regularly. It gives invaluable insight into what's happening in the market—and how to handle it.

When & Where to Find It

The Big Picture is found daily in the *Making Money* section of IBD and on Investors.com.

Step 2: Look for stocks *near a buy point* by quickly scanning the *IBD 50* and *Your Weekly Review*.

30 SOLARWINDS INC (SWI)   Grp 122   o$24.43
51.7M Shares 94 Comp. Rating 95 EPS RS 92 ROE 43%
DEVELOPS NETWORK MANAGEMENT SOFTWARE USED BY COMPA-
NIES TO IDENTIFY AND SOLVE NETWORK PERFORMANCE ISSUES.
+37% Ann. EPS Gro PE 28 Avg. D. Vol 1,027,600 Debt 0%
Last Qtr Eps +29% ▼ Prior Qtr +31% ▲ Last Qtr Sales +29%
18 Qtrs EPS ▷ 15%
Eps Due 10/28
R&D 10%
Acc/Dis C
Sup/Demand 77
JAN 11   APR   JUL   OCT
Forming double bottom with potential 25.72 buy point.

© 2013 Investor's Business Daily, Inc.

Look at the one-line analysis below the chart for each stock. Circle or make note of any stocks said to be nearing or in a potential buying range.

When & Where to Find It

The *IBD 50* is updated every Monday and Wednesday in the *Making Money* section of IBD and *e*IBD.

(The Monday print edition is delivered on Saturdays in most areas so you have it in time for your weekend routine.)

Your Weekly Review is published every Friday in the A section of IBD.

Step 3: Use *IBD Stock Checkup* to see if the stocks you circled pass the Buying Checklist.

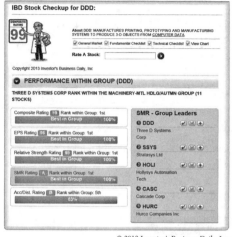

© 2013 Investor's Business Daily, Inc.

In *Stock Checkup*, you'll find pass, neutral or fail ratings for most items on the checklist.

And if you're not familiar with the company and what it does, check out its website and read what IBD and others have written about it. You'll find links to articles in *Stock Checkup*.

You may also find the stock was recently covered in a *Daily Stock Analysis* or *Market Wrap* video on Investors.com.

When & Where to Find It

Stock Checkup is available on Investors.com and updated daily.

Step 4: Add the strongest stocks to your watch list.

My Stock Lists

Show: Near Buy Point (Default)

with: SmartSelect

New | Export | Import | Print | Modify »

Symbol	Company Name	Composite Rating	EPS Rating	RS Rating	SMR Rating	Acc/Dis Rating	Group Rel Str Rating	IBD Tools
DDD	Three D Systems Corp	99	98	99	A	B	A+	✓ ☑
GMCR	Green Mtn Coffee Roastrs	98	99	98	A	A+	B+	✓ ☑
CELG	Celgene Corp	98	98	92	A	A+	A	✓ ☑
CVLT	Commvault Systems Inc	97	98	90	A	B+	C+	✓ ☑
FLT	Fleetcor Technologies	97	98	95	A	B+	C+	✓ ☑
SODA	Sodastream Intl Ltd	99	98	91	A	A-	A	✓ ☑
FNGN	Financial Engines Inc	99	97	94	A	A	A-	✓ ☑
MIDD	Middleby Corp	99	93	93	A	A	A	✓ ☑

Choose »   New | Export | Import | Print | Modify »

© 2013 Investor's Business Daily, Inc.

Make a game plan for each stock that has passed the Buying Checklist and is near a potential buy point:

- What is the ideal buying range? (Chapter 6)
- How many shares will you buy if it breaks out?

Watch to see if any stocks on your list break out in the coming days and weeks. (Make sure each stock still passes the Buying Checklist and the market is in an uptrend at the time of the breakout.)

You can also set up automatic trade triggers with your broker ahead of time (see "Busy During the Day? Set Automatic Trade Triggers" later in this chapter).

Also see "How to Build and Maintain an Actionable Watch List" (Chapter 7).

Tune in to IBD's Weekly Radio Show

 Join Amy Smith and me each week for a look at the current market and how to use CAN SLIM® rules to handle it. For details on how to tune in, visit www.investors.com/radioshow.

• ACTION STEPS •

Time to jump in and try out the routine for yourself! To see how, visit www.investors.com/GettingStartedBook.

1. Watch a short video on how to do the Simple Weekend Routine.

2. Use the routine to see what potential big winners you find. (Remember: Don't invest until you also go through Chapter 5, "Selling Checklist," and set up a selling game plan.)

10-Minute Daily Routine

 10 Minutes

Step 1: Check overall market direction with *The Big Picture.*

MARKET PULSE

Friday's action:
Up in lower volume

Current outlook:
Confirmed uptrend

Distribution days:
4 for Nasdaq and NYSE
composite, 3 for S&P 500

Leaders up in volume:
Google^{GOOG} ARM^{ARMH}
Eastman Chemical^{EMN}
Celgene^{CELG} NeuStar^{NSR}
Tupperware^{TUP} Cree^{CREE}
SodaStream^{SODA}
Thermo Fisher^{TMO}
Icici Bank^{IBN} Expedia^{EXPE}
CommVault^{CVLT}

Leaders down in volume:
Priceline.com^{PCLN}
Alkermes^{ALKS} PVH^{PVH}

© 2013 Investor's Business Daily, Inc.

Scan *The Big Picture* for answers to these questions:

- Any changes in market direction (e.g., from correction to uptrend)?
- Which leading stocks are moving up in big volume?
- What trends are emerging—and how should you handle them?

You can also watch the *Market Wrap* video for a 3–4 minute overview of the day's action and highlights of selected leading stocks.

When & Where to Find It
The Big Picture is found daily in the *Making Money* section of IBD and on Investors.com. The *Market Wrap* video is found daily at Investors.com/IBDtv.

Step 2: Review stocks you own or have on your watch list.

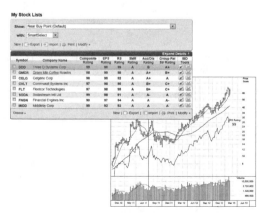

© 2013 Investor's Business Daily, Inc.

Pull up a chart to see how your stocks are faring:

- Any buy or sell signals in the stocks you own?
- Have stocks on your watch list broken out or broken down?

You can also do a search for your stocks on Investors.com to see if IBD wrote about them recently.

If you take a minute to *regularly* check your stocks, you'll become much better at spotting any changes in trend. The more you do it, the faster—and more profitable—it gets.

When & Where to Find It

Use Stock Checkup and *IBD Charts* on Investors.com.

Step 3: As your schedule allows, look for new stock ideas.

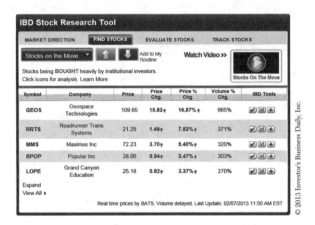

You'll probably do most of your research on the weekend, but if you have time during the week, here are some other places to find timely stock ideas:

- *Sector Leaders*
- *Stock Spotlight*
- *Stocks on the Move*™
- *Daily Stock Analysis* video

See Chapter 7, "More Tips and Tools for Getting Started Right," for how to use these and other features to find winning stocks.

Step 4: **Adjust your game plan and watch list as needed.**

Based on what you find in Steps 2 and 3, add or remove stocks from your watch list, and adjust your buying or selling game plan as needed.

Remember: You can set up automatic trade triggers with your broker ahead of time.

Good Results Start with a *Regular* Routine!

The key to spotting big winners *early* is to have a *regular* routine. Whether you use these routines or something better fitted to your schedule or investing style doesn't matter. What's crucial is that you come up with a plan that works for you and stick to it.

As motivational speaker Brian Tracy has said, **"Successful people are simply those with successful habits."**

• ACTION STEPS •

Time to jump in and try out the routine for yourself! To see how, visit www.investors.com/GettingStartedBook.

1. Watch a short video on how to do the 10-Minute Daily Routine.

2. Start using this routine to stay on top of any stocks you own and build your watch list. (Remember: Don't invest until you also go through Chapter 5, "Selling Checklist," and set up a selling game plan.)

Busy During the Day?
Set Automatic Trade Triggers

If you work during the day and can't watch the market, you can set "conditional orders" ahead of time with your broker.

It can be a great way to catch a big breakout—even as you're plugging away at your day job. And when you're on vacation and can't watch your stocks closely, you also can set conditional sell orders to lock in your gains or cut short any losses if the stock declines.

Important: Talk with your broker before placing a conditional order for the first time. Certain brokers have different ways of setting up these types of trades.

For example, some allow you to set them up based on both price *and* volume, so you can make sure institutional investors are buying heavily as the stock breaks out.

So before you start using trade triggers, call your brokerage service, tell them what your objective for the order is, and have them walk you through the various offerings they have to meet your needs.

Here are some basic examples.

Buy Stop Orders

Purpose: To buy a stock as it breaks out from a proper buy point

Use a buy stop order when you want to buy a stock, but only after it climbs higher and hits a certain price.

Let's say you find a stock on the *IBD 50* that passes the Buying Checklist and is near a potential buy point of $30. But right now, it's trading at $29.50.

On Saturday or Sunday, after you've done your research and set your game plan using the Simple Weekend Routine, you could log in to your online broker's website and set a buy stop order for $30.

If a few days or weeks later the stock hits the target $30 share price, your trade will get triggered automatically. (You can set an expiration date for your conditional order: If it doesn't get triggered within that time frame, the order is cancelled.)

Check the Volume!

If your broker doesn't let you use conditional orders that track both price and volume, be sure to check the volume after your trade has been triggered. You want to see a nice spike in the number of shares traded when a stock breaks out. That confirms institutional investors are buying aggressively. (More on that in Chapter 6, "Don't Invest *Blindly*.")

Stop-Loss Orders

Purpose: To automatically cut short any losses

We've already touched on the cardinal rule of selling: Always sell if a stock drops 7% to 8% below what you paid for it. You can use stop-loss orders to make sure you stick to that rule, and it's very easy to do.

Let's say you bought a stock at $100 a share. If you set a stop-loss order at $93 (i.e., a 7% loss), then the stock will be automatically sold at the market price if it slips to that target.

If you have a hard time selling—if you're afraid you might "freeze" when it's time to get out—having a stop-loss order in place can put your mind at ease.

Trailing Stop-Loss Orders

Purpose: To lock in the bulk of your profits if a stock starts to decline

Trailing stop-loss orders can be very useful but also a little tricky, since there are several different versions. So call your brokerage service and have them show you the right way to set them up.

Here's just one way you can use a trailing stop-loss.

Let's say you bought a stock at $100, and it's now trading at $150. Congrats—you're sitting on a nice 50% gain!

The last thing you want to do is let those profits disappear, so you could set up a trailing stop-loss order to make sure you automatically lock in a good portion of your gains if the stock starts to head south.

Let's say you set a trailing stop of 10%. (You can choose a percentage or dollar amount.)

If the stock drops 10% below the current $150, the sell order would be triggered, and you'd lock in the remaining profits. (Still a nice gain of 35%.)

But let's say the stock *doesn't* decline 10% and instead shoots up to $200—giving you a 100% gain.

Your 10% trailing stop-loss order would be *automatically* adjusted to that new current market price. Pretty convenient, right?

So now if the stock *did* start to decline and dropped 10% below the $200 mark, your sell order would get triggered—locking in the bulk of that big gain.

Use Conditional Orders Wisely

Using automatic trade triggers can be a great way to make sure you don't miss out on a big breakout—and safeguard your profits if a stock begins to drop.

Just make sure you use them correctly. Talk with your broker about how to set them up, and be sure to watch the market as often as you can. Conditional orders are definitely convenient and a big help to busy investors, but remember: There's no substitute for staying engaged and keeping a close eye on your stocks.

Finding Winners Using the Simple Weekend Routine

Here are just a few examples to give you a sense of the kind of big gains you can capture using the Simple Weekend Routine as your starting point.

Keep in mind: Big winners like the ones below emerge in every strong uptrend, and you can find them if you just *regularly* follow that basic game plan.

Green Mountain Coffee Roasters (GMCR)

Here's a day-by-day look at how you could have found Green Mountain Coffee Roasters *before* it broke out and soared over 1,000% from March 2009 to September 2011. The information below is what you would have found if you were doing the routine on the weekend of March 13–15, 2009.

Step 1: **Check overall market direction with *The Big Picture*.**

On March 12, 2009, the *Market Pulse* outlook changed from "Market in correction" to "Confirmed uptrend" (called a "rally" at the time).

That told you a new uptrend was just beginning, following the 2008 bear market.

Follow the market, not the news!

Despite investor fears and bad economic news after the housing and financial crisis, the market action showed it was time to buy.

Step 2: Look for stocks *near a buy point* by quickly scanning the IBD 50 and *Your Weekly Review*.

The same day the market direction changed to "Confirmed uptrend," the analysis for Green Mountain Coffee Roasters in *Your Weekly Review* said: "Cup with handle appears with buy point at 42.99."

Green Mountain was also featured in that day's *Daily Stock Analysis* video.

With the general market in an uptrend and Green Mountain near a potential buying area, it definitely merited further review.

New to charts? Note how *Your Weekly Review* identified the chart pattern *and* buy point. That's a huge help if you're new to chart-reading.

Step 3: Use *IBD Stock Checkup* to see if the stocks you circled pass the Buying Checklist.

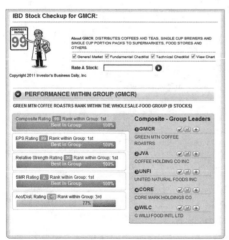

A quick look at *Stock Checkup* showed Green Mountain passed the Buying Checklist:

- Composite Rating: 99
- EPS Rating: 93
- RS Rating: 97
- Return on Equity: 21%
- Last Quarter Sales Growth: 56%
- Last Quarter EPS Growth: 14%*
- 3-Year Annual EPS Growth: 43%

*Green Mountain's earnings growth slipped to 14% in the most recent quarter, but annual EPS growth was 43%, and the previous quarter's gain was 76%.

Plus, it had the "N" in CAN SLIM®: An innovative new product—single-serving K-Cup gourmet coffees—that was revolutionizing the industry.

Step 4: Add the strongest stocks to your watch list.
Over the weekend, you could have added Green Mountain to your watch list, with a game plan to buy if it broke past the 42.99 buy point. And you could have set a trade trigger with your broker before the market reopened on Monday.

You would have been glad you did: On Monday, March 16, 2009, Green Mountain Coffee Roasters broke out and ran up more than 1,000% over the next 2½ years.

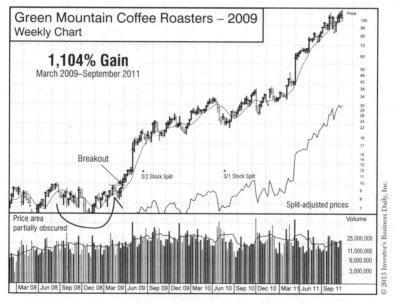

Green Mountain Coffee Roasters is just one example of why it pays to do the Simple Weekend Routine *regularly*.

What if You Missed the First Breakout?

Don't fret. The *IBD 50* and *Your Weekly Review* highlighted Green Mountain as being near a potential buy point **over 20 more times** during its 1,000%+ gain.

Never give up—and keep doing the Simple Weekend Routine. The best stocks will give you *multiple* buying opportunities, and you'll profit from them if you do the routine *regularly*.

SolarWinds (SWI)

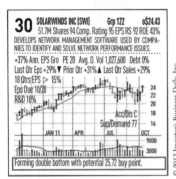

You could have also used the Simple Weekend Routine to spot cloud computing leader SolarWinds *before* it broke out.

On October 17, 2011, the *IBD 50* noted that SolarWinds was "forming double bottom with potential 25.72 buy point."

The stock broke out 10 days later—giving you plenty of time to have it on your watch list and set up your buying game plan. **SolarWinds soared over 130% in just the next 11 months.**

Rackspace Hosting (RAX)

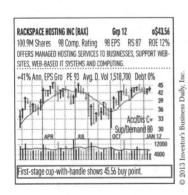

Rackspace Hosting is another cloud computing company you could have found with the Simple Weekend Routine.

On January 20, 2012, *Your Weekly Review* highlighted Rackspace Hosting, saying its "first-stage cup-with-handle shows 45.56 buy point."

Two weeks later, **Rackspace broke out and quickly rose 30% in only 9 weeks.**

Start *Your* Search for the Next Big Winners

Now that you know how powerful this simple routine can be, the next step is to start using it!

If you haven't already, take the Action Steps I've included at the end of the Simple Weekend Routine. Once you've done that, it's time to take a little challenge and find out what a *big* difference you can see in your investing skills in just a couple of weeks.

Take a Simple 2-Week Challenge

You've now seen the kind of money-making opportunities you'll find in every strong market uptrend. And you have a basic routine that shows you, step by step, how to identify them.

So what's next?

Let's turn that new routine into an old—and healthy—habit! And you can do that by taking the IBD 2-Week Challenge.

It's simple: **Try the Simple Weekend Routine and 10-Minute Daily Routine for the next 2 weeks.**

I think you'll be pleasantly surprised at how quickly your confidence grows and the quality of your watch list improves. You'll also find that once you do these routines a few times, you really can go through them in just a matter of minutes. And by combining these routines with the buying and selling checklists, you'll have a clear road map for making money in stocks.

You can do it. You just have to take the first step and start using these routines *regularly.*

To get going with the 2-Week Challenge and start building your watch list, visit www.investors.com/GettingStartedBook.

And while you're there, why not also sign up for free online training and check out the IBD Meetup group near you? Those are two great ways to kick-start your investing skills and start putting these routines and checklists into action—the right and profitable way.

Selling Checklist

Selling Checklist

Time to Sell or Hold?

Use this checklist to lock in your profits and cut short any losses.

While you can learn more advanced selling techniques later, start with these basic rules. They'll give you a sound game plan for achieving both profits and protection.

Offensive Selling: To lock in your profits

❏ Sell *most* stocks if they rise 20%–25% above a proper buy point.
Exception: If a stock rises *over 20% within just 3 weeks* from a proper buy point, hold the stock for at least 8 weeks.

Defensive Selling: To cut short any losses and protect remaining gains

General Market

❏ Take defensive action when *Market Pulse* outlook is "Uptrend under pressure" or "Market in correction."

Your Stock

❏ Always sell if a stock drops 7%–8% below what *you* paid for it. No questions asked!

❏ **Chart Analysis:** Consider selling some or all of your shares if you see these signals:

→ Biggest single-day price decline since start of stock's run on heaviest volume in months

→ Sharp drop below 50-day moving average line on heaviest volume in months

→ Sharp drop—and close—below 10-week moving average line on heavy volume

You can download and print this checklist at www.investors.com/GettingStartedBook.

Want to Invest Well? Learn How to *Sell* Well!

Knowing when to sell is one of the trickier—and most overlooked—aspects of investing.

All too many folks jump into the market thinking only about what to *buy*, without giving much thought to when to *sell*. But as IBD Executive Editor Chris Gessel has said: **"Investing without sell rules is like learning to *fly* without learning how to *land*!"**

Don't think of selling as something negative. It's an essential part of investing that puts *you* in control of your money. Like the brakes on your car, sell rules don't just keep you out of an "accident." They let you stop and get out at your desired destination so you can cash in your profits at the right time.

As we go through the Selling Checklist, you'll see our approach comes back again to the "big rocks"—the essential pillars of successful investing— we've been discussing throughout this book:

- Only buy stocks in a market uptrend. *Take defensive action as a downtrend begins.*

- Buy stocks being heavily bought by institutional investors. *Avoid those they're heavily selling.*

The sell rules we'll cover are easy to follow—*if* you keep those all-too-human emotions of fear, hope and greed on a tight leash.

I'll be the first to admit, that's not always easy to do. So before we go over the specific rules in the Selling Checklist, let's take a look at 8 selling "secrets" that will keep you in the right frame of mind and help you take decisive action when it's time to lock in your profits or cut short any losses.

Check the Chart for Clues on When to Sell or Hold

Would you like an "early warning detection system" for your stocks? Learn to read charts!

Once you understand a few common warning signs, you'll know whether it's time to sit tight—or get out. We'll cover chart-related items on the checklist in Chapter 6, "Don't Invest *Blindly*: Use Charts to *See* the Best Time to Buy and Sell."

---

8 "Secrets" of Successful Selling

1. ***Everyone* makes mistakes! Just be sure to cut all losses short.**

   Even the best investors get hit with a loss from time to time. But they don't dwell on it or wring their hands as the stock drops even lower. They cut their losses *quickly* and move on.

   So leave your ego and pride at the door, and don't let a loss get to you—either mentally or financially. Stay out of trouble by sticking to the rules in the Selling Checklist.

2. **If you don't sell *early*, you'll sell *late*.**

   Don't get greedy. Get disciplined! To lock in solid gains, sell while your stock is still going *up*. As Bill O'Neil has said, "Your objective is to make and take significant gains and not get excited, optimistic, greedy or emotionally carried away as your stock's advance gets stronger."

   I'll show you how to do that with our 20%–25% profit-taking rule.

3. **Have a selling plan in place *before* you buy.**

   If you're a warm-blooded human being like the rest of us, you'll find the real drama kicks in when it comes time to *sell*. And if you don't have sell rules and an exit plan to guide you, it's easy to freeze and not take action when you need to.

   If your stock is soaring higher, you may get a little greedy and want to grab every last nickel—not recognizing certain sell signals that tell you it could be heading for a fall. And if you're sitting on a loss, you may do the old "hold and hope" routine, praying it'll bounce back to break even— while it continues to put you even deeper in the red.

   So make it easy on yourself: Have a clear selling plan in place *ahead of time*. Write down your target sell prices for both locking in your profits and nipping any losses in the bud. How do you do that? Just follow the Selling Checklist. It gives you a sound game plan for staying protected and profitable.

4. **Don't let a decent gain turn into a loss.**

   It's no secret that stock prices fluctuate from day to day. Even if a stock is trending generally higher, it will have down days and weeks along the way. To make money, you need to sit through those swings and give the stock time to climb higher.

But if you have a nice gain of, say, 15%, 20% or better, and the stock begins to trend down, don't let that profit disappear completely.

Look for warning signs like those in the "Defensive Selling" section of the checklist. If institutional investors are clearly starting to sell, you'll want to lock in at least some of your profits. And if the general market uptrend is also starting to run out of steam, that's all the more reason to cash in the gains you have left.

If you choose to hold, have a target sell price in mind. For example, if your former 20% gain falls to, say, 10%, sell. The profit-taking price is up to you. The point is, you never want to "round-trip" a stock by riding it up to a big gain and all the way back down into a loss.

Believe me, it's *much* less frustrating to see a 15%–20% gain turn into a *5%–10% profit* than it is to see it turn into a 5% *loss*. Don't forget: You can always buy back the stock if it rebounds and institutional investors start aggressively buying it again.

Use Trade Triggers to Protect Your Profits

 You can set trailing stop-loss orders and other trade triggers with your broker to make sure a good gain doesn't slip into a loss (Chapter 4).

5. Don't marry your stocks. Just date them!

"For better or for worse, for richer or for poorer" is a noble and time-honored approach to marital fealty, but it's a bad idea when it comes to investing. In most cases, it's better to take a good gain while you have it, then move on to your next conquest. And never hesitate to cut yourself loose from a bad relationship if there are clear signs of trouble. (Remember: Don't try this at home with your significant other . . .)

6. Sell your *losing* stocks first.

If you were trying to build a champion baseball team, would you trade away your top players and keep all your benchwarmers? Of course not!

Yet many investors do just that: They sell stocks in which they have a good gain—and hold on to those showing a loss, thinking a big gain is just around the corner. That's usually wishful thinking. To build a power-house portfolio, you want to do the exact opposite: Sell your losers and use that money to add new winners to your roster or invest more in the top performers you already own.

7. **When *buying* a stock, focus on both fundamentals and the chart action. When *selling*, focus on the chart action.**

They say the view at the top is great, and that often applies to stocks as well. Market leaders will often still be posting stellar earnings and sales growth even as the stock begins to decline. That's because warning signs typically show up in the chart *before* they appear in the fundamentals (i.e., earnings, sales and other *company*-related criteria). It could be that institutional investors see trouble ahead and are starting to take their profits, or the overall market may be weakening. *Whatever the reason, when the chart flashes clear warning signs, you must take defensive action.*

> *"All stocks are bad—except the ones that go up."*
>
> —WILLIAM J. O'NEIL

That may sound funny, but Bill's message is serious. A stock could have phenomenal earnings growth and other outstanding CAN SLIM® traits, but if the share price is clearly tanking, why buy or hold it? It may be a great *company*, but at least right now, it's not a great *stock*. That's a very important distinction.

If fund managers are clearly dumping shares—which you can see by tracking the price and volume action in a chart—don't hold the stock just because it has great earnings. You're fighting a losing battle if you try to hold while institutional investors liquidate their positions.

DryShips was a classic example of this. Even though it was still posting explosive, triple-digit earnings and sales growth, big investors were *dumping* shares, pushing the stock into a clear downtrend. So what happened to investors who "married" the stock because they fell in love with the earnings? They quickly went from "richer" to "poorer," as DryShips dropped from around $130 to $2 over the next 5 years. Something tells me those people now understand why it's so important to cut *all* losses at no more than 7%–8%.

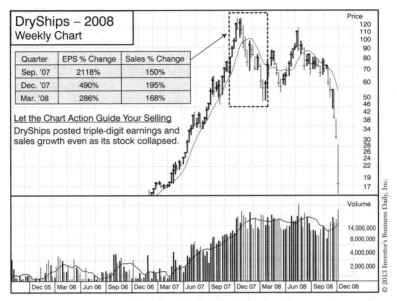

Quarter	EPS % Change	Sales % Change
Sep. '07	2118%	150%
Dec. '07	490%	195%
Mar. '08	286%	168%

DryShips – 2008
Weekly Chart

Let the Chart Action Guide Your Selling
DryShips posted triple-digit earnings and
sales growth even as its stock collapsed.

© 2013 Investor's Business Daily, Inc.

**The fall of DryShips: Focus primarily on chart action,
not earnings, when it comes to selling.**

Bottom line: When you see clear sell signals in the chart, just *sell*—even if the earnings look great. You may not know *why* institutional investors are dumping shares, but who cares?! You can find that out later, *after* you've protected your money by moving safely to the sidelines.

8. **The most important sell rule is to *buy* at the right time.**

Several years ago I had an epiphany that sounds incredibly obvious in hindsight, but it made a big difference for me: I realized that most of my mistakes came down to one simple problem—I was buying at the *wrong* time. I had a tendency to jump in a little early or chase stocks if I missed the breakout. So instead of starting with a nice gain, I often started with one foot already below the thin ice I was trying to walk on.

Fixing that one problem has made a huge difference, enabling me to launch new stock positions on more stable and solid ground.

Psychologically, it's *much* easier to make sell or hold decisions when you're sitting on a gain. When you have a loss, self-doubt—plus a mix of *hope* for a quick rebound and *fear* of an even bigger loss—can creep in and prevent you from making a level-headed, objective decision.

While not every trade will work out the way you want, if you always run a stock through the Buying Checklist before you buy, you'll be investing in quality stocks being bought heavily by institutional investors as they break out of a proper buy point during a market uptrend. That *greatly* increases the likelihood that you'll start off in the right frame of mind—and with a profit in your stock.

> *"Nothing ever becomes real 'til it is experienced."*
>
> —JOHN KEATS

Unfortunately, I think there's a lot of truth to what Keats said. I say "unfortunately" because I'm afraid many people will just quickly read through these 8 "secrets" and move on before they really sink in.

Then down the road, they'll suffer a loss and realize, "By gosh, Matt was right! I *should* have cut my losses sooner!" or "Why did I let that big gain disappear?!"

In case you're wondering . . . Yes, I'm speaking from experience. I did indeed learn many of these "secrets" the hard way.

But that doesn't mean *you* have to! Reread this chapter from time to time to reinforce these key points and make sure you really take them to heart. They'll spare you a lot of unnecessary grief and help you experience a great deal of investing joy.

A Simple Selling Game Plan

The Selling Checklist covers the basics. There are more advanced sell signals to look for, and you can learn more about them in Bill O'Neil's classic work, *How to Make Money in Stocks*, or by attending an IBD workshop and your local IBD Meetup group.

My goal here is to make sure you start out with a clear, easy-to-use plan—one you can begin using immediately to both grow your money and avoid any serious mishaps. Here it is.

• YOUR SIMPLE SELLING GAME PLAN •

- Sell *most* stocks when they go up 20%–25% from a proper buy point.
- *Always* sell if a stock drops 7%–8% below what you paid for it.
- Take defensive action as a market downtrend begins.

These 3 simple rules—both offensive and defensive—will serve you well. We'll also get into other warning signs and sell signals, but when in doubt, stick to these 3 core principles.

3-to-1 Profit-and-Loss Ratio

The first step to making money in the market is to protect the money you already have, and sticking with this selling formula will help you do that.

Notice how the first 2 sell rules above give you roughly a 3-to-1 ratio: 20%–25% profits vs. losses of no more than 7%–8%. If you stick to this basic selling plan, you can be *wrong* on 2 out of 3 stocks and still come out slightly ahead or with just a minor loss. The next table shows how that works.

Use a 3-to-1 Profit-and-Loss Ratio to Grow—and Protect—Your Portfolio

Trade	Amount Invested	% Gain/Loss	$ Profit/Loss	Total Value
#1	$5,000	−7%	−$350	$4,650
#2	$4,650	−7%	−$326	$4,324
#3	$4,324	+25%	+$1,081	$5,405 (8% overall gain)

As I noted earlier, everyone makes mistakes and takes a loss sometimes. But if you cut *all* your losses short, you won't make any *big* mistakes.

And look what happens when your batting average improves. The table below shows how if you were right just 60% of the time (3 winners and 2 losers), you could walk away with a solid 69% profit.

Compound Your Gains and Minimize Any Losses

Trade	Amount Invested	% Gain/Loss	$ Profit/Loss	Total Value
#1	$5,000	−7%	−$350	$4,650
#2	$4,650	+25%	+$1,163	$5,813
#3	$5,813	+25%	+$1,453	$7,266
#4	$7,266	−7%	−509	$6,757
#5	$6,757	+25%	$1,689	$8,446 (69% overall gain)

So be sure to use the Buying Checklist to get into quality stocks at the right time, then follow this basic selling game plan to lock in your gains and limit any losses.

By doing that, you can start delving into the market with confidence, knowing you're safeguarding your money from undue risk while also laying a solid foundation for compounding your profits over time.

Offensive Selling to Lock in Your Profits

A quick note on charts before we jump in.

As we go through the Selling Checklist, I'll touch on chart-related terms like "base pattern," "cup-with-handle," "ideal buy point" and "proper buying range." If you're not familiar with those concepts, don't worry. We're going through this one step at a time—and we'll cover all that in due course.

For now, just stay focused on the basic selling game plan: Take most profits at 20%–25%; cut all losses at no more than 7%–8%; and take defensive action as a market downtrend begins.

We'll get into chart-based sell signals in Chapter 6, "Don't Invest *Blindly*: Use Charts to *See* the Right Time to Buy and Sell."

Selling Checklist

Offensive Selling: **To lock in your profits**

❏ Sell *most* stocks if they rise 20%–25% above a proper buy point.
Exception: If a stock rises *over 20% within just 3 weeks* from a proper buy point, hold the stock for at least 8 weeks.

 Sell most *stocks if they rise 20%–25% above a proper buy point*

Especially when you're new to investing, this rule will help you hit the kind of singles and doubles that will grow your money—and your confidence. It's tempting to think you should swing for the fences and only try to hit home runs and grand slams, but that's not likely to happen. And fortunately, it doesn't have to. You can generate very impressive profits by stringing together a few 20%–25% gains. Here's why.

The Rule of 72

I first came across this rule when I read *Beating the Street* by legendary mutual fund manager Peter Lynch in the mid-1990s. It's a handy calculation to see how quickly you can basically double your money.

Here's how it works: Take the gain you have in a stock (or any other investment), described as a percentage. Then divide 72 by that number. The answer tells you how many times you have to compound that gain to essentially double your money.

For example, let's say you nailed down a 24% gain in a stock. 72 divided by 24 is 3. That means if you reinvested that same money (including your 24% profit) and got two more 24% gains, you'd nearly double your money.

You'll find it's easier to get three 20%–25% gains in a few different stocks than it is to score a 100% profit in one. As the following table shows, if you compound those gains, those smaller wins turn into major profits.

How Smaller Gains Can Lead to Big Profits

Trade	Amount Invested	% Gain	$ Profit	Total Value
#1	$5,000	24%	$1,200	$6,200
#2	$6,200	24%	$1,488	$7,688
#3	$7,688	24%	$1,845	$9,533 (91% overall gain)

Why Sell at 20%–25%?

In a word, history. We've studied all the top stocks since 1880, and here's what typically happens: When a stock breaks out of a proper buy point and rises 20%–25%, it usually pulls back and forms a new chart pattern, like a cup-with-handle, double bottom or flat base.

So rather than sit through that correction (i.e., decline) and watch some or all of your profits disappear, it can be a good opportunity to lock in those gains. That ties into one of the 8 "secrets" of successful selling we saw earlier: "If you don't sell early, you'll sell late." In other words, take your gains on the way *up*, before the stock comes back down and takes a big chunk of your profits with it.

See the following charts for two examples of how the 20%–25% profit-taking rule helps you nail down some nice gains.

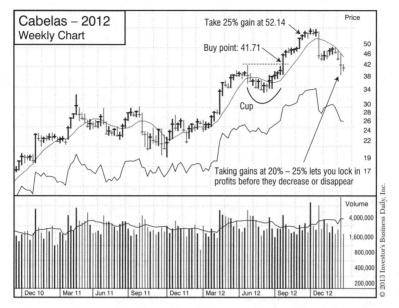

Cabelas – 2012
Weekly Chart

Take 25% gain at 52.14

Buy point: 41.71

Cup

Taking gains at 20% – 25% lets you lock in profits before they decrease or disappear

Price

50
46
42
38
34
30
28
26
24
22
19
17

Volume

4,000,000
1,600,000
800,000
400,000
200,000

Dec 10   Mar 11   Jun 11   Sep 11   Dec 11   Mar 12   Jun 12   Sep 12   Dec 12

© 2013 Investor's Business Daily, Inc.

Taking most gains at 20%–25% helps build your portfolio and your confidence.

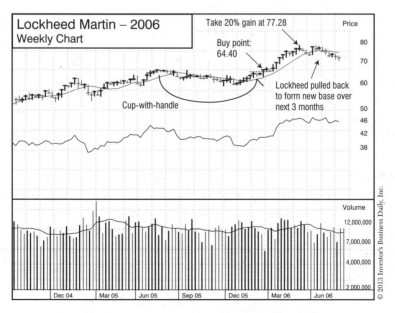

Lockheed Martin – 2006
Weekly Chart

Take 20% gain at 77.28

Buy point:
64.40

Cup-with-handle

Lockheed pulled back to form new base over next 3 months

Price

80
70
60
50
46
42
38

Volume

12,000,000
7,000,000
4,000,000
2,000,000

Dec 04   Mar 05   Jun 05   Sep 05   Dec 05   Mar 06   Jun 06

© 2013 Investor's Business Daily, Inc.

Don't let a good gain slip away. Following the 20%–25% sell rule
helps you lock in and compound your profits.

Important Note About the 20%–25% Rule

The 20%–25% gain is calculated from the stock's ideal buy point. That may be different from your own purchase price.

As you'll see later when we discuss chart patterns, the buying range for a stock is from the ideal buy point up to 5% above that. So let's say you bought 4% above the *ideal* buy point. If the stock then rose 20% above the ideal buy point, *your* profit would be 16%.

Below is an example of how to properly apply the 20%–25% sell rule.

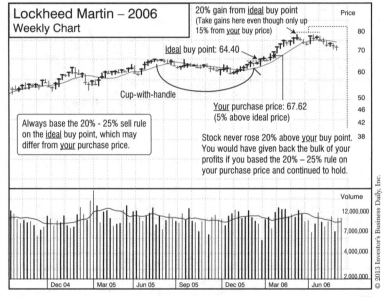

Always buy as close as possible to the ideal buy point. One way to do that is to set automatic trade triggers to buy stocks right when they break out (see Chapter 4).

I'm emphasizing this because I misunderstood this rule when I was starting out—and it cost me money. I thought I should sell a stock when *my gain* was 20%–25%. On more than one occasion, I'd be up 15% or so, just waiting for the stock to hit that 20% benchmark. But it would pull back before reaching that target, and I'd end up taking a much smaller gain or in some cases a loss. (Apparently, I had to take some lumps before I took to heart the idea that you should "never let a decent gain turn into a loss.")

It wasn't until I reviewed some past trades that I realized my mistake. I was buying 4%–5% above the ideal buy point, but I was basing the 20%–25% rule on *my purchase price* instead of on the stock's ideal buy point. (That's just one example of why reviewing your trades is so important. See Chapter 7 for how to do a profitable post-analysis and fix any bad habits.)

Don't Ignore a Winning Stock After You Sell It!

The Best Stocks Give You *Multiple* Money-Making Opportunities

The best stocks will typically form multiple base patterns as they double or triple in price. Like a hiker, they'll go up for awhile, rest (or maybe slide down the hill a bit), then continue the climb.

So when you sell a stock that hits that 20%–25% benchmark, it's not necessarily the end of the story. Watch to see what happens next. Does it pull back and form a new cup-with-handle or other base pattern? Or does it climb higher, then move sideways to form a 3-weeks tight or flat base? These and other scenarios can give you another opportunity to buy the stock and profit again.

It's absolutely critical that you continue to track these winning stocks. They have the CAN SLIM® traits, and they've proven they have the power to break out of a good chart pattern and make a nice gain. If they do repeat that winning process, why not grab another piece of those *additional* profits?

The chart for Chipotle Mexican Grill shows an example of how that can work.

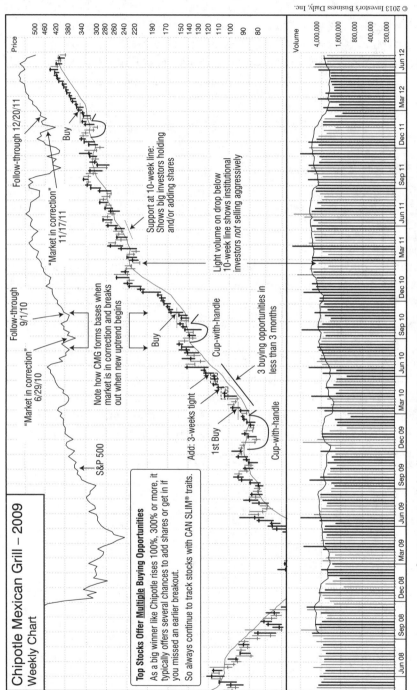

Chipotle Mexican Grill – 2009
Weekly Chart

Top Stocks Offer Multiple Buying Opportunities

As a big winner like Chipotle rises 100%, 300% or more, it typically offers several chances to add shares or get in if you missed an earlier breakout.

So always continue to track stocks with CAN SLIM® traits.

Note how CMG forms bases when market is in correction and breaks out when new uptrend begins

Support at 10-week line: Shows big investors holding and/or adding shares

Light volume on drop below 10-week line shows institutional investors *not* selling aggressively

3 buying opportunities in less than 3 months

Cup-with-handle

Add: 3-weeks tight

1st Buy

Cup-with-handle

Buy

Buy

Follow-through 12/20/11

"Market in correction" 11/17/11

Follow-through 9/1/10

"Market in correction" 6/29/10

S&P 500

Price

Volume

© 2013 Investor's Business Daily, Inc.

Continue to track leading stocks: *IBD 50, Your Weekly Review* and other features alert you to multiple buy points as the top stocks make their big moves.

Also keep this in mind: Since you've already owned the stock once, you know its story, and if you're using charts, you know its trading "personality." That makes it easier to handle the stock properly and spot any changes in trend.

It also makes it easier to capture a sizable chunk of a big winner's gains—without the stress of having to sit through major sell-offs that may happen along the way.

When a stock like Apple, Priceline.com or Green Mountain Coffee Roasters goes up 1,000% or more, you probably won't capture that whole gain. But by following the 20%–25% rule—and continuing to track a winner even after you sell—you can certainly grab multiple 20%+ profits in that stock. And the "Rule of 72" shows how a few of those gains can very quickly increase the size of your portfolio.

Don't Forget the General Market!

Stocks don't operate in a vacuum. Like the moon's effect on the tides, the direction of the general market has an enormous pull on individual stocks.

You'll often find that stocks hit that 20%–25% target, then pull back to form new bases at the same time the *overall* market uptrend is starting to run out of steam.

See the connection?

Winning stocks make their climbs when the overall market is trending higher, and they'll start to pull back when the market weakens. That's why it's important to be on the lookout for any changes in market direction by regularly checking the *Market Pulse* in *The Big Picture* column.

We'll get into the role of the general market more when we talk about "defensive selling," but for now, just make a mental note of how closely the 20%–25% sell rule is tied to the ebb and flow of the *overall* market.

Important Exception to the 20%–25% Sell Rule

If a stock rises *over 20% within just 3 weeks* from a proper buy point, hold the stock for at least 8 weeks.

Stocks that show that kind of power have the potential to go on to even bigger gains. It's an indication that institutional investors are aggressively establishing new positions or increasing existing ones, and that's what fuels a big, sustained climb.

But it's unlikely the stock will go straight up without some bumps along the way. In fact, soon after a stock makes that initial jump, it may pull back sharply as some investors take their short-term profits. If the stock is exceptionally strong, it will shake off that temporary setback and continue its upward move.

The purpose of the 8-week rule is to help you sit through any sudden pullbacks so you can hold on for potentially much larger profits. Without such a rule, it's easy to get scared out of the stock and sell too early.

See the following charts for 2 examples of how the 8-week rule can help investors hold on for big gains.

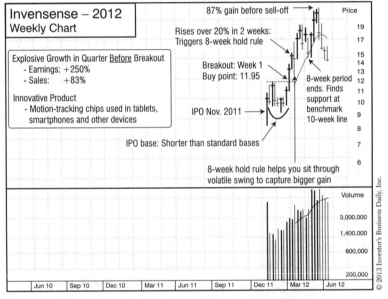

The 8-week hold rule helped investors sit tight and grab a bigger chunk of Invensense's 87% gain.

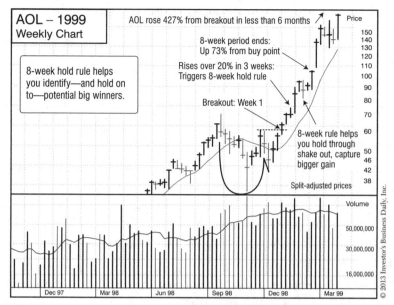

AOL – 1999
Weekly Chart

AOL rose 427% from breakout in less than 6 months

Price

8-week hold rule helps you identify—and hold on to—potential big winners.

8-week period ends:
Up 73% from buy point

Rises over 20% in 3 weeks:
Triggers 8-week hold rule

Breakout: Week 1

8-week rule helps you hold through shake out, capture bigger gain

Split-adjusted prices

Volume

© 2013 Investor's Business Daily, Inc.

Without the 8-week hold rule, it's easy to get nervous and sell a big winner too soon.

3 Notes on the 8-Week Hold Rule

1. Don't apply this rule to just any old stock. Make sure it is a true market leader with superior earnings and sales growth, solid institutional sponsorship and other CAN SLIM traits.

2. Note that the week of the breakout counts as week #1 in the 8-week count. See the examples in the previous two charts.

3. This rule only applies to stocks that have just broken out of a proper base. Do *not* apply this rule to a stock that suddenly shoots up 20% or more *without* first breaking out of a cup-with-handle or other chart pattern. For example, a stock may shoot up 20% or more on a good earnings report, but that only triggers this rule if the move comes as it breaks out of a base (see Chapter 6 for more on bases and chart-reading).

What to Do When the 8 Weeks Are Up

After the 8-week holding period ends, you have a choice to make: Sell or hold the stock?

Here are a few questions to help you decide:

- Has the stock climbed substantially higher during those 8 weeks, or have you given back most of your gains? Is your former good gain on the verge of turning into a loss?

- If the stock has pulled back, did it find support at key areas, such as the 10-week moving average line or a former area of resistance? That would show big investors are holding onto their shares. Or has it been falling *below* those key benchmarks on heavy volume? That shows fund managers could be liquidating their positions—and it may be time for you to do the same.

- Is the overall market still in a confirmed uptrend, or has the outlook changed to "uptrend under pressure" or "market in correction"?

When you combine your answers to those questions with your own risk tolerance, the decision to sell or hold should become fairly easy. Keep in mind: You don't have to sell *all* your shares. You could choose to sell just a portion. That lets you lock in some of your profits but still keep a position in case the stock shoots higher. And if the stock is forming a new base or running into trouble, you can always sell now and buy it back if the stock rebounds and again passes the Buying Checklist.

Profits Come to Those Who Grab Them

Not every stock you buy will be the next Priceline.com, Netflix or Lululemon Athletica—with a 100%, 500% or 1,000%+ gain.

And even when you do latch on to big winners (and you *will* if you stick to these checklists and routines), those stocks don't go straight up. They take breathers along the way—and if the market is particularly weak, they may drop *sharply* before they (hopefully) resume their climb.

That's why you need *offensive* sell rules to cash in your profits while you still have them.

You can do that if you just follow the key points we've discussed here:

- Take most profits at 20%–25%.

- Be ready to lock in at least some of your gains when the market weakens.

- Use a 3-to-1 Profit-to-Loss Ratio to systematically grow and protect your money.

As you improve your stock-picking and chart-reading skills, you'll become even more adept at capturing multiple 20%–25% gains from the same stock—and at holding "monster" stocks for even bigger profits.

But the key right now is to start right. And if you stick to this simple selling game plan, you'll grow your portfolio—and your confidence—by hitting safely for a lot of singles and doubles.

• ACTION STEPS •

Here are some quick *To Dos* to help you start capturing profits using the Selling Checklist. To take these steps and start improving your selling skills, visit www.investors.com/GettingStartedBook.

- Watch 2 short videos on offensive selling:
  - *Take Most Profits at 20%—25%*
  - *Use the 8-Week Hold Rule to Help Capture Bigger Gains*

Defensive Selling to Cut Short
Any Losses and Protect Your Gains

I think this is true for just about any investor: We start out with 2 basic emotions—hope and fear. We *hope* we'll make a ton of money ASAP. But we also *fear* we'll lose our shirts.

Wouldn't it be nice to have a little peace of mind—some simple guidelines that will make sure you don't get burned?

That's where the "Defensive Selling" segment of the checklist comes in.

To avoid any serious damage, just follow these basic sell rules. If you do that, even when a severe bear market hits like it did in 2008, you can rest easy, knowing you've proactively protected yourself by sticking to a sound game plan.

Let's start with a look at the first two "Defensive Selling" criteria. Then we'll get into the chart-related items in Chapter 6, "Don't Invest *Blindly*: Use Charts to *See* the Best Time to Buy and Sell."

Selling Checklist

Defensive Selling: To cut short any losses and protect remaining gains

General Market

❏ Take defensive action when *Market Pulse* outlook is "Uptrend under pressure" or "Market in correction."

Your Stock

❏ Always sell if a stock drops 7%–8% below what *you* paid for it. No questions asked!

Notice how I've divided this part of the checklist into "General Market" and "Your Stock."

As we keep emphasizing, individual stocks don't operate in a vacuum—most get pulled in whatever direction the general market is currently heading.

While it's ultimately the behavior of your stock that determines whether you should sell or hold, you should *always* take into account what's happening in the overall market.

You may drive a finely tuned luxury sports car, but if the road is covered in oil slicks and ice, you might want to slow down! It's the same with investing: How you "drive" your portfolio depends on current market conditions.

So let's start there.

Selling Checklist

Defensive Selling: **To cut short any losses and protect remaining gains**

General Market

 Take defensive action when the Market Pulse *outlook is "Uptrend under pressure" or "Market in correction"*

By now, I think this point is clear: **You *must* protect yourself when the market comes under pressure and begins to fall into a correction.**

Remember: **You do *not* have to be invested in the market at all times.** Your goal is to make money when the market is trending higher and protect those profits when it heads south.

How Do You Know When the Market is Running into Trouble?

Check the *Market Pulse* in *The Big Picture* column.

We covered this earlier in the section on Big Rock #1 in Chapter 3, so we'll just do a quick recap here and focus on what steps you can take to protect yourself in a weak market.

IBD's 3-stage approach lets you know if selling pressure is rising, which could mean the current uptrend is on the verge of falling into a correction. Think of it like a traffic light that goes from green ("Confirmed uptrend") to yellow ("Uptrend under pressure") to red ("Market in correction").

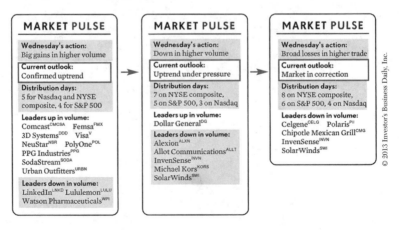

Distribution Days Alert You to Mounting Trouble

When the market is in an uptrend, we watch for "distribution days"—days of heavy selling in at least one of the major indexes, primarily the Nasdaq, S&P 500 or Dow Jones Industrial Average (see Big Rock #1, Chapter 3).

If the number of distribution days starts to rise, watch out! That shows institutional investors are moving to the sidelines, which may mean the current uptrend is running out of steam.

If you get 6 distribution days over any 4- to 5-week span, the general market almost always falls into a correction.

You can easily track the number of distribution days just by checking the *Market Pulse* (see examples above). If the count continues to grow, the outlook will shift from "Confirmed uptrend" to "Uptrend under pressure" and finally to "Market in correction." (The number of distribution days needed to turn the market into a correction may change over time. Regularly read *The Big Picture* to stay aware of any adjustments.)

Think about how valuable that 3-stage progression is.

While some markets are more volatile, **changes in market trend typically happen over a few weeks, giving you time to protect your money.**

Earlier, we saw how distribution days mounted in March–April 2012 as the market rolled over into a correction (Big Rock #1, Chapter 3). We also noted how shifts in the *Market Pulse* helped investors avoid any serious damage when the financial and housing crisis pushed the market into a severe bear market starting in November 2007 (Big Rock #1, Chapter 3). Let's take a closer look at how that latter episode played out—and how you can use distribution days to help safeguard your portfolio whenever future downtrends emerge.

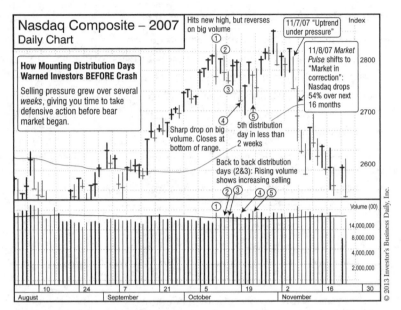

Nasdaq Composite – 2007 Daily Chart

How Mounting Distribution Days Warned Investors BEFORE Crash

Selling pressure grew over several *weeks*, giving you time to take defensive action before bear market began.

Hits new high, but reverses on big volume ①

②

11/7/07 "Uptrend under pressure"

Index

11/8/07 *Market Pulse* shifts to "Market in correction": Nasdaq drops 54% over next 16 months

2800

2700

③

④ ⑤ 5th distribution day in less than 2 weeks

Sharp drop on big volume. Closes at bottom of range.

Back to back distribution days (2&3): Rising volume shows increasing selling

2600

② ③   ④ ⑤

①

Volume (00)

14,000,000
8,000,000
4,000,000
2,000,000

| 10 | 24 | 7 | 21 | 5 | 19 | 2 | 16 | 30 |
| August | | September | | October | | November | | |

© 2013 Investor's Business Daily, Inc.

Regularly checking the distribution day count in the *Market Pulse* in *The Big Picture* column will help you know when it's time to play defense and protect your gains.

What Action Should You Take as Distribution Days Mount?

First and foremost, make sure you're following your selling game plan.

- **Look for opportunities to lock in some profits.** If you have a stock that's gone up 20%–25% from a buy point, why not cash in some or all of those gains? If the number of distribution days continues to rise, there's a good chance your stocks will also get dragged down.

- **Cut any losses short.** Even in a *strong* market, if a stock drops 7%–8% below what *you* paid for it, sell immediately. In a *weakening* market, you can cut your losses even sooner—at, say, 3%–4%. Better to be safe than sorry.

Here's a basic guideline for how to handle a rising number of distribution days:

# of Distribution Days	Action
1	No special action needed
2	No special action needed
3	Start watching your stocks even more closely
4	Look for something to sell
5 or 6	Proactively take defensive action if your gains are threatened or you have small losses

You can see from the table above that 1 or 2 distribution days is not a cause for concern. But when you get a third day, take note. Make sure you're keeping a close eye on each of your stocks and following your selling game plan. That way you'll be ready to act decisively if we get even more distribution days.

When the distribution day count reaches 4, look for something to sell. Selling pressure is on the rise, so it's an opportunity to shed your *weaker* holdings. Remember one of the 8 "secrets" of successful selling: Sell your *losing* stocks first! Don't make the mistake of selling your winners while holding your laggards.

Why should you look to sell something when you have 4 distribution days?

Because by the time the general market has 5 or 6 distribution days, many leading stocks may have already taken a hit. So be proactive and reduce your exposure by selling any stocks showing weakness. For example, a stock may be dropping lower on increasingly heavy volume—a sign institutional investors are selling.

See the next chart for an example of how you could have locked in your gains using the *Market Pulse* and basic sell rules.

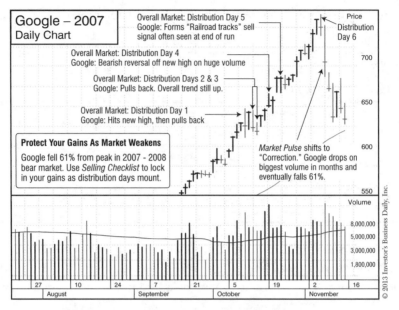

Stay profitable and protected: Take defensive action as distribution days mount and the market weakens.

One Important Caveat

If an uptrend is already established (i.e., at least a few weeks old) and rolling along just fine, you don't need to worry about the first couple of distribution days. However, *if you see distribution right after a new uptrend begins, that is definitely cause for concern.* It could mean the nascent uptrend is not taking hold and will quickly fall back into a correction.

The Big Picture column alerts you to those types of warning signs, so be sure to read it regularly as part of your investing routine.

Beware the Double Whammy!

If your stock is flashing warnings signs *and* the overall market is coming under increasing selling pressure, that's two strikes against you. Big investors are getting out of the market in general and out of your stock in particular. The classic double whammy.

Why hold on and take the chance of striking out completely? Why leave yourself at the mercy of the market?

It's your money—take control and protect it by sticking to the Selling Checklist.

Take Your Profits—and Cut Your Losses—Even Sooner in a Weak Market

The basic selling game plan says you should:

- Take *most* profits at 20%–25%
- Cut *all* losses at no more than 7%–8%

But you can—and should—adjust that in a weak market. As a rule of thumb, keep the 3-to-1 Profit-to-Loss Ratio we discussed in "Offensive Selling."

For example, you could take your profits at 10%–15% and cut any losses at no more than 3%–5%. It's just like slowing down and driving more cautiously in heavy fog: The normal speed limit may be 65 mph, but do you drive that fast when you can't see the road?

So always adjust your game plan based on current market conditions. That's how you arrive safely at your destination.

---

3 Tips on How to Handle a Market Correction

By the time the outlook in the *Market Pulse* changes from "Confirmed uptrend" to "Uptrend under pressure" to "Market in correction," you've probably already sold at least some of your positions. Either you hit your target profit goals and locked them in, or your stocks triggered sell rules found in the Selling Checklist.

But keep in mind: *You do not have to automatically sell all your stocks when the market is in a correction.* If you have a large gain in a particularly strong leader that is holding up relatively well, you may choose to sit tight.

(Note: Holding *some* stocks is fine, but if you're still *fully* invested during a market correction, you probably need to take a closer look at your portfolio. Make sure you're properly following the selling game plan and taking heed of the 8 "secrets" we discussed earlier.)

Here are 3 proven ways to stay safe in a market downturn—and get ready to make more money in the next uptrend.

1. **Don't make new buys.**

   You now know that most stocks move down when the market is in a correction, so why risk it? Wait for a new uptrend to begin before making any new purchases.

2. **Protect yourself.**

   Remember your primary goal: Make money in an uptrend—and safeguard those gains when the market weakens.

What's the point of scoring nice gains in a strong rally, if you're only going to give them all back when the market direction changes? You can easily avoid "round-tripping" your stocks simply by following the Selling Checklist.

If you do hold stocks during a correction, understand that the market tide *is* against you. You need to remain vigilant and ready to protect yourself if your stocks start to seriously weaken. Here's how to do that:

- **Make sure you have a large enough gain** to "cushion" yourself against a potential drop. It's risky to hold in a downtrend if you're at breakeven or just sitting on a small gain.

- **Set a target sell price.** Decide how much of your profit you're willing to give back if the stock sells off. For example, if you have a 75% gain, you might be willing to ride that down to 50% but no further. If the stock hits that price, cash in your remaining profits.

  You can set automatic trade triggers to make sure you stick to your target sell price (Chapter 4).

- **Consider selling at least a *portion* of your shares.** That's a way to nail down guaranteed profits, but still have a position in the stock if it continues to climb.

3. **Prepare *now* to profit in the next uptrend.**

We touched on this earlier, but I want to make sure it really sinks in: If you stop doing your investing routine while the market is *down*, you won't be ready to make big money when it moves back *up*!

In the stock market, good things don't come to investors who just wait. Good things—and stellar profits—come to those who *prepare*.

Now you may be wondering: Why should I keep doing my routine and look for winning stocks if I'm not even supposed to make new buys in a correction? Here's the answer . . .

Why You Must Stay Engaged During a Market Downtrend

- **The market direction can change very quickly.**

When we're in a correction, the market is never more than 4 days away from a potential new uptrend. That's all it takes for a "follow-through day" to kick off a new rally (Big Rock #1, Chapter 3).

And remember: New uptrends often begin when the news is terrible. So if you stay focused on the doom and gloom headlines and ignore the

Market Pulse outlook, you probably won't realize—until it's too late—that a new rally has begun.

- **Most stocks form new bases—the chart patterns that launch big new moves—during market corrections.**

  If you're *not* checking the *IBD 50* or other lists for top-rated stocks forming bases, you won't have them on your watch list when a new uptrend begins.

- **The big money is made in the *early* stages of a new uptrend.**

  What typically happens after the *Market Pulse* outlook changes from "Market in correction" to "Confirmed uptrend"?

  The strongest CAN SLIM® stocks shoot out of the gate. They break out of the cup-with-handle or other chart pattern they formed during the correction, and generate nice profits for those investors who were paying attention and staying alert.

The following chart shows just some of the money-making opportunities that always pop up in the early stages of a strong new uptrend.

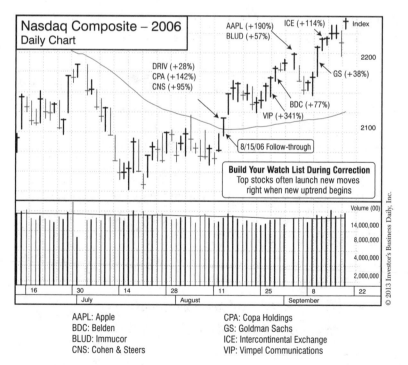

Be prepared: The best stocks launch new moves right when a new uptrend begins.

This is a critical point to understand, so be sure to go back and look at the other examples we saw earlier for uptrends that started in 2003, 2010 and 2011 (see Big Rock #1, Chapter 3).

And remember: This is *not* a case of 20-20 hindsight. You'll find many of these leading stocks on the *IBD 50*, *Your Weekly Review*, *Sector Leaders*, *Stock Spotlight* and other lists before they break out if you regularly use the daily and weekend routines we went through in Chapter 4.

Protect. Prepare. Profit.

I don't know what your perception of the stock market was before you started reading this book, but I hope by now you realize these 2 things:

- **You do *not* have to be at the mercy of the market.** You *can* see the right time to get in—and out.

- **You should *not* get frustrated by a downtrend—even a severe one.** Protect yourself by following the Selling Checklist, then prepare to profit from the huge money-making opportunities that *will* appear in the next strong uptrend by sticking to the Buying Checklist and simple routines.

Next up: Now that you know how to handle a *weak* market, let's talk about how to handle weakness in your own *stocks*.

• ACTION STEPS •

Here are some quick *To Dos* to learn more about how to spot weakness in the general market—and what to do about it. To take these steps, visit www.investors.com/GettingStartedBook.

1. Read *The Big Picture* column.

- Is the market currently in an uptrend—or correction?

- What else does it say about current market conditions?

2. Watch short videos on:

- *Sell or Hold? How to Review Your Stocks in a Weakening Market*

- *How to Handle a Market Correction*

- *What to Do After a Follow-Through Day*

Selling Checklist

Defensive Selling: To cut short any losses and protect remaining gains

---

Your Stock

☑ *Always sell if a stock drops 7%–8% below what* you *paid for it. No questions asked!*

Whether it's the dot-com crash in 2000 or the financial crisis in 2008, we hear horror stories of people who lose 30%, 50% or more of their money in a severe bear market. That's heart-wrenching—especially because it's so easy to avoid.

Just follow this one simple rule: **Cut all losses at no more than 7%–8%.**

It's extremely effective and easy. No charts to read, no fancy technical indicators to look for. If the stock drops 7%–8% below what you paid for it, just get out!

So why doesn't *everybody* follow this rule?

I think the first reason, frankly, is ignorance. Millions of people simply don't understand how market cycles work. And they don't have any sell rules to protect themselves.

The second reason is emotions.

We're all human, and we don't like to admit when we're wrong. So instead of quickly cutting a loss, the natural inclination for many investors is to hold and hope it bounces back.

Big mistake! That's how a little loss becomes a big one.

And here's a paradox about selling: *If you have a hard time selling a loss when it's small, it'll be that much harder to sell as it gets bigger.* That's when denial and delusion start to really kick in.

Believe me, I've been there. The following chart shows how I stubbornly held on to a former leader called Namtai Electronics when I was just starting out.

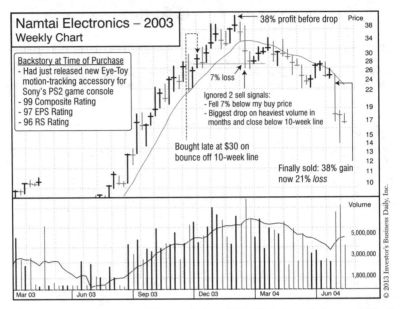

Namtai Electronics – 2003
Weekly Chart

38% profit before drop

Price
38
34
30
28
26
24
22

Backstory at Time of Purchase
- Had just released new Eye-Toy
  motion-tracking accessory for
  Sony's PS2 game console
- 99 Composite Rating
- 97 EPS Rating
- 96 RS Rating

7% loss

Ignored 2 sell signals:
- Fell 7% below my buy price
- Biggest drop on heaviest volume in
  months and close below 10-week line

19
17
15
14
13
12
11
10

Bought late at $30 on
bounce off 10-week line

Finally sold: 38% gain
now 21% *loss*

Volume

5,000,000

3,000,000

1,800,000

© 2013 Investor's Business Daily, Inc.

Mar 03   Jun 03   Sep 03   Dec 03   Mar 04   Jun 04

I learned my lesson: Always sell if a stock drops 7%–8% below what *you* paid for it.

I made two mistakes:

1. I let a decent gain disappear and turn into a loss.

2. I let a small loss become a big one.

Here's a very important point: I *knew* the rules but chose not to *follow* them.

I think we all come face to face with that issue at some point, especially when starting out. It's one thing to *have* rules. It's quite another to actually stick to them in the heat of battle.

There can be a big difference between how you *think* you'll behave and what you actually *do* when you have money on the line. It's like playing poker for peanuts or potato chips: It's just not the same unless you have skin in the game.

I know the 7%–8% sell rule sounds obvious and sensible, so it's easy to just read this and move on. But it is absolutely essential that you take this rule to heart. It will be an *indispensable* part of your success.

There's a great scene in the movie *Good Will Hunting* where Robin Williams, a psychiatrist, confronts Matt Damon, a troubled but brilliant student who comes from a broken family. In an effort to get Damon to realize he's not responsible for what his family did, Williams looks at him and says, "It's not your fault." Damon half-heartedly accepts that, but it's clearly not really sinking in. So Williams physically grabs Damon and keeps repeating, "It's not your fault, it's not your fault," until Damon truly gets the message.

So, this is my way of grabbing you by the lapel to say again and again: "You *must* cut all your losses short."

> *"When you find yourself in a hole, stop digging."*
>
> —WILL ROGERS

When you start investing you have 2 choices:

1. You can jump in *without* a "protection plan" and no limit on how much money you might lose.

2. Or you can set a specific limit and cap any potential losses.

Pretty straightforward decision, right? And all you have to do to limit your losses is just follow the 7%–8% sell rule.

The following graph shows why that's so important.

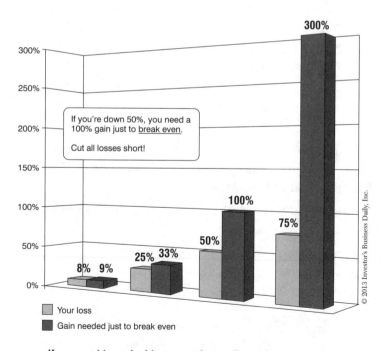

If you're down 50%, you need a 100% gain just to <u>break even</u>.

Cut all losses short!

□ Your loss

■ Gain needed just to break even

© 2013 Investor's Business Daily, Inc.

If you want to make big money, keep all your losses small.

If you cut a loss at 8%, you only need a 9% gain to get back to breakeven. But the deeper your loss becomes, the harder it is to make yourself whole again. If you take a 50% loss, you need to *double* your money just to break even. It's not that often you grab a 100% gain, and when you do, you want to *profit*—not just make up for a past *loss*!

(Buy and) Holder Beware!

This is a good time to recall 2 key facts we touched on earlier. If *they* don't reveal the dangers of "buy and hold" investing, I don't know what will.

- **Once leading stocks eventually peak, they decline 72% on average.**

  Here's what happened to selected leaders in the 2007–2008 bear market. It's a vivid reminder that even leading CAN SLIM stocks eventually peak and must be sold.

  Declines of Selected Leading Stocks in 2007–2008 Bear Market

Company Name	% Decline
Apple	−56%
Baidu	−67%
China Mobile	−63%
Dick's Sporting Goods	−71%
Google	−61%
Intuitive Surgical	−71%

  That may look scary, but remember: You can easily avoid that damage. **Lock in the bulk of your profits and cut short any losses by following the Selling Checklist.**

- **Only about 1 in 8 stocks that led in the prior bull market go on to lead again in the next one.**

  Those are not good odds.

  Now you may be thinking, "What about stocks like Apple or Priceline.com or Monster Beverage? They made big gains in multiple bull markets."

  Yes, there are exceptions. But they're relatively rare. And as a former leader is dropping 72% or so, do you really want to take that loss and bet the farm it'll be one of those rare exceptions? Even if it does bounce back, do you want to start that new run with the profits you locked in when the downtrend began—or *down* 72%?

Look again at the chart above that shows the gains you need to make up for past losses. If you hold on as a former leader drops 75%, you need a *300%* gain just to break even! So if that stock falls to $20, you won't make a dime in profit until it climbs back *above* $80.

So let's review . . .

You can hold as your stock loses most of its value, with only a 1 in 8 chance it'll come back to be a big winner again.

Or you can lock in your profits using simple sell rules.

I wish all choices in life were that easy!

Don't Forget the Opportunity Costs

Holding a stock as it sheds a large percentage of its value does more than just hand you a big loss. You also have to consider the opportunity costs.

- **Your goal is to compound profits, not recoup losses.**

  Let's say you made a 25% gain on a $10,000 position. You'd now have $12,500 to invest in another stock. If you make 20% on your next trade, you now have $15,000—a total gain of 50%. That's the beauty of compounding.

  But . . . you'd be in a very different position if you ignored *both* the 20%–25% profit-taking rule and the 7%–8% sell rule and took a 50% loss before you sold. You'd now only have $5,000 to invest (a 50% loss)—and you'd need a 100% gain just to recoup your losses. Investors who do that take a loss *and* forfeit the opportunity to compound good gains.

- **The big money is made in the *new* crop of leading stocks.**

  If only 1 in 8 former leaders comes back to lead again, what does that tell you? That in every bull market cycle, *new* names appear. And these new leaders—not the old ones—are the stocks most likely to double or triple in price.

  So if you take a big loss in a former leader and continue to hold it, it could take *years* before you recoup that loss—if you *ever* do. And in the meantime, you'd be missing out on the huge profits the current leaders are serving up.

That's an opportunity cost none of us can afford to pay.

Consider the case of DryShips we saw earlier: From November 2006 to November 2007, the stock soared from around $14 to $131—an 835% gain in just one year. Even if you only got a small piece of that move, it could still mean a big profit.

But if you kept holding that stock as the financial crisis pushed the market into a sharp downtrend, you would have seen DryShips drop from $131 to under $2 over the next 5 years.

That loss is painful enough, but it gets worse. Investors who sat there holding DryShips would have missed all the *new* big winners that emerged in the 2009 bull—stocks that surged 100%, 200% or much more: Chipotle Mexican Grill, Apple, Ulta Beauty, Lululemon Athletica, Watson Pharmaceuticals, Tractor Supply, Ross Stores, Dollar General, Panera Bread, Intuitive Surgical, SolarWinds, Rackspace Hosting, Priceline.com, TDG, Mellanox Technologies, Michael Kors, 3D Systems and dozens more.

All of this just brings us back to that one simple concept: Make money in an uptrend by following the Buying Checklist. Then lock in those profits—and cut short any losses—when the market weakens by using the Selling Checklist.

That's how you make money in stocks.

How to Properly Apply the 7%–8% Sell Rule

Note that this rule is only triggered when a stock drops 7%–8% below *your purchase price*. For example, if you buy a stock at $100 a share and it drops to $92, sell.

But let's say you buy a stock at $100, and it goes up to $150. If it then drops 8% from there to $138, that does *not* trigger this sell rule.

Start Out Right: Stick to the Plan

As I said at the very beginning of this book: Keep it simple. Don't overcomplicate what you need to do.

If you regularly check current market conditions and follow both the *offensive* and *defensive* sell rules in the checklist, you'll be in good shape to make good money.

And if you find it hard to sell when your stocks trigger these rules, or if you can't watch the market during the day, set up trade triggers with your broker *ahead of time* (Chapter 4). It's a good way to make sure you stick with the selling game plan and stay profitable and protected.

Check the Chart for More Warning Signs and Sell Signals

 See how to spot other signs of weakness in Chapter 6, "Don't Invest *Blindly*: Use Charts to *See* the Best Time to Buy and Sell."

• ACTION STEPS •

Here are some quick *To Do*s to learn more about how to apply the rules on the Selling Checklist. To take these steps, visit www.investors.com/GettingStartedBook.

1. Use the Selling Checklist to check current market conditions and any stocks you own right now.

   • Is the market currently in an uptrend—or correction?

   • Are you up 20%–25% on any of your stocks—or nearing a 7%–8% loss?

2. Watch a short video on how to apply the 7%–8% sell rule.

Don't Invest *Blindly*: Use Charts to *See* the Best Time to Buy and Sell

Why Use Charts?

"Just as doctors would be irresponsible not to use X-rays on their patients, investors are just plain foolish if they don't learn to interpret the price and volume patterns found on stock charts."

—WILLIAM J. O'NEIL

I couldn't imagine making any buy or sell decision without first checking the chart. It would be like driving blindfolded: If I can't see what's going on around me, how do I know if I should hit the gas—or the brakes?

Charts truly are *that* important. And here's why.

Think back to one of the "Big Rocks" we've been discussing:

Buy stocks being heavily bought by institutional investors. Avoid those they're heavily selling.

We spent an entire section hammering home that key point: Fund managers and other professionals ultimately determine the fate of *your* stocks.

By using charts, you can literally see what these big investors are doing. And it's not hard to do once you demystify what's in a chart and understand one simple fact . . .

Charts Tell You a "Story"

When I was starting out, charts seemed overly "technical" to me. My epiphany came when I finally realized all those lines and bars aren't so mysterious after all. They actually do just one simple thing: They tell you a story. As you'll soon see, charts paint a behind-the-scenes picture of what is *really* going on with the stock:

- Are fund managers enthusiastically buying? Or are they heading for the exits, unloading shares as fast as they can?

- Despite some recent price declines, have institutional investors actually been stepping in to support the stock and pick up more shares—meaning it could be heading for even bigger gains?

- How have big investors reacted to recent news about the stock? Did they *sell* even though the news was *good*? Or did they *buy* more shares even though the news was *bad*?

By understanding that story and looking for certain signals, you'll know if now is a time to buy, sell or hold.

Start with the Basics

At workshops and IBD Meetup events, I've worked with countless investors looking at stock charts for the very first time. From that experience—and my own—I've boiled down the basics of chart-reading into a few key concepts.

The goal here isn't to get into *advanced* techniques. It's about getting started: By the end of this chapter, you'll have everything you need to run your stocks through the "Chart Analysis" items on the buying and selling checklists.

Here's how we'll do that one step at a time:

- **Chart-Reading 101:** You'll learn what's in a chart and 3 ways to "see" if institutional investors are heavily buying or selling a stock.

- **3 Telltale Patterns That Launch Big Moves and Alternative Buy Points:** You'll see that spotting "bases" and "buy points" is really not that hard—and can be immensely profitable.

- **Using Charts to Go Through the Checklists:** I'll show you how to start using the "Chart Analysis" items on the buying and selling checklists to help capture—and keep—solid gains.

Stick with It

Even if it seems a little confusing at first, don't give up. Watch the videos and take the Action Steps. You'll soon get the hang of it and realize that chart-reading truly is a lifelong money-making skill.

As Bill O'Neil has said: **"Fortunes are made every year by people who learn to properly read charts."**

Improve Your Chart-Reading with the Simple Weekend Routine

As you're getting started, do the **Simple Weekend Routine** (see Chapter 4).

- Check the *IBD 50* and *Your Weekly Review* for highlights of stocks near potential buy points.
- Pull up a chart on Investors.com. Can you spot the pattern and buy point?

It's a good way to improve your chart-reading skills and build a timely watch list at the same time.

17 CHIPOTLE MEX GRILL (CMG) Grp 43 o$153.03
14.6M Shares 99 Comp. Rating 97 EPS RS 96 ROE 19%
OPERATES 956 CASUAL FRESH MEXICAN FAST FOOD RESTAURANTS IN 36
STATES WITH PLANS TO OPEN 120-130 MORE (13%-14%) IN 2010.
+38% Ann. EPS Gro PE 32 Avg. Daily Vol 688,900 Debt 1%
Last Qtr Eps +33%▼ Prior Qtr +53%▼ Last Qtr Sales +20%
6 Qtrs EPS > 15%
Eps Due 10/22

Acc/Dis B+
Sup/Demand 89

Shapes handle in cup base; potential buy point at 154.53.

© 2013 Investor's Business Daily, Inc.

See the Routine in Action

Watch a short video at www.investors.com/GettingStartedBook.

Chart-Reading 101: What's in a Chart?

To understand the "story" a chart reveals, we'll cover 3 basic concepts:

- What's the trend?
- Always check price *and* volume.
- Is the stock finding support or hitting resistance?

Once you understand those, all the other things on the buying and selling checklists—chart patterns, buy points, sell signals, etc.—will fall into place.

But first, we need to answer an even more basic question: What's in a chart?

Basic Elements of Daily and Weekly Charts

Important: Be sure to use *both* daily and weekly charts. The weekly chart helps you see longer-term trends, while the daily chart helps you pinpoint specific buy and sell signals. (Throughout this book, each chart is identified as being either weekly or daily in the top left corner.)

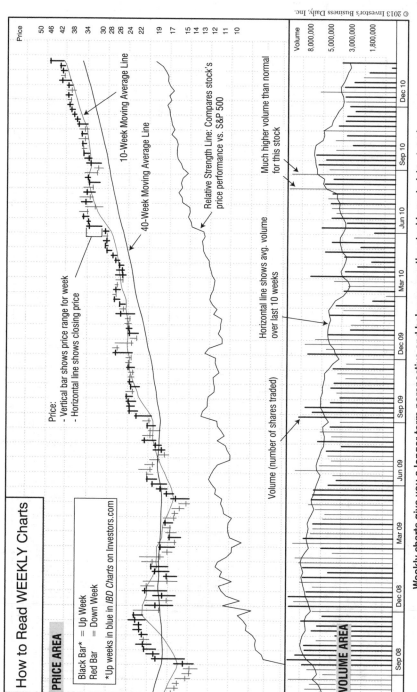

How to Read WEEKLY Charts

PRICE AREA

Black Bar* = Up Week
Red Bar = Down Week
*Up weeks in blue in *IBD Charts* on Investors.com

Price:
- Vertical bar shows price range for week
- Horizontal line shows closing price

10-Week Moving Average Line

40-Week Moving Average Line

Relative Strength Line: Compares stock's price performance vs. S&P 500

Volume (number of shares traded)

Horizontal line shows avg. volume over last 10 weeks

Much higher volume than normal for this stock

VOLUME AREA

© 2013 Investor's Business Daily, Inc.

Weekly charts give you a longer term perspective and help you see the stock's underlying trend.

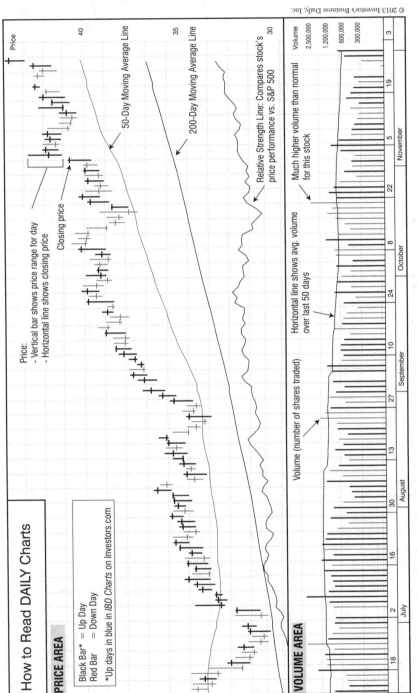

How to Read DAILY Charts

PRICE AREA

Black Bar* = Up Day
Red Bar = Down Day
*Up days in blue in *IBD Charts* on Investors.com

Price:
- Vertical bar shows price range for day
- Horizontal line shows closing price

Closing price

Price

40

50-Day Moving Average Line

35

200-Day Moving Average Line

Relative Strength Line: Compares stock's
price performance vs. S&P 500

30

VOLUME AREA

Volume (number of shares traded)

Horizontal line shows avg. volume
over last 50 days

Much higher volume than normal
for this stock

Volume

2,500,000

1,200,000

600,000

300,000

3

19

November

5

22

8

October

24

10

September

27

13

August

30

16

2

July

18

Daily charts help you spot specific buy points and early warning signs.

- **Black bars vs. red bars:** IBD charts are color-coded to make them easy to read: Black (blue on Investors.com) indicates the share price for that day or week closed higher. Red means the share price closed lower.

- **Long price bars vs. short price bars:** In the price area (upper half) of the chart, the bars may be long or short. The bars show the price range for that day or week. So a longer price bar indicates a wider swing in price, while a shorter price bar means the stock traded in a tighter range.

- **Above-average vs. below-average volume:** In the volume area (lower half) of the chart, you'll see a black horizontal line. That shows the average volume (i.e., the number of shares traded) for that stock over the last 50 days on a daily chart or 10 weeks on a weekly chart.

  If the volume bar is above that line, it means volume for that particular stock was *above* average for that day or week. As you'll soon see, sharp spikes in volume reveal what institutional investors are really up to, and this line helps you see if volume is unusually heavy or light.

- **Moving average lines:** These horizontal lines, found in the price area (upper half) of the chart, simply track the average share price over the specified time period.

  On a weekly chart, the red horizontal line shows the 10-week moving average, and the black line shows the 40-week moving average. On a daily chart, the red line tracks the 50-day moving average, while the black line tracks the average share price over the last 200 trading days.

  You'll soon understand why it's extremely important to see how a stock behaves when it is trading around these benchmark lines.

- **Relative strength line:** In the price area (upper half) of the chart, the horizontal relative strength line compares the share price movement over the last 52 weeks of that particular stock to the price movement of the S&P 500.

  If the line is trending up, the stock is outperforming the S&P 500—a positive sign that tells you that stock is a market leader in terms of price action. If the relative strength line is trending down, it tells you the stock is lagging the overall market.

Next up: Let's look at 3 ways you can tell what "story" the chart is telling—and see if institutional investors are heavily buying or selling.

Chart-Reading 101: What's the Trend?

This "story" is fairly obvious, but very important: Which direction is the stock heading in right now?

There are basically just 3 possibilities.

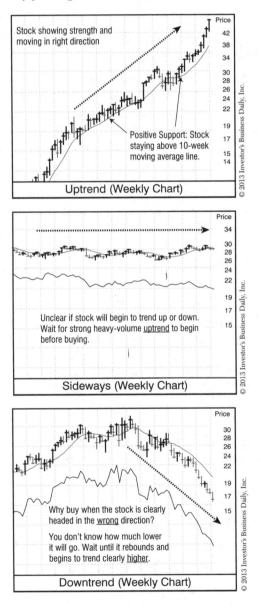

You want to buy a stock when it's showing strength, not weakness. "Strength" means the stock is trending higher and finding support at key moments—both signs that institutional investors are buying shares.

Look at the example of a downtrend. Does that look like strength or weakness? How much lower will that stock go before it finds an area of support (a "floor") and starts coming back up? Will it *ever* come back up? No one knows! It might start a big run tomorrow; it might keep going lower.

That's the point: **Why take on all that risk and uncertainty when you don't have to?**

Don't get suckered into "bargain hunting" for beaten down stocks that are on the decline. Remember what we learned earlier: **Stocks hitting new lows tend to go lower. Stocks hitting new highs tend to go higher.**

So only buy stocks that are *already* showing strength and moving in the right direction—up!

Chart-Reading 101:
Always Check Price *and* Volume

Some people write off charts as too complicated—or as some type of modern day fortune-telling tea leaf. But the fact is, *charts are nothing more than a visual representation of price and volume action.*

And the picture a chart paints is very revealing: That *combination* of price *and* volume clearly shows you what big investors are up to.

Here's how it works . . .

Institutional investors are like the proverbial elephant in the bathtub—they can't hide. When they jump in or get out, you can't miss it *if you use charts.*

That's because a stock chart will clearly show any significant spike (or drop) in *volume* as the share price changes. That change in volume tells you how serious the buying or selling by institutional investors actually is.

The scenarios in the following charts give you a *basic* look at how price and volume work together. Other factors may come into play, but for now these outline the key concepts to keep in mind.

Now *That's* Unusual!

As you go through these scenarios, understand that you're looking for *unusual* volume—either unusually heavy or unusually light.

For example, if a stock that normally trades 1 million shares a day suddenly trades 2 million, you need to pay attention. That's not your Uncle Fred buying or selling 100 shares. That's *institutional* trading—and you have to find out what "story" it's telling.

Take a few minutes to carefully review the notes inside the following charts. Pay special attention to the spikes in volume that are highlighted and the "story" they reveal about what fund managers and other big investors are up to. Knowing how to spot *unusual* volume—and understanding what it means—will be key to your investing success.

Institutional Buying: Big Price Gains on Unusually Heavy Volume

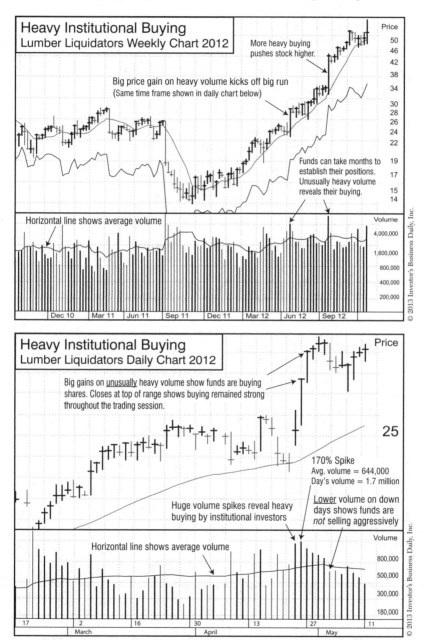

Heavy Institutional Buying
Lumber Liquidators Weekly Chart 2012

More heavy buying pushes stock higher.

Big price gain on heavy volume kicks off big run
(Same time frame shown in daily chart below)

Funds can take months to establish their positions. Unusually heavy volume reveals their buying.

Horizontal line shows average volume

Price
50
46
42
38
34
30
28
26
24
22
19
17
15
14

Volume
4,000,000
1,600,000
800,000
400,000
200,000

Dec 10 Mar 11 Jun 11 Sep 11 Dec 11 Mar 12 Jun 12 Sep 12

© 2013 Investor's Business Daily, Inc.

Heavy Institutional Buying
Lumber Liquidators Daily Chart 2012

Big gains on <u>unusually</u> heavy volume show funds are buying shares. Closes at top of range shows buying remained strong throughout the trading session.

170% Spike
Avg. volume = 644,000
Day's volume = 1.7 million

<u>Lower</u> volume on down days shows funds are *not* selling aggressively

Huge volume spikes reveal heavy buying by institutional investors

Horizontal line shows average volume

Price

25

Volume
800,000
500,000
300,000
180,000

17   2   16   30   13   27   11
     March   April   May

© 2013 Investor's Business Daily, Inc.

Big price gains on unusually heavy volume show institutional investors are buying aggressively. It's also a bullish sign when the stock's *closing price* is in the *top* part of the range for that day or week.

Institutional Selling: Big Price Drops on Unusually Heavy Volume

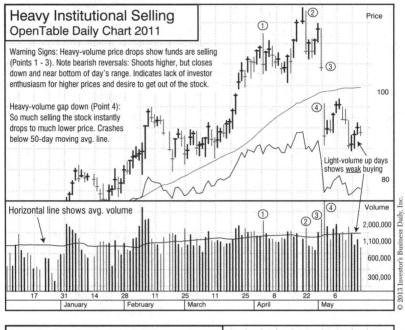

Heavy Institutional Selling
OpenTable Daily Chart 2011

Warning Signs: Heavy-volume price drops show funds are selling (Points 1 - 3). Note bearish reversals: Shoots higher, but closes down and near bottom of day's range. Indicates lack of investor enthusiasm for higher prices and desire to get out of the stock.

Heavy-volume gap down (Point 4): So much selling the stock instantly drops to much lower price. Crashes below 50-day moving avg. line.

Light-volume up days shows <u>weak</u> buying

Horizontal line shows avg. volume

Price
100
80

Volume
2,000,000
1,100,000
600,000
300,000

17 31 14 28 11 25 11 25 8 22 6
January February March April May

© 2013 Investor's Business Daily, Inc.

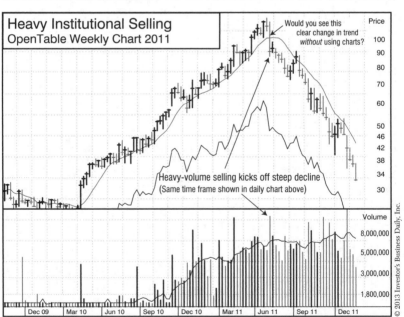

Heavy Institutional Selling
OpenTable Weekly Chart 2011

Would you see this clear change in trend *without* using charts?

Heavy-volume selling kicks off steep decline
(Same time frame shown in daily chart above)

Price
100
90
80
70
60
50
46
42
38
34
30

Volume
8,000,000
5,000,000
3,000,000
1,800,000

Dec 09 Mar 10 Jun 10 Sep 10 Dec 10 Mar 11 Jun 11 Sep 11 Dec 11

© 2013 Investor's Business Daily, Inc.

Big price drops on unusually heavy volume show institutional investors are selling aggressively. It's also a bearish sign when the stock's *closing price* is in the *bottom* part of the range for that day or week.

Price Gain on Light Volume

Light volume on *up* days or weeks could mean big investors are *not* enthusiastic about the stock. May be a sign the stock will start to sell off.

Price Drop on Light Volume

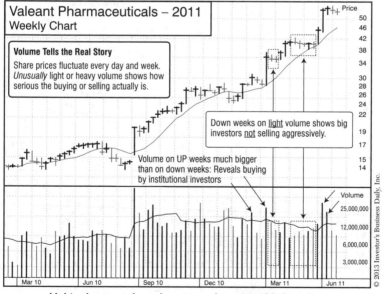

Light volume on *down* days or weeks means big investors are sitting tight and not selling aggressively.

Bullish vs. Bearish Reversals

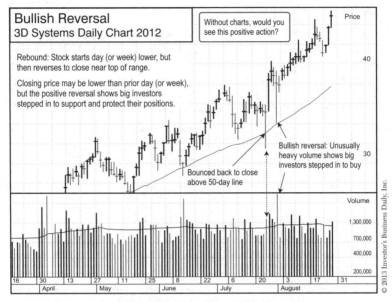

Bullish reversal shows investors stepped in to support the stock.

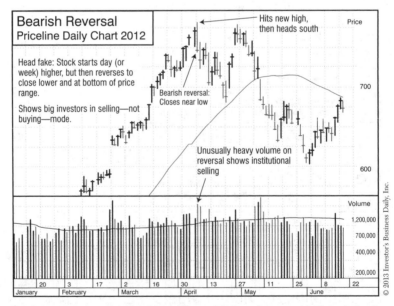

Bearish reversal on heavy volume: Shows big investors used initial price gain as opportunity to sell. Rather than support the stock and push it higher, they sold and pushed it down.

And the Survey Says . . .

Here's another way to think about volume.

Let's say you run a small clothing store and you have to decide what clothes to buy for the summer season. In a trade magazine, you see a survey that says "70% of women plan on buying a red swimsuit this year." Your initial reaction might be, "Wow, I'd better fill my shelves with red swimsuits."

But then you dig a little deeper and find out there were only 10 respondents to that survey!

Would you still base your inventory on the opinions of 10 people? Of course not. Now, if the survey was properly sampled, professionally conducted and had *10,000* respondents, you might lend the results more credence.

It's the same with volume. If a stock's share price goes up 2% one day, that doesn't tell you all that much—until you also check the volume. Was it unusually heavy? Or was volume well *below* average?

Without that information, there's no way to understand what the price change actually means. Are big fund managers showing real enthusiasm and heavily buying the stock? Or is it just a head fake?

It still amazes me that so many financial news programs and publications will just say "IBM closed 1% higher today" and say nothing about the *volume*. It's essentially the same as a pollster saying "7 out of 10 women love red swimsuits" without explaining how many people they surveyed (i.e., the volume) to come to that conclusion.

They say real estate is all about "location, location, location." You'll find that when it comes to using charts to see the right time to buy and sell a stock, it's all about "volume, volume, volume." So to understand what the changes in share price are *really* telling you, **always check the volume.**

Chart-Reading 101: Is the Stock Finding Support or Hitting Resistance?

Now that you have a basic sense of the important relationship between share price and trading volume, let's take a look at another key chart-reading concept: Support and resistance.

Think of it like a floor (support) and ceiling (resistance).

The chart patterns and "buy points" we'll discuss are all based on this simple idea: To make sure the stock is more likely to go up than down when you buy it, first make sure it has already established a solid floor (support) from which it can move higher. Then wait for the stock to show real power by smashing through the ceiling (resistance), clearing the way for a new upward move.

Here again, let's go through some common scenarios so you understand the basic concepts.

Turn Up the Volume

Be sure to pay attention to changes in volume in these scenarios. For example, when a stock is punching through an area of resistance, you want to see *unusually heavy* volume kick in. That shows institutional investors are buying enthusiastically and aggressively. Light volume would show more hesitation and a lack of conviction—which could mean the stock will fail to climb higher and soon fall back below that same area of resistance.

Support or Resistance at 10-Week
or 50-Day Moving Average Line

*It's very important to watch how your stock behaves around the moving
average lines*—particularly the 10-week line on the weekly chart and the 50-
day line on a daily chart. The reason is simple: Professional investors use
these lines as key benchmarks. So you can see if fund managers and other
big players are supporting or selling the stock by watching how it behaves
around those key moving average lines.

- **Support:** If institutional investors still have a positive outlook on the
  stock, they'll often step in to buy more shares and protect their positions
  when the stock pulls back to or dips below the moving average line.

  In that scenario, you'll typically see the stock pull back to the 50-day or
  10-week line on *light* volume (showing that institutions are *not* selling
  aggressively), then bounce back above that line on *heavy* volume (showing that fund managers are stepping in to buy more shares).

- **Sell-off:** If the stock fails to find support at the benchmark lines and
  crashes below them on heavy volume, what does that tell you? That big
  investors may now be less interested in shoring up their positions and
  more interested in just getting out of the stock.

  Again, the key is to watch the *volume*: If trading is particularly *heavy* as
  the stock breaks through the moving average line, that's a definite warning sign. If volume is *light*, it could mean the selling is less serious.

As you can see in the following chart for F5 Networks, it's not unusual for
a stock to move below the 10-week or 50-day moving average line for a few
days or weeks, even as its overall trend is still headed higher. So a drop
below one of these key benchmark lines does not mean you should automatically sell the stock. We'll talk more about that and specific sell signals in
the Selling Checklist.

Support at 10-Week Moving Average Line

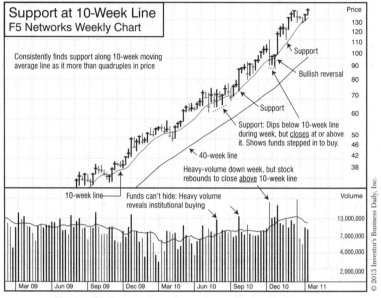

Looking for support at the 10-week and 50-day moving average lines
can help you hold a stock for potentially bigger gains.

Sell-Off at 10-Week Moving Average Line

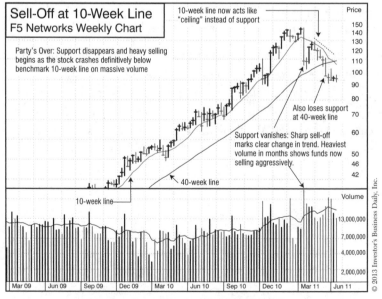

Watch out when a stock crashes through and closes sharply below
the 10-week line on heavy volume. It could mean more selling is on the way.

Support or Resistance at Specific Price Points

In addition to watching how a stock behaves around the moving average lines, you also want to look for signs of support and resistance at certain price areas. This is a vital part of understanding how and why the telltale chart patterns we'll discuss later help you pinpoint the best time to buy a stock.

And after you buy, this concept will also help you know whether you should *hold* the stock because it's building "stepping stones" by finding support at key areas—or if it's time to sell because it crashed right through the "floor."

The following examples show you what support and resistance look like on a chart. As you look at the notes in each example, pay particular attention to that all-important relationship between price and volume.

Resistance at Key Price Points

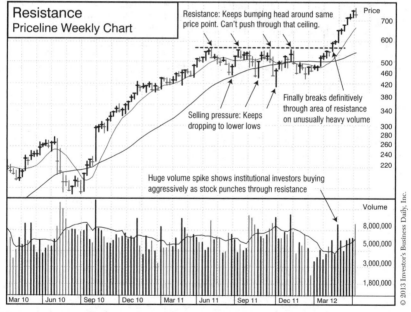

**An area of resistance is a key testing ground:
Make sure the stock can punch through it on *heavy* volume.**

Former Area of Resistance Becomes Area of Support

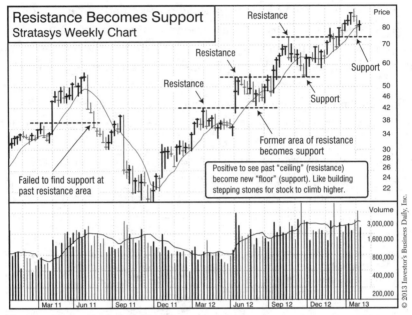

Stepping stones: Watch to see if a prior area of resistance becomes an area of support. That can help you hold a stock as it climbs higher, one step at a time.

Next up: Let's use the 3 concepts we just learned to spot the telltale patterns that launch big price moves.

3 Telltale Patterns That Launch Big Moves

As a political history buff, I'm always struck by how little things change from decade to decade, even century to century. New players and issues come and go, but the core arguments and debates remain essentially the same. Why? Because it all comes back to human nature, and human nature never changes.

It's the same with the stock market. And if you understand and accept human nature for what it is, the seemingly chaotic behavior of the market will make more sense—and *you* can make more money.

I'm bringing this up because as we go through the 3 main patterns that alert you to a potential big move, I want you to keep in mind that these are not random shapes on a chart. They're a reflection of human emotions: Hope, fear and greed. And just like the price and volume action, they have a story to tell.

The Patterns Don't Change

Because human nature doesn't change, the shapes of these telltale patterns also remain the same.

At the beginning of *How to Make Money in Stocks*, Bill O'Neil showed the charts of 100 of the top-performing stocks over the last 100+ years. Whether it was General Motors in 1915, Coca-Cola in 1934 or Priceline.com in 2006, those patterns (also known as "bases") were identical. You'll find the same shapes today and the same patterns decades from now.

By learning to spot these bases, you'll be able to get in early on the best stocks—year after year.

Think of a chart pattern like a "launching pad": It's the *starting point* for the stock's big new move. So once you learn to spot these 3 common bases, you'll be right there for "takeoff." That's why it's so profitable to use chart patterns to time your buys.

As I said before, it takes some time and effort to read charts properly. But stick with it. It's not as hard as you may think, and as the table below shows, the payoff can be life-changing.

How These Telltale Patterns Launched Major Gains

Company	Year Run Started	Type of Pattern	Subsequent % Gain
Apple	2004	Cup-with-Handle	1,528% in 199 weeks
Intuitive Surgical	2004	Cup-with-Handle	1,826% in 180 weeks
CME Group	2005	Double Bottom	224% in 113 weeks
Deckers Outdoor	2007	Flat Base	173% in 46 weeks
Baidu	2009	Cup-with-Handle	401% in 93 weeks
Chipotle Mexican Grill	2010	Cup-with-Handle	186% in 84 weeks
Lululemon Athletica	2010	Double Bottom	196% in 44 weeks
Lumber Liquidators	2012	Cup-with-Handle	167% in 48 weeks
Regeneron Pharmaceutical	2012	Cup	136% in 45 weeks
3D Systems	2012	Cup	178% in 40 weeks

We'll talk first about the 3 main patterns that launch the big gains of virtually all big winners: **Cup-with-handle**, **double bottom** and **flat base**. Once we see how to spot the basics, we'll also take a look at some additional clues you want to keep an eye on in the "Go Beyond Just the Shapes" section of this chapter.

Then we'll go over 2 alternative buying opportunities that can deliver some nice gains: **3-weeks tight** and a **pullback** to the 50-day or 10-week moving average line.

There are other patterns and price actions to look for, but these are by far the most common and, frankly, the most profitable. So as you're getting started, keep it simple and just focus on these.

As we go through these patterns, keep in mind what we just discussed about the "story" that *price and volume* and *support and resistance* reveal. That provides the backstory for what's going on in these chart patterns and why it's important.

Cup-with-Handle

Most Common and Profitable Pattern

- Winning stocks often *start* their big runs by forming this pattern
- Resembles a teacup viewed from the side

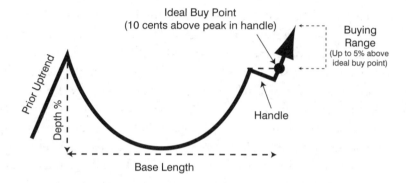

What to Look For

How do you find winning stocks in the *early* stages of a major move? Learn to spot a cup-with-handle. Year after year, the biggest winners often launch their runs as they break out of this same pattern.

We'll go through several examples below, but first let's see what to look for in a proper cup-with-handle.

As we do that, we'll also take a look at what "story" the chart is telling as the base forms. That will help you understand how chart patterns and buy points work—and see how emotions and human nature play a big role.

Watch Your Chart-Reading Skills Grow with IBD TV

Tune in to free *Daily Stock Analysis* and *Market Wrap* videos to see how to analyze charts—and build a timely watch list. See how at www.investors.com/GettingStartedBook.

☑ *Prior uptrend: 30% or more*

To form a proper "base" or chart pattern, you have to have a prior uptrend. The idea behind a base is that after making a decent run, the stock is now digesting those gains as it catches its breath in preparation for an even higher climb. In other words, it's forming the "stepping stones" we discussed in the section on support and resistance.

Backstory

The prior uptrend typically happens when the overall market is moving higher. When that uptrend starts to slip into a correction, even the top CAN SLIM® stocks will likely pull back and start forming a new base.

When that happens, savvy investors who got in *early* on that uptrend will start to cash in their gains. You'll probably see your 20%–25% profit-taking rule kick in around this time.

But it's a very different story for people who did *not* get in early and ended up buying at the end of that prior uptrend. Because they didn't have proper buy rules like the ones in the Buying Checklist, they bought just as the overall market weakened and the stock itself started to decline. And since they probably don't have proper sell rules either, they'll soon be sitting on a big loss.

☑ *Base Depth: 15%–30%*

The depth of the base—measured from the peak on the left side of the cup to the lowest point (the "bottom") of the cup—should be between 15%–30%. In a severe bear market, the depth may be 40%–50%. As a general rule, look for stocks that held up relatively well during the market correction. So if one stock on your watch list dropped 35% while another's base depth is only 20%, all else being equal, the stock with the 20% decline could be forming a stronger base.

Backstory

Remember those folks who bought too late in the prior uptrend? They're now sitting on significant losses, just hoping and praying to somehow get back to breakeven.

In the meantime, the stock has found a bottom and is now starting to form the right side of the cup. Why did that happen? Because *institutional investors* stopped selling and started buying. That's what stops the bleeding and allows the stock to start moving higher again.

 Base length: At least 7 weeks
  * The first down week in the base counts as Week #1

The minimum length for a cup-with-handle is 7 weeks, but some can last much longer—several months or even a year or more. Be wary of any pattern that has the *shape* of a cup-with-handle but is only, say, 5 weeks long. That's typically not enough time for the stock to consolidate the prior gains, and that base has a higher chance of failing.

Backstory

The length of a cup-with-handle is usually affected by the length of the general market correction. In a long, deep bear market, you'll likely have a lot of long, deep cup-with-handle formations. And in shorter and shallower interim corrections, you'll see the bases mirror that same action.

 The Handle
  * Volume in handle should be *light*
  * Depth of the handle should be around 10%–12%
  * Should form in *upper* half of base
  * Peak of handle should be within 15% of old high on left side of cup

The handle should be a *mild* pullback on relatively *light* volume. It's a "shakeout" of weaker holders—those not committed to holding the stock longer term. A sharp decline of more than 12%–15% on *heavy* volume could indicate a more serious sell-off that might prevent the stock from launching a successful move.

The handle should form in the *upper* half of the base. If it begins forming too soon (i.e., in the lower half of the base), it could mean institutional buying, right now, is not as strong as it needs to be to push the stock higher.

"N" Also Means "New High"

As we saw earlier, the "N" in CAN SLIM stands for a "new" product or industry trend, but it also refers to a new 52-week price high.

For each of these telltale patterns—cup-with-handle, double bottom and flat base—a key requirement is that the stock be at or near a new high as it breaks out. That's a sign of strength—and an important reminder of this historical market fact:

- Stocks hitting new price *highs* tend to go *higher.*
- Stocks hitting new price *lows* tend to go *lower.*

So save the bargain bin, clearance sales for the shopping mall! When it comes to buying *stocks*, focus on those showing strength as they climb into new high territory and break out of a sound chart pattern.

Backstory

Who are the weaker holders getting shaken out in the handle? Those folks who bought late at the end of the prior uptrend and suffered big losses. Getting a *profit* is no longer their goal. They just hope to recoup some of their losses. So as the stock nears that old high—and the weaker holders' breakeven points—they start to sell.

Here's why that shakeout is healthy: If you have a lot of "weak holders" in a stock, whenever the share price rises, they jump in to sell, which pushes the price back down. Once they're out of the picture, it's easier for the stock to move higher.

And what about the big investors who've been picking up shares as the stock formed the right side of the cup?

They're more committed and are holding onto their shares. That's why the volume in the handle is *light:* Only the weak holders are selling. The big institutions are sitting tight in expectation of a new upward move.

 Ideal buy point
- 10 cents above the peak in the handle
- Buying range: Up to 5% above ideal buy point
- *Always buy as close as possible to the* ideal *buy point!*

If the peak in the handle is, say, $30, then you add 10 cents to get the *ideal buy point* of $30.10.

The *buying range* would be from $30.10 to $31.60—5% above the ideal buy point.

You want to buy as close to the ideal buy point as possible. If you're not able to watch the market during the day, you can set trade triggers ahead of time (Chapter 4).

Once a stock climbs more than 5% above the ideal buy point, it's considered "extended" or beyond the proper buying range. **Don't buy extended stocks.**

Stocks often pull back a bit after a breakout. If you buy too late, there's a higher chance you'll get "shaken out" of the stock because it triggers the 7%–8% sell rule we covered in the Selling Checklist.

Backstory

Note how the peak in the handle is the most recent area of *resistance*: The stock bumped its head against that ceiling and fell back down.

So that's our new testing ground—and that's why we use that to determine the buy point.

Can the stock punch through that area on heavy volume? That would mean institutional investors are enthusiastically buying the stock and willing to push it higher.

For all bases, we add 10 cents to the most recent area of resistance to determine the ideal buy point. That's just to make sure the stock is truly punching through that resistance and not just bumping up against it.

 *Volume on day of breakout:* At least *40%–50% above average*

On the day a stock breaks past its ideal buy point, volume should be at least 40%–50% higher than normal for that stock. That shows strong institutional buying. On many breakouts, you'll see volume spike 100%, 200% or more above average. *Light* or below-average volume could mean the price move is just a head fake, and the stock is not quite ready for a big run.

Be on the Lookout During Earnings Season

 Whether it's from a cup-with-handle or other pattern, many breakouts happen when companies release their latest quarterly earnings report. So stay alert—but also cautious: The stock may *drop* sharply instead. See Chapter 3 for more on how to handle earnings season.

Why Not Buy at the *Bottom* of the Cup-with-Handle?

Hindsight is indeed 20-20.

After a stock has completed the pattern, it's easy to *retroactively* say, "I would have made more money if I'd bought at the bottom." That's true—that one time—in hindsight. But when the base is still forming, how do you know if the stock has really hit bottom?

If you try to buy *before* the pattern is complete, you're just taking on unnecessary risk.

If you wait for the stock to finish the base and break out on heavy volume, you *dramatically* reduce your risk and still leave plenty of potential for *major* gains.

Launching Big Gains with the Cup-with-Handle

Below are examples of winning stocks that launched big runs from a cup-with-handle pattern. Both the daily and weekly charts are included. The weekly charts show the longer term trend, while the daily charts show the action on the actual day of the breakout. Be sure to use both!

Don't rush through the following examples. Take some time to study the notes and see how these patterns met the key requirements of a proper cup-with-handle. And as always, pay close attention to the price and volume action within the base, and see how the concept of "support and resistance" comes into play.

Also remember that IBD does a lot of the work for you. You'll find highlights of stocks forming cup-with-handles and other patterns as you review *IBD 50, Your Weekly Review, Stock Spotlight* and other features as part of your daily and weekend routines (Chapter 4).

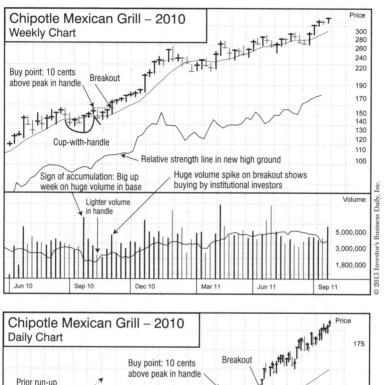

Chipotle Mexican Grill – 2010
Weekly Chart

Buy point: 10 cents above peak in handle
Breakout
Cup-with-handle
Relative strength line in new high ground
Sign of accumulation: Big up week on huge volume in base
Huge volume spike on breakout shows buying by institutional investors
Lighter volume in handle

Price
300
280
260
240
220
190
170
150
140
130
120
110
100

Volume
5,000,000
3,000,000
1,800,000

Jun 10   Sep 10   Dec 10   Mar 11   Jun 11   Sep 11

© 2013 Investor's Business Daily, Inc.

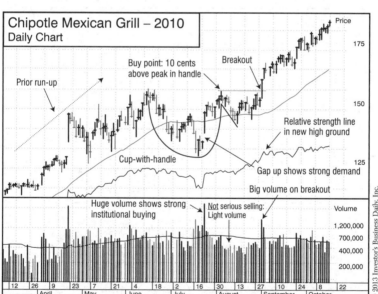

Chipotle Mexican Grill – 2010
Daily Chart

Buy point: 10 cents above peak in handle
Breakout
Prior run-up
Relative strength line in new high ground
Cup-with-handle
Gap up shows strong demand
Big volume on breakout
Huge volume shows strong institutional buying
Not serious selling: Light volume

Price
175
150
125

Volume
1,200,000
700,000
400,000
200,000

12 26 9 23 7 21 4 18 2 16 30 13 27 10 24 8 22
April   May   June   July   August   September   October

© 2013 Investor's Business Daily, Inc.

Chipotle Mexican Grill increased 186% from September 2010–April 2012.

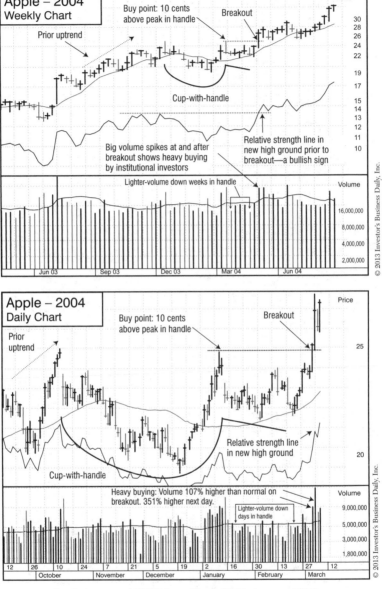

Apple – 2004
Weekly Chart

Buy point: 10 cents above peak in handle

Breakout

Prior uptrend

Cup-with-handle

Big volume spikes at and after breakout shows heavy buying by institutional investors

Relative strength line in new high ground prior to breakout—a bullish sign

Lighter-volume down weeks in handle

Price
30
28
26
24
22
19
17
15
14
13
12
11
10

Volume
16,000,000
8,000,000
4,000,000
2,000,000

Jun 03   Sep 03   Dec 03   Mar 04   Jun 04

© 2013 Investor's Business Daily, Inc.

Apple – 2004
Daily Chart

Prior uptrend

Buy point: 10 cents above peak in handle

Breakout

Relative strength line in new high ground

Cup-with-handle

Heavy buying: Volume 107% higher than normal on breakout. 351% higher next day.

Lighter-volume down days in handle

Price
25

20

Volume
9,000,000
5,000,000
3,000,000
1,800,000

12 26 10 24 7 21 5 19 2 16 30 13 27 12
October   November   December   January   February   March

© 2013 Investor's Business Daily, Inc.

Apple increased 596% from March 2004–January 2006.

Faulty Cup-with-Handles

Sometimes the best way to see what works is to study what *fails*.

Take a look at the following chart patterns, and see how they stack up against the traits of proper—and successful—cup-with-handle formations.

Learning to spot these kinds of flaws will help significantly improve your stock-picking batting average.

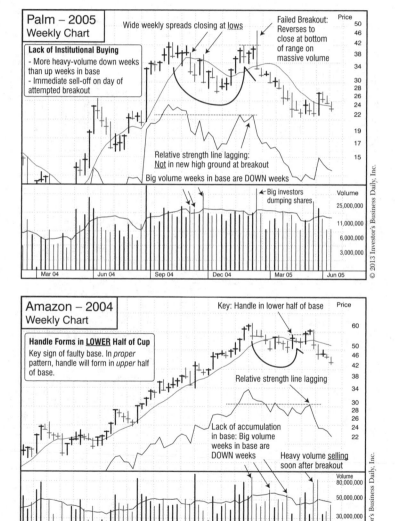

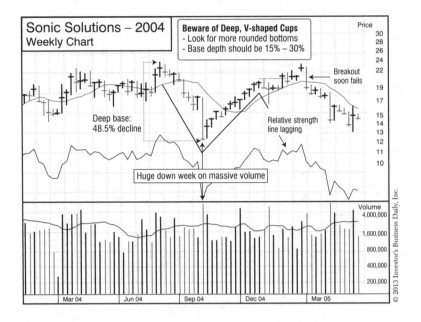

Sonic Solutions – 2004
Weekly Chart

Beware of Deep, V-shaped Cups
- Look for more rounded bottoms
- Base depth should be 15% – 30%

Price
30
28
26
24
22

Breakout
soon fails

19

17

Deep base:
48.5% decline

Relative strength
line lagging

15
14
13
12
11
10

Huge down week on massive volume

Volume
4,000,000

1,600,000

800,000

400,000

200,000

Mar 04   Jun 04   Sep 04   Dec 04   Mar 05

© 2013 Investor's Business Daily, Inc.

Finding Flaws

In the *IBD 50* and *Your Weekly Review*, you'll find alerts to warning signs and potential flaws in a base. That'll also help you learn to spot them on your own.

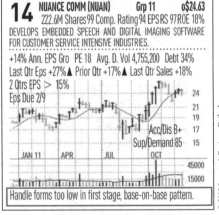

14 NUANCE COMM (NUAN)   Grp 11   o$24.63
222.6M Shares 99 Comp. Rating 94 EPS RS 97 ROE 18%
DEVELOPS EMBEDDED SPEECH AND DIGITAL IMAGING SOFTWARE
FOR CUSTOMER SERVICE INTENSIVE INDUSTRIES.

+14% Ann. EPS Gro PE 18 Avg. D. Vol 4,755,200 Debt 34%
Last Qtr Eps +27%▲ Prior Qtr +17%▲ Last Qtr Sales +18%
2 Qtrs EPS > 15%
Eps Due 2/9

24
21
19

Acc/Dis B+   17
Sup/Demand 85   15

JAN 11   APR   JUL   OCT

45000

15000

Handle forms too low in first stage, base-on-base pattern.

© 2013 Investor's Business Daily, Inc.

Cup-without-Handle

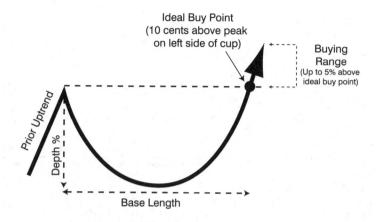

The cup-without-handle—also called a cup-shaped base or simply a cup—is a variation on the cup-with-handle pattern. As the name implies, it's essentially the same, except it doesn't have a handle. All the attributes, except for the buy point, are identical.

The buy point in a cup-shaped base is calculated by adding 10 cents to the peak on the left side of the cup—the most recent area of resistance.

Next is an example of how Google formed a cup-shaped base that launched a 119% gain in less than 10 months.

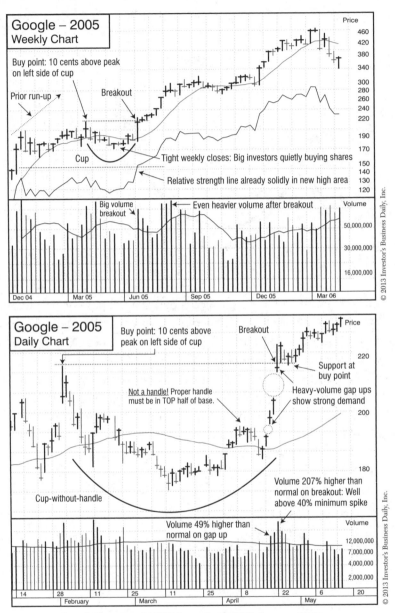

Google – 2005
Weekly Chart

Buy point: 10 cents above peak on left side of cup

Prior run-up

Breakout

Cup

Tight weekly closes: Big investors quietly buying shares

Relative strength line already solidly in new high area

Big volume breakout

Even heavier volume after breakout

Price: 460, 420, 380, 340, 300, 280, 260, 240, 220, 190, 170, 150, 140, 130, 120

Volume: 50,000,000, 30,000,000, 16,000,000

Dec 04, Mar 05, Jun 05, Sep 05, Dec 05, Mar 06

© 2013 Investor's Business Daily, Inc.

Google – 2005
Daily Chart

Buy point: 10 cents above peak on left side of cup

Breakout

Support at buy point

Not a handle! Proper handle must be in TOP half of base.

Heavy-volume gap ups show strong demand

Cup-without-handle

Volume 207% higher than normal on breakout: Well above 40% minimum spike

Volume 49% higher than normal on gap up

Price: 220, 200, 180

Volume: 12,000,000, 7,000,000, 4,000,000, 2,000,000

14, 28, 11, 25, 11, 25, 8, 22, 6, 20
February, March, April, May

© 2013 Investor's Business Daily, Inc.

Google increased 119% from April 2005–January 2006.

See How to Spot a Cup-with-Handle

 Watch a short video at www.investors.com/GettingStartedBook.

Double Bottom

Second Most Common Pattern

- Looks like a lopsided "W"
- Often occurs when overall market is choppy and volatile
- Can also set the stage for huge price gains

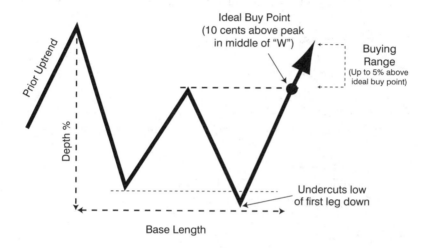

What to Look For

While the shape is different than a cup-with-handle, the core concepts and backstory of double bottoms are the same.

- **Mirroring the Market:** Double bottoms tend to form while the overall market is volatile, and that's reflected in the shape. You have one down leg, then the stock tries to rally but hits resistance and ends up pulling back to form a second down leg. The stock rebounds one more time and is finally able to punch through and move higher. The breakout typically occurs when the overall market has also bounced back from a correction into a new uptrend.

- **Support and Resistance:** Like the cup-with-handle and all other bases, the buy point for a double bottom is calculated by adding 10 cents to the most recent area of resistance. That's the peak in the middle of the "W."

Breaking through that resistance on unusually heavy volume shows institutional investors are back in the game, aggressively scooping up shares.

- **Shakeout:** Remember how the handle in the cup-with-handle shook out the weaker holders? You have the same concept here, just in a different place. Note how the bottom of the second leg in a double bottom undercuts the bottom of the first leg. That gets rid of the weaker holders, leaving more committed investors who create support for the stock's new run.

Here's a quick list of the key traits to look for in a double bottom.

☑ *Prior uptrend: 30% or more*

☑ *Base depth: 40% or less*

☑ *Base length: At least 7 weeks*
  - The first down week in the base counts as Week #1

☑ *Peak in middle of "W"*
  - Should form in upper half of base
  - Should be *below* left-side peak

☑ *Undercut: Bottom of second leg down should be* lower *than bottom of first leg down*

☑ *Ideal buy point*
  - 10 cents above the peak in the middle of the "W"
  - Buying range: Up to 5% above the ideal buy point
  - *Always buy as close as possible to the* ideal *buy point!*

☑ *Volume on day of breakout: At least 40%–50% above average*

Launching Big Gains with the Double Bottom

Below are examples of winning stocks that launched big runs from a double bottom.

Again, don't rush through these examples. Study what the patterns look like on both the daily and weekly charts, and look for big spikes in volume on the breakouts.

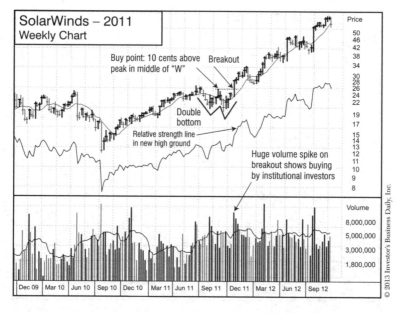

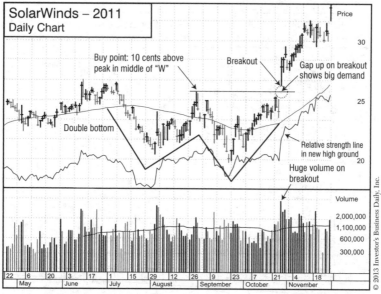

SolarWinds increased 137% from October 2011–September 2012.

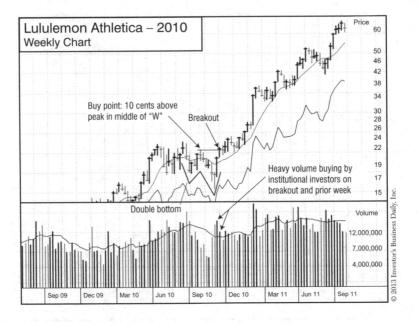

Lululemon Athletica – 2010
Weekly Chart

Buy point: 10 cents above peak in middle of "W"

Breakout

Heavy volume buying by institutional investors on breakout and prior week

Double bottom

Volume

© 2013 Investor's Business Daily, Inc.

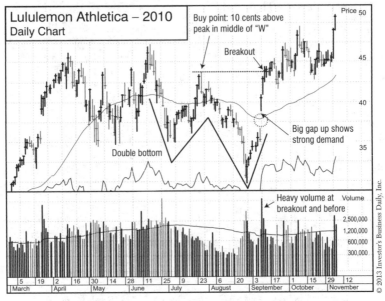

Lululemon Athletica – 2010
Daily Chart

Buy point: 10 cents above peak in middle of "W"

Breakout

Big gap up shows strong demand

Double bottom

Heavy volume at breakout and before

Volume

© 2013 Investor's Business Daily, Inc.

Lululemon Athletica increased 196% from September 2010–July 2011.

Faulty Double Bottoms

Here are some common flaws to look out for when reviewing a potential double bottom pattern.

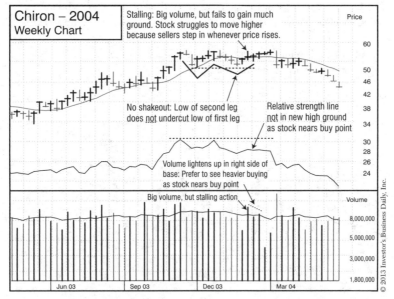

Chiron – 2004
Weekly Chart

Stalling: Big volume, but fails to gain much ground. Stock struggles to move higher because sellers step in whenever price rises.

Price

60

50

46

42

No shakeout: Low of second leg does not undercut low of first leg

Relative strength line not in new high ground as stock nears buy point

38

34

30

28

Volume lightens up in right side of base: Prefer to see heavier buying as stock nears buy point

26

24

Big volume, but stalling action

Volume

8,000,000

5,000,000

3,000,000

1,800,000

Jun 03   Sep 03   Dec 03   Mar 04

© 2013 Investor's Business Daily, Inc.

In a double bottom, make sure the low in the second leg down undercuts the low in the first leg.

See How to Spot a Double Bottom

 Watch a short video at www.investors.com/GettingStartedBook.

Flat Base

Usually a Second-Stage Base

- Often occurs *after* a stock forms a cup-with-handle or double bottom
- Can offer another opportunity to start a new position or add shares to an existing one
- Milder decline than cup-with-handle and double bottom
- Shorter time frame (minimum 5 weeks)

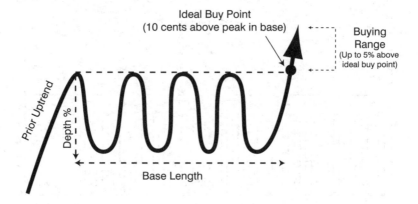

What to Look For

Remember how we mentioned the best stocks will form "stepping stones" as they make their big moves? They'll go up for a while, pull back to form a new base, then resume their climb—giving you *multiple* opportunities to make money.

The flat base is a classic example of that. They typically form *after* a stock has made a nice gain from a cup-with-handle or double bottom breakout. That's why they're often considered "second-stage" bases. (We'll get into that later in this chapter in "Go Beyond Just the Shapes.")

Here are the key concepts to understand.

- **Trading Sideways to "Digest" Earlier Gains:** Stock will often break out of a cup-with-handle or double bottom pattern, run up at least 20%, then go sideways to form a flat base. It's a milder decline than what you see in other patterns—no more than 15%.

The price range will usually remain fairly tight throughout the base. That may mean institutional investors—who have to buy tens of thousands or more shares to establish their large positions—are quietly buying within a certain price range. That's how they increase their holdings without significantly driving up their average cost-per-share.

- **Support and Resistance:** Here again the buy point is determined by adding 10 cents to the most recent area of resistance—the highest price point within the flat base. Until the stock breaks through that "ceiling" (preferably on heavy volume), it won't be able to launch the next leg of its climb.

- **Shakeout:** Flat bases also have a way of shedding those weaker holders we keep mentioning. Instead of a sharper sell-off like the handle in a cup-with-handle or the second-leg undercut in a double bottom, the flat base shakeout is more of a slow grind. The weaker holders just get worn out by the indecisive, sideways action and eventually lose patience and sell.

Here's a quick list of the key traits to look for in a flat base.

☑ *Prior uptrend: 30% or more*

☑ *Base depth: 15% or less*

☑ *Base length: At least 5 weeks*
  - The first down week in the base counts as Week #1

☑ *Ideal buy point*
  - 10 cents above the peak within the base
  - Buying range: Up to 5% above the ideal buy point
  - *Always buy as close as possible to the* ideal *buy point!*

☑ *Volume on day of breakout: At least 40%–50% above average*

Launching Big Gains with the Flat Base

Here are just two examples of winning stocks that launched big runs from a flat base.

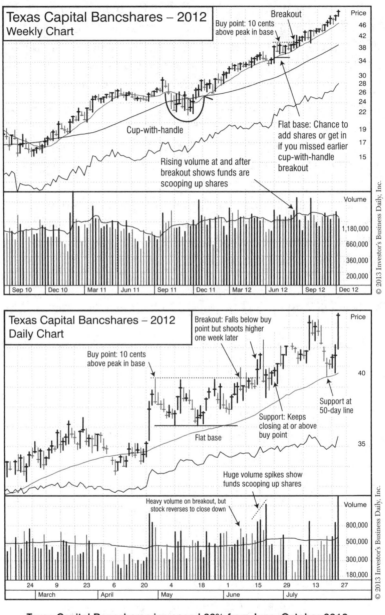

Texas Capital Bancshares increased 33% from June–October 2012.

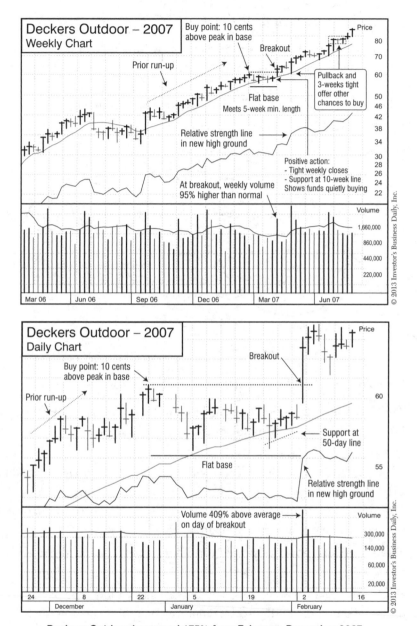

Deckers Outdoor increased 175% from February–December 2007.

More Second Chances with the "Base-on-Base"

Sometimes a stock will break out from a cup-with-handle or double bottom but fail to make the typical 20%–25% gain before starting to form a *new* pattern.

When that happens, we call it a "base-on-base" formation—and it can lead to some powerful moves.

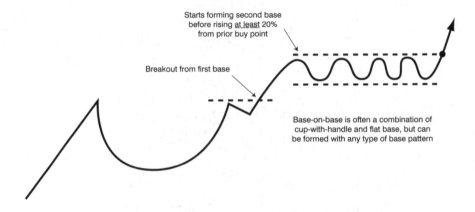

Starts forming second base
before rising <u>at least</u> 20%
from prior buy point

Breakout from first base

Base-on-base is often a combination of
cup-with-handle and flat base, but can
be formed with any type of base pattern

Here are the 2 key things to understand about a base-on-base:

- **The stock must begin forming a new base *before* rising at least 20% from the ideal buy point in the prior pattern.**

  Here's how that works.

  Say a stock breaks out of a cup-with-handle with an ideal buy point of $100. If it starts forming a flat base after climbing to just $115—only a 15% rise—the prior cup-with-handle *and* the new flat base would be considered one "base-on-base" formation.

- **The ideal buy point depends on what type of pattern the *second* base is.**

  While the *second* base in the base-on-base can be any type of pattern, it often ends up being a flat base. Whatever type of formation it is, all the normal criteria for that pattern still apply.

  So if it's a flat base, the ideal buy point would be 10 cents above the peak in that flat base.

  If the second pattern in the base-on-base is a cup-with-handle, then the buy point would be 10 cents above the peak in the handle.

Mirroring the Market Once Again

Just as double bottoms typically form when the overall market is volatile, base-on-base patterns often appear when there is uncertainty or significant selling pressure.

You'll see stocks make that initial breakout from the prior pattern, but then the overall market weakens and they quickly pull back to form that second base.

The good news is, once the heavy "weight" of a market downturn or selling pressure is removed, leading stocks break out from these base-on-base and other patterns and quickly spring higher to new gains.

Here are examples of the kind of profits base-on-base patterns can deliver.

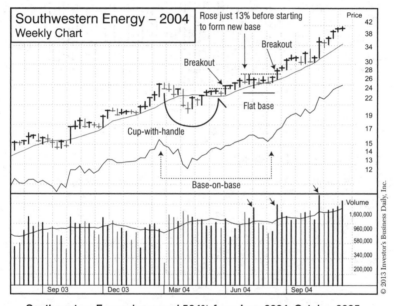

Southwestern Energy increased 504% from June 2004–October 2005.

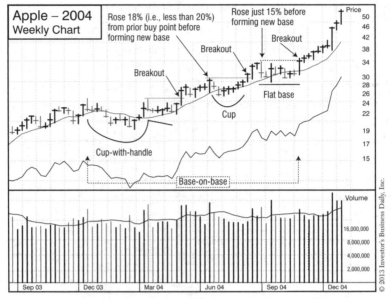

Apple increased 402% from August 2004 to January 2006.

See How to Spot a Flat Base

 Watch a short video at www.investors.com/GettingStartedBook.

Go Beyond Just the Shapes

Once you spot the *shape* of a chart pattern, also look for signs of "accumulation" (institutional buying) and support within the base. That's how you separate sound patterns from potentially faulty ones.

This comes back to Big Rock #3 we discussed earlier: Buy stocks being heavily bought by institutional investors. Avoid those they're heavily selling.

Look for "Clues" in the *Daily Stock Analysis* Videos

 Regularly watching these free videos in the *IBD TV* section of Investors.com is an easy way to improve your chart-reading skills. See how at www.investors.com/GettingStartedBook.

Signs of Institutional Buying

These signals further confirm that big institutional investors are enthusiastic about the stock and are buying up shares, providing the fuel for a higher climb.

- More up weeks on heavy volume than down weeks on heavy volume in the base

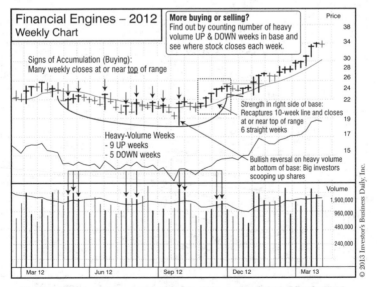

Financial Engines increased 48% from November 2012–March 2013.

- Gap ups on heavy volume

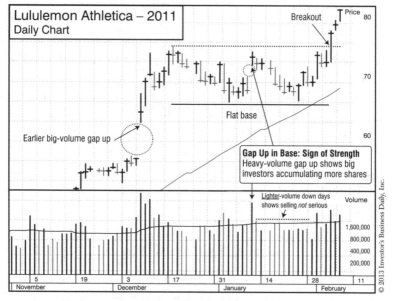

Lululemon Athletica increased 72% from February–July 2011.

- Positive reversals, and closes in the upper half of the range

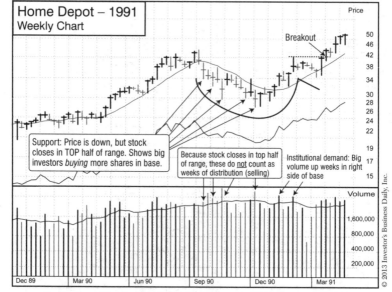

Home Depot increased 275% from January 1991–January 1993.

Warning Signs

When you see these signs of institutional selling or uncertainty in a cup-with-handle or other pattern, proceed with caution. That base is less likely to launch a big move and is more likely to fail.

- Too many down weeks on heavy volume

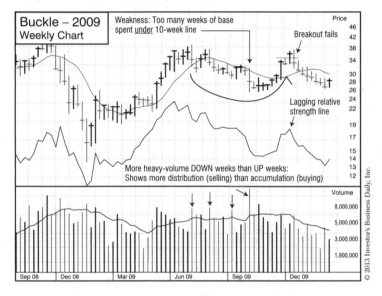

- Gap downs on heavy volume

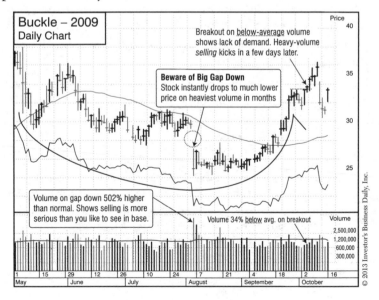

- Wide and loose, volatile trading action

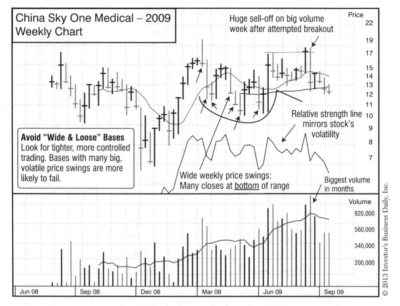

China Sky One Medical – 2009 Weekly Chart

Huge sell-off on big volume week after attempted breakout

Price

Avoid "Wide & Loose" Bases
Look for tighter, more controlled trading. Bases with many big, volatile price swings are more likely to fail.

Relative strength line mirrors stock's volatility

Wide weekly price swings: Many closes at <u>bottom</u> of range

Biggest volume in months

Volume

© 2013 Investor's Business Daily, Inc.

Compare China Sky's wide and loose action to the tighter, healthier trading in the chart for Financial Engines we saw earlier in "Signs of Institutional Buying."

Beware of Late-Stage Bases

Nothing goes up forever.

As we saw earlier, the big money is made in the *early stages*—usually the first 1–2 years—of a new bull market. That's when the prior *bear* market has wiped the slate clean, and a new crop of leading stocks break out from a chart pattern and soar higher.

As they continue to climb higher, these stocks will likely take a breather and form another chart pattern along the way—maybe a flat base. That would be a second-stage base.

The Reset Button

Generally, a bear market resets the "base count"–the number of chart patterns the stock has formed since the start of its big run. So the first breakout in a new bull market is considered a first-stage base. Note: Milder "interim corrections" do *not* reset the count (Big Rock #1, Chapter 3).

By the time a stock starts forming a third- or fourth-stage base, it could be getting a little long in the tooth. Here's why:

- **The stock itself has already made a big move.** It could be up 100% or more. How much higher can it really go before institutional investors cash in their profits and put the stock into a deep decline?

- **The overall market may be running out of steam.** When you get into the third year of a bull cycle, the market tends to get more volatile and choppy. That impacts the leading stocks, and they may also struggle to move higher.

That's the basic reason you want to be careful about buying stocks as they break out of a third- or even later-stage base.

Late-stage patterns *can* work and sometimes do lead to nice gains. But successful investing is about keeping the odds in your favor. So just understand that late-stage bases involve more risk. If you buy a stock on a late-stage breakout, you might cut your losses sooner—say, at 3%–4%—if the stock fails to gain traction.

See How to "Count" Bases

 This is easier to "show" than "tell," so if you'd like to learn more about late-stage bases, check out a short video on that topic at www.investors.com/GettingStartedBook.

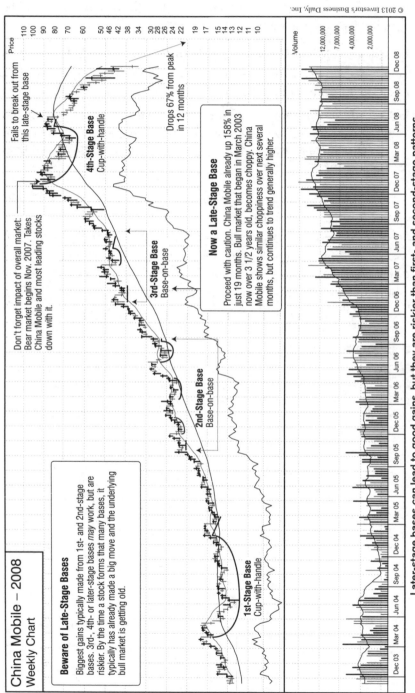

© 2013 Investor's Business Daily, Inc.

China Mobile – 2008
Weekly Chart

Beware of Late-Stage Bases

Biggest gains typically made from 1st- and 2nd-stage bases. 3rd-, 4th- or later-stage bases *may* work, but are riskier. By the time a stock forms that many bases, it typically has already made a big move and the underlying bull market is getting old.

Don't forget impact of overall market: Bear market begins Nov. 2007. Takes China Mobile and most leading stocks down with it.

Fails to break out from this late-stage base

4th-Stage Base
Cup-with-handle

Drops 67% from peak in 12 months

3rd-Stage Base
Base-on-base

2nd-Stage Base
Base-on-base

1st-Stage Base
Cup-with-handle

Now a Late-Stage Base

Proceed with caution. China Mobile already up 158% in just 19 months. Bull market that began in March 2003 now over 3 1/2 years old, becomes choppy. China Mobile shows similar choppiness over next several months, but continues to trend generally higher.

Price
110
100
90
80
70
60
50
46
42
38
34
30
28
26
24
22
19
17
15
14
13
12
11
10

Volume
12,000,000
7,000,000
4,000,000
2,000,000

Dec 03   Mar 04   Jun 04   Sep 04   Dec 04   Mar 05   Jun 05   Sep 05   Dec 05   Mar 06   Jun 06   Sep 06   Dec 06   Mar 07   Jun 07   Sep 07   Dec 07   Mar 08   Jun 08   Sep 08   Dec 08

Later-stage bases *can* lead to good gains, but they are riskier than first- and second-stage patterns.

See a Pattern Here?

Now it's time to put what you've learned to the test!
Here's how to do it:

1. Go through the examples below and see if you can spot a pattern within each chart. If you do, can you name the type of base and see the ideal buy point?

2. Once you spot the pattern, look for the "clues" we discussed in "Go Beyond Just the Shapes." Do you see any? What do they tell you about the stock and chart pattern? Is the relative strength line in or near new high territory?

3. See how you did by checking the markups I've included for the same chart on a different page.

The More You Practice, The More You Profit

Don't expect to learn all of this in one sitting! Take chart-reading one step at a time, and you'll see it all come together very soon.

Here's what I suggest: **Before and/or after you take this quiz, watch the videos I included at the end of each chart pattern description and do the Simple Weekend Routine.** That will help you improve your own chart-reading skills—and see where to find stocks forming these 3 telltale patterns *right now*.

Don't Forget to Take Advantage of Free Investor Training

Have you done the "Must-Do" steps I mentioned in the Introduction?

- Check out the local **IBD Meetup** group near you.
- Sign up for online **IBD Product Training**.

Both are free—and both will help you improve your chart-reading skills and get answers to any questions you may have. You can take both steps right now at www.investors.com/GettingStartedBook.

Can You Spot the Patterns?

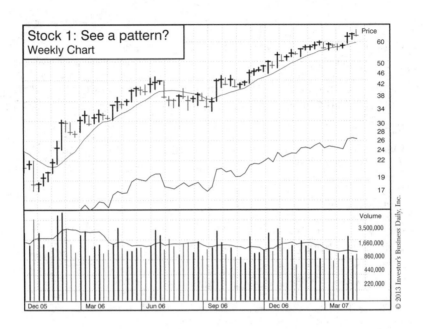

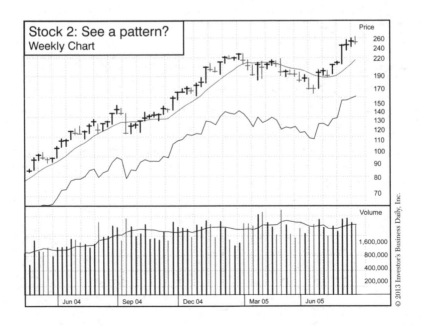

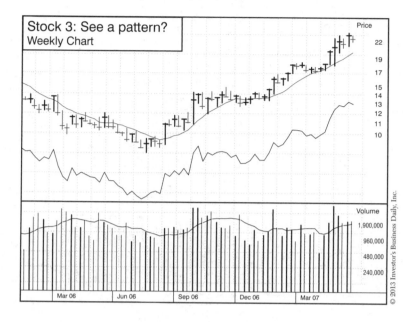

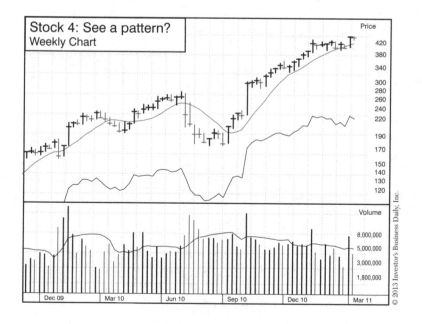

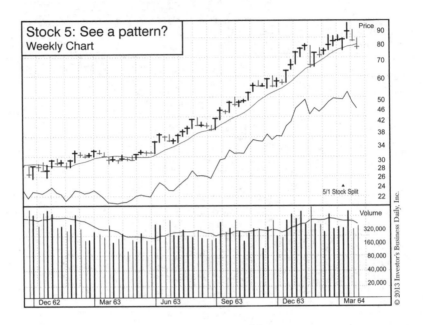

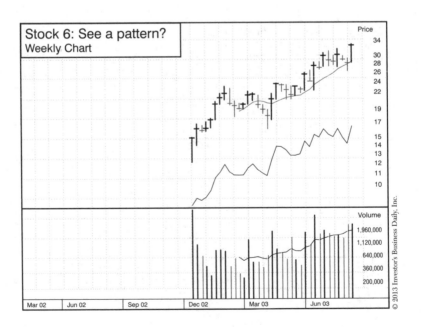

See How You Did by Checking These Markups

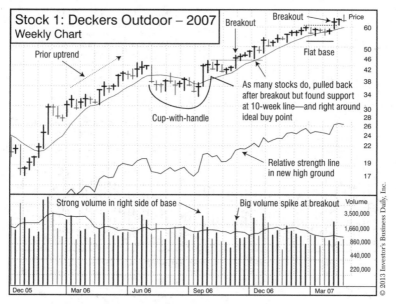

Deckers Outdoor increased 151% from September 2006–August 2007.

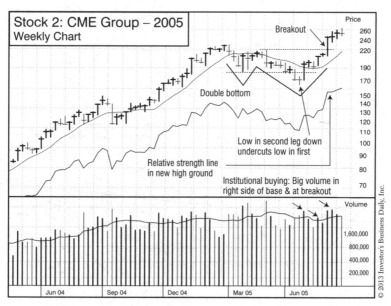

CME Group increased 224% from June 2005–December 2007.

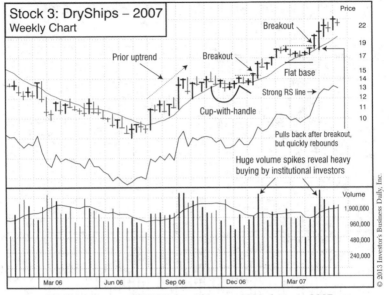

DryShips increased 815% from January 2006–January 2007.

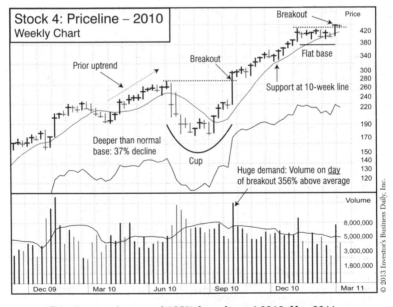

Priceline.com increased 105% from August 2010–May 2011.

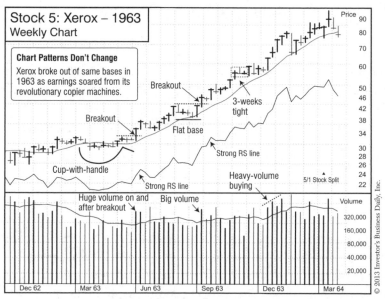

Xerox increased 660% from April 1963 to April 1966.

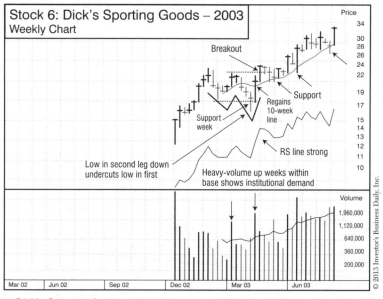

Dick's Sporting Goods increased 181% from February 2003–April 2004.

Stick with It!

Keep improving your chart-reading skills—while also building a timely watch list—by regularly watching the *Daily Stock Analysis* and *Market Wrap* videos at Investors.com/IBDtv.

Alternative Buy Points

The cup-with-handle, double bottom and flat base are the main patterns that launch big runs. But what if you miss those breakouts? Don't worry. All is not lost!

The big winners will typically form alternative buying opportunities. You can use these to initiate a position in the stock—or *add* to your position if you *did* catch the breakout.

Less Is More

Since these are secondary buy points, it's a good idea to buy a smaller position than you would from, say, a cup-with-handle. That's especially true if you're buying more shares in a stock you already own. In that case, you always want to buy fewer shares than you purchased in the initial breakout. That keeps you from running up your *average* purchase price too much.

Here are two of the most common alternative buying opportunities.

3-Weeks Tight

Like a flat base, this occurs after a stock breaks out, goes up for a while, then pauses to digest those gains.

As the name implies, it only takes 3 weeks to form. Here are the key points:

 Each weekly close *should be within about 1% of the prior week's close.*

That's what creates the "tight" range you see in the chart. Remember to focus on the weekly *closing prices*. During the week, the share price may move around a bit, but you're focused on where it *closes* on Friday.

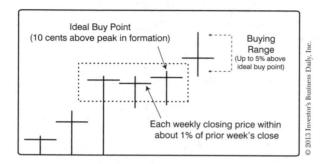

What do the tight weekly closes tell you? That institutional investors are holding onto their shares.

Fund managers and other professionals expect more from the stock, so they're not taking their profits off the table. In fact, they're quietly accumulating *more* shares, and that's what keeps the stock in that tight and narrow price range.

☑ *Ideal buy point*
- 10 cents above the peak in the formation (i.e., the most recent area of resistance)
- Buying range: Up to 5% above the ideal buy point
- *Always buy as close as possible to the* ideal *buy point!*

☑ *Volume on day of breakout: At least 40%–50% above average*

As with all bases, you want volume to be at least 40%–50% higher than normal on the breakout to show that fund managers and other professional investors are jumping in.

Next are just 2 examples of how a 3-weeks tight can give you an opportunity to pick up shares as a winning stock continues its run.

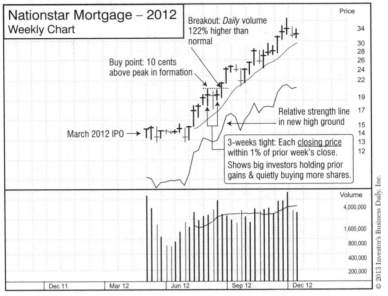

Nationstar Mortgage increased 82% from June–October 2012.

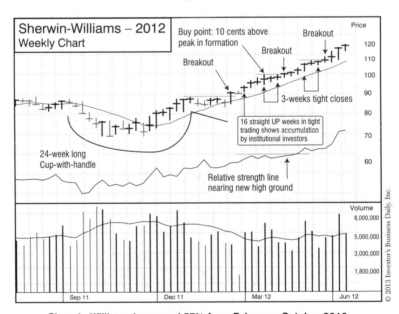

Sherwin-Williams increased 57% from February–October 2012.

See How to Spot a 3-Weeks Tight Pattern

 Watch a short video at www.investors.com/GettingStartedBook.

Pullback to 10-Week or 50-Day Moving Average Line

After a stock has broken out of a proper chart pattern, it may pull back to the benchmark 10-week or 50-day moving average lines we discussed earlier. *If the stock bounces off the moving average line and shoots higher on heavy volume, it can offer a chance to buy shares.*

That type of behavior shows institutional investors are stepping in to "support" and defend the stock. It happens around these moving average lines simply because professional investors use those lines as key benchmarks (see "Chart-Reading 101" in this chapter).

Don't "Buy on the Dips"

You'll often hear pundits talk about "buying on the dips"—that is, buying a stock just because its share price is now lower and appears to be a "bargain." That's an *extremely* risky strategy. A stock going down in price is going down for a reason.

Depending on how heavy the volume is, one of those reasons may be that fund managers are dumping shares and moving out of the stock. Remember "Big Rock #3": Buy stocks being heavily bought by institutional investors. Avoid those they're heavily selling.

So how is buying on a "pullback" different?

Simple: You wait for the stock to find support and move *up* on *heavy* volume before you buy. In other words, don't buy it if it keeps going *down*!

Here are some basic guidelines for how to properly buy on a pullback:

This shows professional investors are *not* aggressively selling shares. Volume may be above average certain days or weeks during the pullback, but overall it should be "drying up" or getting lighter as the stock nears the moving average line.

☑ *Make sure the stock bounces off the moving average line and heads higher on heavy volume*

You want the stock to rebound and show strength, not weakness, before you buy. Never buy a stock as it's moving *down*.

☑ *Buy as close to the moving average line as possible*

As the stock bounces off the 50-day or 10-week moving average line, you want to buy as close to that line as possible. The farther away from the line you buy, the riskier it gets.

☑ *Focus on the first 2 pullbacks*

The best gains typically come from the first 2 pullbacks to the 10-week line. By the time a stock's third or fourth retreat occurs, it likely has already had a good move. Chances are now higher that the pullback is actually the start of a more serious sell-off.

Study the following weekly and daily charts for Netflix. They show how a pullback can be an opportunity to add shares to a winning position, or a second chance to buy into a stock if you missed an earlier breakout.

That's also a good reminder of why you want to continue to track winning stocks as they make a big move. They'll typically offer multiple opportunities for you to get in and profit.

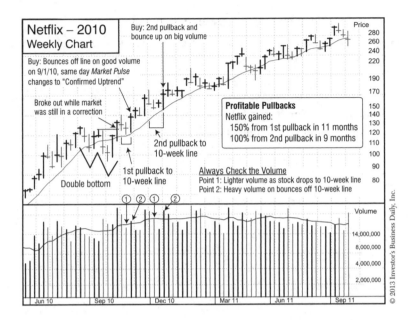

Netflix – 2010
Weekly Chart

Buy: 2nd pullback and bounce up on big volume

Buy: Bounces off line on good volume on 9/1/10, same day *Market Pulse* changes to "Confirmed Uptrend"

Broke out while market was still in a correction

Profitable Pullbacks
Netflix gained:
150% from 1st pullback in 11 months
100% from 2nd pullback in 9 months

2nd pullback to 10-week line

1st pullback to 10-week line

Double bottom

Always Check the Volume
Point 1: Lighter volume as stock drops to 10-week line
Point 2: Heavy volume on bounces off 10-week line

Price
280
260
240
220
190
170
150
140
130
120
110
100
90
80

Volume
14,000,000
8,000,000
4,000,000
2,000,000

Jun 10   Sep 10   Dec 10   Mar 11   Jun 11   Sep 11

© 2013 Investor's Business Daily, Inc.

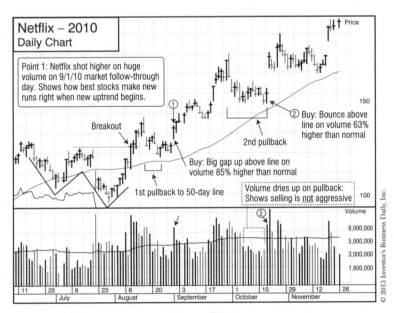

Netflix – 2010
Daily Chart

Point 1: Netflix shot higher on huge volume on 9/1/10 market follow-through day. Shows how best stocks make new runs right when new uptrend begins.

Breakout

Buy: Big gap up above line on volume 85% higher than normal

Buy: Bounce above line on volume 63% higher than normal

2nd pullback

1st pullback to 50-day line

Volume dries up on pullback: Shows selling is *not* aggressive

Price

150

100

Volume
8,000,000
5,000,000
3,000,000
1,800,000

11   25   9   23   6   20   3   17   1   15   29   12   26
July   August   September   October   November

© 2013 Investor's Business Daily, Inc.

Netflix increased 150% from September 2010–July 2011.

5 Quick Guidelines for How to Buy on a Pullback

 Watch my *2-Minute Tip* video on the right way to buy on a pullback at www.investors.com/GettingStartedBook.

Next up: Now that we've gone through Chart-Reading 101 and how to spot profitable chart patterns, let's see how to check off the "Chart Analysis" items on the buying and selling checklists.

Using Charts to Go Through the Checklists

In the Buying Checklist and Selling Checklist sections we covered earlier, you saw how to quickly run through most of the buying and selling criteria using *Stock Checkup* and some basic rules.

Now that we've also covered the basics of chart-reading, let's see how to go through the **"Chart Analysis"** items on both checklists.

It Pays to Practice

If you're brand new to charts, I'm sure you're still trying to absorb all the patterns and concepts we just went through. As I keep saying—and as I know from personal experience—it takes a little time for it all to sink in and come together. But whatever you do, *don't give up on chart-reading!*

The practice you put in now *will* pay off down the road. So stick with it. Keep doing the Simple Weekend Routine, and keep watching the *Daily Stock Analysis* and other *IBD TV* videos. Spotting buy and sell signals in a chart will soon become second nature.

Let's start right now with a quick run through the Buying Checklist.

Buying Checklist

Chart Analysis: Buy stocks as they break out of the common patterns that launch big moves.

❑ Breaking out of sound base or alternative buy point

❑ Volume at least 40% to 50% above average on breakout

❑ Relative strength line in new high ground

❑ Within 5% of ideal buy point

As we go through this, don't forget *why* we put so much emphasis on following sound buy rules:

Stocks that pass the Buying Checklist have the greatest potential to make a *big* gain.

And by making each stock prove itself *before* you buy, you significantly increase your chances of starting out right—with a nice profit instead of a loss. That's why you want to always use this checklist as your starting point: Less risk, more reward.

☑ *Breaking out of a sound base or alternative buy point*

Is the stock nearing the ideal buy point in a cup-with-handle, double bottom or flat base—or an alternative buying area like a 3-weeks tight or pullback to the 10-week line?

To help with your analysis, do a search on Investors.com to see what IBD has written about the stock's latest chart action. And if the stock is on the *IBD 50, Your Weekly Review, Sector Leaders* or *IBD Big Cap 20*, check the latest chart analysis. Does that analysis match what you're seeing?

If the stock is *not* forming any recognizable pattern or buy point, what does that tell you?

It means you need to stay patient. Stick to your rules and wait for a *proper* buying opportunity to emerge. A little discipline goes a *long* way to keeping you profitable and protected!

Is the Pattern Sound—or Suspect? Find Out with the Base Checklist

 Download and print this little "cheat sheet" to help you quickly evaluate a cup-with-handle or other pattern. You'll find the Base Checklist at www.investors.com/GettingStartedBook.

☑ *Volume on day of breakout:* At least *40%–50% above average*

If volume is *below* or just barely above average, that makes the breakout more suspect. Look for a big spike to show *enthusiastic* institutional buying.

Remember: 40%–50% is the *minimum* benchmark. On a strong breakout, you'll often see volume come in 100%, 200% or more above average.

How Can You Tell if Volume Is Unusually Heavy or Light?

● **Check the "Volume % Change" feature.**

IBD's unique "Volume % Change" tells you *throughout the trading day* if volume is trending above or below average. You'll see it when you pull up a stock quote on Investors.com.

So as a stock breaks out, you'll find the *projected* Volume % Change based on the trading volume up to that point, letting you easily see if it's on track to hit the 40%–50% benchmark.

You'll find "Volume % Change" in *Stock Checkup* and the quotes pages on Investors.com and in *IBD Smart NYSE + Nasdaq Tables* (Chapter 7).

- **Check the *daily* chart.**

  You can also see how heavy volume is on the day of the breakout with a quick glance at the daily chart.

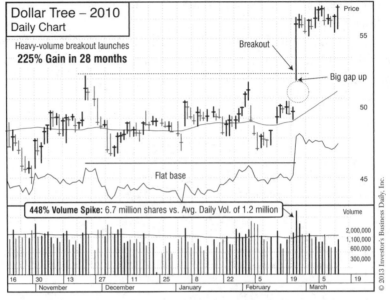

Dollar Tree – 2010
Daily Chart

Heavy-volume breakout launches
225% Gain in 28 months

Breakout

Big gap up

Flat base

448% Volume Spike: 6.7 million shares vs. Avg. Daily Vol. of 1.2 million

Volume

Price

55

50

45

2,000,000
1,100,000
600,000
300,000

16 30 13 27 11 25 8 22 5 19 5 19
November December January February March

© 2013 Investor's Business Daily, Inc.

Unusually heavy volume on a breakout shows strong institutional demand.

In some cases, you may find volume falls short of the 40%–50% benchmark on the day of the breakout, but heavy volume kicks in a day or two later. That's not ideal, but if the stock has the CAN SLIM® traits, is still within buying range (i.e., less than 5% above the ideal buy point) and volume comes in particularly strong, you could still buy it.

✔ *Relative strength line in new high ground*

The relative strength (RS) line compares the price performance of your stock over the last 52 weeks to that of the S&P 500.

- If the RS line is trending *higher*, the stock is outperforming the overall market.
- A *downward* trending line means the stock is lagging the market.

It's bullish to see the RS line already moving into new high territory as a stock completes its base and breaks out. It confirms the stock has bounced back from its correction and is now showing market-leading power.

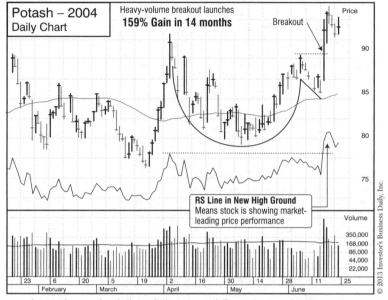

Make a point to always check the relative strength line when evaluating a chart pattern.

☑ *Within 5% of ideal buy point*

As we saw earlier, the buy points and buying ranges of base patterns are all essentially calculated the same way:

- **Ideal Buy Point:** 10 cents above the most recent area of resistance
- **Buying Range:** Up to 5% above the ideal buy point

Your goal is to buy as close to the ideal buy point as possible, but the stock can still be bought up to 5% past that price.

Don't chase "extended" stocks—those beyond the 5% buying range.

It just exposes you to unnecessary risk. Stocks often pull back after they break out, and the farther away from the ideal buy point you make a purchase, the higher chance you have of getting "shaken out" by the 7%–8% sell rule.

So if you miss a breakout, resist the temptation to chase that train down the tracks. Instead, wait for it to pull into the next station by forming a new base or alternative buy point like a pullback or 3-weeks tight. That allows you to board the train more safely and sensibly.

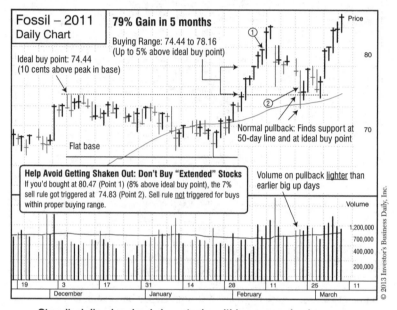

Stay disciplined and only buy stocks within a proper buying range.

Checking the Chart for Buy Signals

 See a short video on how to run your stock through the "Chart Analysis" elements of the Buying Checklist at www.investors.com/GettingStartedBook.

Next up: Let's use charts and the Selling Checklist to look for early warning signs in a stock.

Using Charts to Go Through the Checklists

Selling Checklist

❏ **Chart Analysis:** Consider selling some or all of your shares if you see these signals:

→ Biggest single-day price decline since start of stock's run on heaviest volume in months

→ Sharp drop below 50-day moving average line on heaviest volume in months

→ Sharp drop—and close—below 10-week moving average line on heavy volume

We've already covered the basic selling game plan:

- Take most profits at 20%–25%.
- Cut all losses at no more than 7%–8%.
- Take defensive action as a market downtrend begins.

That's a simple and effective way to nail down some good profits and avoid any serious losses.

And now that you've added charts to your investing toolbox, you can tap into *additional* ways to spot early warning signs in your stocks—signs that someone who does *not* use charts simply *cannot* see. Over time, it will become increasingly clear what a huge, money-making advantage that gives you.

As you become more comfortable with charts, you'll discover other techniques that help you move to the sidelines and safeguard your profits. But to get started, let's take a look at 3 common signs of trouble.

 Biggest single-day price decline since start of stock's run on heaviest volume in months

Let's see: A *huge decline* on the *heaviest volume* in months . . .

There's no mystery to that "story." Institutional investors are aggressively dumping shares!

Some fund managers may be liquidating their positions, and that spells serious trouble for the stock—and for *you* if you continue to hold.

The stock may bounce back down the road, but that type of sudden sell-off is a trend-changer: Chances are high the stock will continue to move farther south.

In the context of this sell rule, let's revisit the charts we saw for OpenTable earlier in "Chart-Reading 101." The company had carved out a profitable niche with a new platform that lets restaurants take online reservations and market to their customers. It was a young, innovative company and a market leader—until its trajectory changed sharply in the spring of 2011.

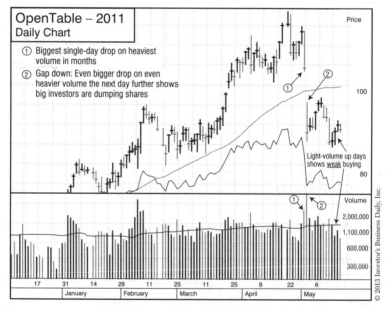

A huge price drop on heavy volume shows big investors are aggressively selling.

Here's what that looked like on OpenTable's weekly chart.

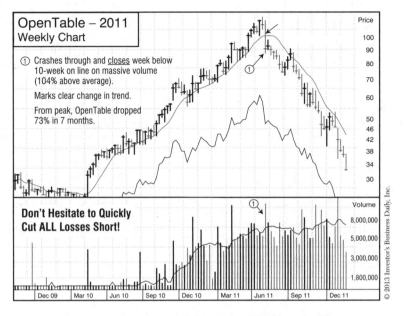

OpenTable – 2011
Weekly Chart

① Crashes through and <u>closes</u> week below 10-week on line on massive volume (104% above average).

Marks clear change in trend.

From peak, OpenTable dropped 73% in 7 months.

Don't Hesitate to Quickly Cut ALL Losses Short!

© 2013 Investor's Business Daily, Inc.

Do you see how the trend changed on that big sell-off?

As briefly noted in the charts for OpenTable in "Chart-Reading 101," there were other warning signs even *before* the stock flashed this sell signal. Learning to spot those is definitely helpful, but as you're getting started, at a minimum, stick to this rule. If a stock makes this kind of sharp downward shift on the heaviest volume in months, it's time to sell at least some of your shares.

What About Overall Market Conditions?

A vital part of the Selling Checklist is to make sure you take defensive action when the overall market starts to weaken. As the following examples for Fossil show, warning signs and sell signals often appear in individual stocks as distribution days mount and the market uptrend slips into a correction. Paying attention to those signs can help you lock in your profits and move to the sidelines before any serious damage hits.

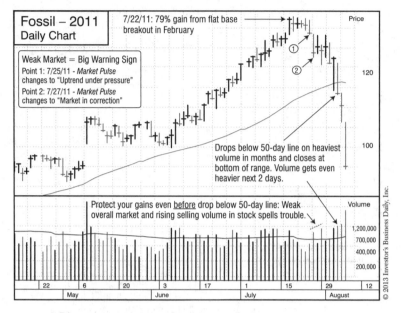

Fossil – 2011
Daily Chart

7/22/11: 79% gain from flat base breakout in February

Price

Weak Market = Big Warning Sign
Point 1: 7/25/11 - *Market Pulse* changes to "Uptrend under pressure"
Point 2: 7/27/11 - *Market Pulse* changes to "Market in correction"

① ②

120

Drops below 50-day line on heaviest volume in months and closes at bottom of range. Volume gets even heavier next 2 days.

100

Protect your gains even <u>before</u> drop below 50-day line: Weak overall market and rising selling volume in stock spells trouble.

Volume

1,200,000
700,000
400,000
200,000

22   6   20   3   17   1   15   29   12
May   June   July   August

© 2013 Investor's Business Daily, Inc.

Be ready to lock in profits as the overall market weakens.

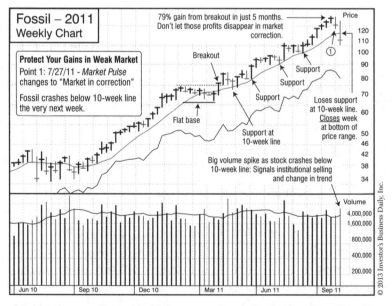

Fossil – 2011
Weekly Chart

79% gain from breakout in just 5 months. Don't let those profits disappear in market correction.

Price
120
110
100
90

Protect Your Gains in Weak Market
Point 1: 7/27/11 - *Market Pulse* changes to "Market in correction"
Fossil crashes below 10-week line the very next week.

Breakout

Support

80

Support

Support

70

Loses support at 10-week line. <u>Closes</u> week at bottom of price range.

60

Flat base

50
46

Support at 10-week line

42
38

Big volume spike as stock crashes below 10-week line: Signals institutional selling and change in trend

34

Volume

4,000,000
1,600,000
800,000
400,000
200,000

Jun 10   Sep 10   Dec 10   Mar 11   Jun 11   Sep 11

© 2013 Investor's Business Daily, Inc.

Double whammy: The market is in a correction and your stock is selling off on heavy volume. Time for defensive action.

The Trend Is No Longer Your Friend

Take another look at the weekly charts for OpenTable and Fossil—and recall what we learned earlier about support and resistance.

In the months leading up to the sharp sell-off, both stocks had been making a relatively steady upward climb, finding nice support at their 10-week moving average lines.

Do you see how that changed when the stocks suddenly made those exceptionally sharp declines on unusually heavy volume? Don't ignore such a change in trend—it's usually a sign of even more trouble ahead.

☑ *Sharp drop below 50-day moving average line on heaviest volume in months*

As we saw in the section on support and resistance, professional investors often use the 50-day moving average line as a key benchmark. That's why it's so important to watch how a stock behaves when it trades near that line.

- If the stock stays *above* the 50-day line, that means professional investors are stepping in to support the stock and protect their positions.

- If the stock crashes sharply *below* the 50-day line on *unusually heavy* volume, that could mean institutions are reducing their holdings, and more selling will follow.

A drop below the 50-day line does *not* necessarily mean you should automatically sell your entire position. However, it is a definite warning sign, particularly if the stock:

- Slices *sharply* below the line (especially on a huge gap down)
- Closes at the very bottom of the day's price range
- Declines on unusually heavy volume

Also, if the general market is weakening and the *Market Pulse* outlook has changed to "Uptrend under pressure" or "Market in correction," that's all the more reason to take defensive action and protect yourself.

Next is an example of a heavy-volume drop below the 50-day line.

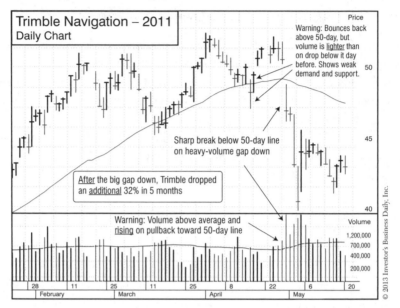

Trimble Navigation – 2011
Daily Chart

Price

Warning: Bounces back above 50-day, but volume is <u>lighter</u> than on drop below it day before. Shows weak demand and support.

Sharp break below 50-day line on heavy-volume gap down

After the big gap down, Trimble dropped an additional 32% in 5 months

Warning: Volume above average and rising on pullback toward 50-day line

Volume
1,200,000
700,000
400,000
200,000

28 11 25 11 25 8 22 6 20
February March April May

© 2013 Investor's Business Daily, Inc.

Support or sell-off? Always watch how a stock behaves around the 50-day line.

Beware the Gap Down!

In "Go Beyond Just the Shapes," we saw why a big gap *up* on heavy volume is a good thing. It shows there's so much demand for a stock that, instead of moving up incrementally, it instantly jumps to a much higher price.

But a heavy-volume gap *down* is a completely different story. It tells you institutions are so eager to *sell* that the stock instantly drops down to a much *lower* price.

Take a minute and go back to the *daily* charts above for OpenTable and Trimble. Do you see the heavy-volume gap downs they had—and how the stocks went even farther south after that? If you ever see that behavior in one of *your* stocks, it's definitely a sign to reduce your exposure and sell some or all of your shares.

 *Sharp drop—and **close**—below 10-week moving average line on heavy volume*

The 10-week moving average line found on weekly charts is roughly equivalent to the 50-day line found on daily charts. While professional investors use both lines as benchmarks (and you should too!), the 10-week line makes it easier to see the longer-term trend.

As we just saw, if a stock drops sharply below the 50-day line on extremely heavy volume and closes at the bottom of its range, that's a serious sign of trouble. On the other hand, if volume is light and the stock bounces back to close near the *top* of the day's range and at or just below that benchmark line, it could mean funds are buying shares to prop up the stock and protect their positions.

To gauge how serious the selling is, also check the *weekly* chart.

Where Does the Stock *Close* for the Week?

You may find that after a day or two of selling, fund managers step in to buy shares, and by the end of the week, the stock closes above or just under the 10-week line. That's a sign of *support*.

However, if the stock breaks sharply below the 10-week line and *closes* under it on *heavy* volume, that's a sign of institutional *selling*, not support. It's often a precursor to *more* selling, meaning it's time to protect yourself.

Here are two examples. The first shows a stock that did *not* find support and *closed* below the 10-week line on heavy volume. The second shows one that bounced back by the end of the week.

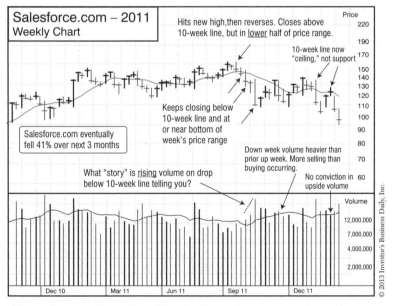

Salesforce.com did not find support at 10-week line, and continued lower.

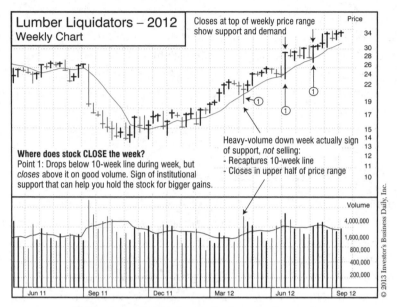

Lumber Liquidators – 2012
Weekly Chart

Closes at top of weekly price range show support and demand

Price

Where does stock CLOSE the week?
Point 1: Drops below 10-week line during week, but *closes* above it on good volume. Sign of institutional support that can help you hold the stock for bigger gains.

Heavy-volume down week actually sign of support, *not* selling:
- Recaptures 10-week line
- Closes in upper half of price range

Volume

© 2013 Investor's Business Daily, Inc.

Waiting to see where the stock *closes* for the week can help you hold on for bigger profits.

Checking the Chart for Sell Signals

See a short video on how to spot signs of trouble using daily and weekly charts at www.investors.com/GettingStartedBook.

· CHAPTER ·

More Tips and Tools for Getting Started Right

How Many Stocks Should You Own?

*"**Many investors over-diversify.** The best results are usually achieved through concentration, by putting your eggs in a few baskets that you know well and watching them carefully."*

—WILLIAM J. O'NEIL, IBD CHAIRMAN AND FOUNDER

There is no magic formula that determines exactly how many stocks you should own. But here are some basic guidelines to keep in mind.

☑ *Don't own more stocks than you can handle* properly *and watch* carefully.

I remember talking with an investor at a Money Show years ago who told me she owned over 60 stocks! Who has time to keep tabs on 5 *dozen* different positions? Not me! And not anyone else I know at Investor's Business Daily either—including Bill O'Neil.

So before you jump in and start buying a bunch of stocks, ask yourself a simple question: *How much time will you realistically spend on investing each week?*

Let's say you only have 10–20 minutes a day and some more time on the weekend. That is *definitely* enough to go through the simple routines (Chapter 4) and start generating good profits—*if* you limit yourself to a *few* top-rated stocks.

Remember what I keep saying about keeping it simple. That also goes for the number of stocks you own.

Start small. If you find you can handle more stocks down the road, fine. But definitely don't buy more stocks than you can manage successfully when you're just getting started.

☑ *Diversify for the* right *reasons.*

Diversification is not a bad thing, per se. The problem is, too many investors diversify for all the *wrong* reasons—and that's what gets them into trouble. Here are some examples.

- **Diversification can dilute your results.** Your goal is to have your biggest *winners* also be your biggest *positions*. If you get a 100% gain in a stock that is only 1 of 20 different positions in your portfolio, it's a nice percentage gain—but it doesn't make you any significant *money*.

- **Over-diversification can lead to buying some stocks with less potential or lower quality.** Will you really achieve *superior* results by buying *inferior* stocks? Be picky, and only invest in top-rated stocks that pass the Buying Checklist.

- **Over-diversification does *not* protect your portfolio.** Here's why the idea of "safety in numbers" doesn't apply to your portfolio.

  First, it's *much* harder to spot early warning signs if you have to constantly track 15 or 20 stocks. But you can do it very quickly if you only need to check in on 3 or 4 positions.

  Second, when you *own* a lot of stocks, you also have to *sell* a lot of stocks to protect your overall portfolio. If you own 20 stocks, will you really sell 10 or 15 of them quickly enough to avoid serious damage?

  Remember: A market downtrend will take 3 out of 4 stocks down with it. Owning a bunch of stocks doesn't change that fact—it just makes it that much harder to reduce your risk.

  On the other hand, if you own 3 or 4 stocks, you only need to sell 1 or 2 to quickly safeguard a significant portion of your money.

So What Are the *Right* Reasons to Diversify?

The main one is to avoid putting all your money into *one* industry.

For example, if you own nothing but semiconductor stocks or nothing but housing stocks—both of which are cyclical industries—you're taking on undue risk. If bad news or an economic downturn suddenly rocked the industry, *all* of your stocks might instantly sell off.

Stocks move in *groups*. If institutional investors start pumping money into a particular industry, stocks in that business will generally go up. And when fund managers decide they want out, *all* stocks in that group are at risk.

In Bill's quote at the beginning of this chapter, he didn't say put *all* your eggs in *one* basket. The point is that you don't want to diversify just because people say diversification is "good" or "safe." Instead, concentrate on a few stocks in a "few" baskets—and watch them very carefully.

A General Guideline for How Many Stocks to Own

Based on the concepts above, here is a basic rule of thumb for how many stocks to have in your portfolio.

Portfolio Size	Suggested Number of Stocks
Under $20,000	2–3 Stocks
$20,000–$200,000	4–5 Stocks
$200,000–$1 million	5–6 Stocks
$1 million–$5 million	6–8 Stocks
Over $5 million	7–10 Stocks

Set a Maximum Number, and Stick to It

As part of your investing game plan, decide the maximum number of stocks you'll own at one time. When you reach that cap, stay disciplined: Before you buy another—presumably *better* stock—sell your *weakest* holding to make room for it.

Bottom line: Be selective and only buy a few top-rated CAN SLIM® stocks that pass the Buying Checklist, then watch them very closely. That's a more manageable way to grow your portfolio.

How to Build and Maintain an Actionable Watch List

"It takes as much energy to wish as it does to plan."

—ELEANOR ROOSEVELT

Superior results start with a superior watch list. So here are 4 steps you can take to build and regularly refresh *your* list.

Keep in mind: This is just one possible approach you can use to get started. Find whatever approach works best for you.

 *Create 2 watch lists.*

- **Near Buy Point:** For stocks near a potential buy point or in buying range *right now*.

    To keep this list actionable, be sure to prune it regularly so it doesn't get cluttered with stocks *not* currently near a buy point.
- **Radar Screen:** For stocks with CAN SLIM® traits that are *not* near a buy point right now.

    You want to keep any eye on these because they could offer a buying opportunity later.

How Do I Set Up a Watch List?

Most people set them up using tools from their online broker or trading platform. Ask your brokerage service what watch list tools they offer.

How Many Stocks Should I Have on My Lists?

Set a limit on how many stocks you'll have on each list. For a watch list to be valuable, it has to be actionable. So stick to a *manageable* number of stocks. You might limit your Near Buy Point list to 5–10 stocks and your Radar Screen list to 15–20. The number depends on how much time you have to spend on research.

Don't hesitate to be picky! Only keep stocks that pass the Buying Checklist with flying colors on your list. Over the long term, focusing on the strongest stocks will generate the biggest returns.

☑ *Use the Simple Weekend Routine and IBD tools to find quality stocks.*

- See "Simple Routines for Finding Winning Stocks" (Chapter 4) and "More Ways to Find Winning Stocks" (later in this chapter).
- Run the most promising stocks through the Buying Checklist. If they pass, add them to your Near Buy Point list. If a stock has the CAN SLIM traits but is not currently near a buy point, you can add it to your Radar Screen list.

☑ *Make a game plan for stocks on your Near Buy Point list.*

To catch a stock as it breaks out, you need to make your game plan *ahead of time*. It'll often be too late if you wait until *after* the stock has begun its move.

At a minimum, be sure to note:

- The ideal buy point
- How many shares you'll buy if the stock breaks out on heavy volume

Trade triggers: You can also set up automatic trade triggers ahead of time if you can't watch the market during the day (Chapter 4).

Earnings season: Check when a stock you're tracking is scheduled to report. Stocks can make a big move—up or down—when they release their latest numbers (Chapter 3).

☑ *Review and refresh your watch list regularly.*

Your watch list will only be actionable and effective if you keep it focused and up to date.

- Regularly refresh your list as part of your weekend and/or daily routine.
- If you've reached the maximum number of stocks you set for your list, be sure to remove your weakest stock before you add a new one.

- When in doubt about what to keep or cut, focus on the "big rocks":

  - Which stock has the biggest earnings growth?

  - Which company has the most innovative product or service dominating its industry?

  - Which stock is being most heavily bought by institutional investors?

Maintain Your Watch List in Strong *and* Weak Markets

Keep building and refreshing your watch list *even if the market is in a downtrend*. The best stocks form bases during a correction, then *quickly* shoot higher when a new uptrend begins. To catch these winners and make big money when the market is *up*, you need to prepare while the market's *down*.

• ACTION STEPS •

To take these steps, visit www.investors.com/GettingStartedBook.

- Watch my *2-Minute Tip* video: *5 Steps to Building & Maintaining a Profitable Watch List*.

- Create your watch lists: Near Buy Point and Radar Screen (or whatever setup works for you).

- Start *regularly* doing the simple routines to find new stock ideas (Chapter 4).

- Make a game plan for stocks on your Near Buy Point list.

How to Do a Profitable Post-Analysis

"The only way you get a real education in the market is to invest cash, track your trade, and study your mistakes."

—JESSE LIVERMORE, LEGENDARY INVESTOR

Even the best investors make mistakes—but they learn from them. That's why after decades of investing, IBD founder Bill O'Neil and his portfolio managers *still* regularly do a post-analysis of their trades. It's simply the best (perhaps, the *only*) way to become a successful investor over the long term. So make sure you keep good records of your trades and review them at least once a year.

We'll get into 2 ways to help you do that:

- 5 questions to help you do a profitable post-analysis
- Improve your returns by improving your records

Finding and fixing *just one or two common mistakes* can have a huge impact on the amount of profits you make. Maybe you're buying stocks when the overall market is weak or holding your stocks a little too long.

Whatever the issue, *don't get discouraged*. Each time you address one of yesterday's pitfalls, you add that much more to tomorrow's profits.

Start with—and Stick to—Basic Rules

 You can easily avoid many common pitfalls from the start simply by following the buying and selling checklists found in this book.

5 Questions to Help You Do a Profitable Post-Analysis

These basic questions will help you pinpoint any habits that need to be addressed.

1. **Was the market in an uptrend when you bought the stock?**

   Don't fight the market! When the market is in a correction, it will take most stocks down with it. So keep the odds in your favor: Only buy stocks when the *Market Pulse* outlook says "Confirmed uptrend."

   See Big Rock #1 (Chapter 3).

2. Did the stock have CAN SLIM® traits when you bought it?

Always start your search for tomorrow's big winners by looking for stocks that have the 7 CAN SLIM traits and the "big rocks" we discussed: Focus on stocks that have big earnings growth, new innovative products and are being heavily bought by institutional investors.

See the Buying Checklist (Chapter 3).

3. Did you buy at a proper buy point?

Most winning stocks launch their big moves as they break out of a cup-with-handle, double bottom or flat base. If you don't use charts to identify those money-making opportunities, you're putting yourself at a serious disadvantage. Charts prove that "timing really *is* everything."

If you ran into trouble with the stock, go back and see if it passed the Buying Checklist *at the time you bought it*:

- Did you buy too *late*—after the stock was already over 5% past the ideal buy point?

- Did you buy too *early*—trying to *anticipate* a breakout?

- Was volume at *least* 40%–50% above average at the breakout?

- Was it a late-stage base?

- Were there serious flaws in the base, such as wide and loose action or excessive distribution (selling)?

- Did you hold a stock because it had good earnings growth and a great product—even as the stock fell lower and the chart flashed clear sell signals?

Whatever the issue is, don't *dwell* on your mistake—*fix* it! A good starting point is to always make sure a stock passes the Buying Checklist before you buy.

See the Buying Checklist (Chapter 3) and *Don't Invest Blindly* (Chapter 6).

4. Did you follow sound sell rules?

Maybe your emotions took over, and you let a little loss become a big one. Or maybe you sold too *soon*—and a stock you used to own went on to huge gains without you.

That's frustrating, but here's the good news: All those issues can be fixed by following some time-tested sell rules. And you can start applying the most important ones right now by using the Selling Checklist.

See the Selling Checklist (Chapter 5).

5. **Did you continually weed out laggards and focus your money on your best-performing stocks?**

One common—and costly—mistake many investors make is they sell their *winning* stocks and hold onto their *laggards*. That's exactly the *opposite* of what you want to do. To build a winning portfolio, always shed your weak or losing stocks first.

Cut all losses short, and look for chances to steer money into your best-performing stocks when they form a 3-weeks tight or other alternative buy point. In other words: Maximize your returns by making your *biggest gainers your biggest positions*.

See the 8 *"Secrets" of Successful Selling* (Chapter 5) and *Alternative Buy Points* (Chapter 6).

Turn Your Past Mistakes into Future Profits

If you ask these questions for each of your trades—and answer them honestly!—you'll avoid making the same mistakes in the future. That's how you generate even bigger profits for the rest of your investing career.

• ACTION STEPS •

To take these steps, visit www.investors.com/GettingStartedBook.

- Watch my *2-Minute Tip* video: *5 Questions to Help You Do a Profitable Post-Analysis*.

- Use the questions above to review any trades you've made in the last 12 months.

Improve Your Results
by Improving Your Records

"You can't manage what you don't measure."

—W. EDWARDS DEMING

Your online broker keeps a basic record of your trades—purchase price, number of shares, etc. But to systematically improve your skills and returns, you'll want to personally keep a more detailed account of every buy and sell. As you'll see, it's *very* easy to do, and the payoff is definitely worth the extra little effort.

As we just saw, regularly reviewing your trades is essential to your success. Having good records of your trades makes doing that review *so much* easier and faster.

Plus, *writing down* your reasons for the trade at the time you make it will help prevent rash buy and sell decisions. It forces you to step back and make sure you're sticking to the buying and selling checklists. Trust me—you'll be a lot more confident and comfortable if you have a sound rationale for making that trade *before* you make it.

Here's a simple way to keep a snapshot of what each stock looked like when you bought or sold it. If you follow these steps, you can always go back and see what the chart action, ratings, earnings and other key criteria looked liked at the time of your trade.

Tracking Your Buys

Every time you make a buy, print out the following for each stock:

- *Daily* and *weekly* chart
- Current *IBD Stock Checkup*

You can print these out and keep them in a binder. I prefer to create PDF documents and store them on my computer. I find that easier to organize, but the format doesn't matter. Do whatever works best for you. What's important is that you keep a detailed record of what was happening with the stock at the time of your purchase.

Here's the nice thing about printing out *Stock Checkup*: It does most of the work for you! Just print it out, and you have a permanent snapshot of what was happening at the time you bought the stock.

You'll find pass, neutral or fail ratings for:

- Market direction: Uptrend or correction?

- Your stock's fundamental performance (earnings and sales growth, return on equity, etc.)

- Your stock's technical performance (fund ownership, Relative Strength Rating, etc.)

It takes all of about 2 seconds and makes doing a post-analysis *much* easier.

Here are some other things you want to note. I add them as "comments" on the chart PDFs I create, but you could also just grab a pen and write them down on your printouts.

- **Basic info**
  - Date of purchase, number of shares purchased, cost per share.
- **Base and buy point**
  - Note the type of base (e.g., cup-with-handle) or other buy point (e.g., pullback to 10-week moving average line), and *draw it on the chart*.
- **Any yellow flags?**
  - Examples: Lower than ideal sales growth, a slightly weak industry group ranking, etc.
- **Primary reasons for buying**
  - Examples: Breakout from cup-with-handle on heavy volume; new innovative product; emerging industry trends, etc.
- **Target sell prices**
  - Offensive: Typically 20%–25% above *ideal* buy point
  - Defensive: Typically 7%–8% below *your* purchase price

Tracking Your Sells

Just like when you buy a stock, print out the following every time you sell:

- *Daily* and *weekly* chart
- Current *IBD Stock Checkup*

Selling is one of the toughest parts of investing. But if you follow the Selling Checklist and get in the habit of keeping good records, you'll be surprised how quickly you become more adept at locking in profits at the right time.

Be sure to write down the following:

- **Basic info**
  - Date of trade, your sell price, number of shares sold, number of shares you still own *after* the sale (if any), your % gain or loss
- **Reasons for Selling**
  - Examples: Hit target of 20%–25% above ideal buy point; fell 7% below what you paid for it; crashed below 50-day moving average line on the heaviest volume in months, etc.

Good Records Lead to Good Habits

To make money over the long term, you need good habits and routines. You can do that just by following the simple routines and checklists we covered earlier and by keeping detailed records so you're able to properly review your results.

Just as athletes watch past games to improve their skills, as investors, we all need to review our past trades. But to do that, you need to have the "game tape"—and you will if you follow the steps above. Then you'll be ready to do a quick and profitable post-analysis to minimize any mistakes and build on your successes.

• ACTION STEPS •

For more information on how to keep good records and do a regular post-analysis, visit investors.com/GettingStartedBook.

- Set up a binder or other filing system for keeping records of your trades.
  - If you're going to create PDF documents instead, set up a folder on your computer to store the records.
- Start keeping records of *all* your trades!

More Ways to Find Winning Stocks

IBD's stock lists, ratings and other features all have one common goal: To alert you to today's best stocks.

You'll find today's top performers in IBD's lists because they screen the entire market, looking for stocks with CAN SLIM® traits—the 7 characteristics the biggest winners typically have just *before* they launch a major price move. Those are the same traits found on the Buying Checklist (Chapter 3).

Keep It Simple

We've already touched on some of the features we'll get into here—*IBD 50*, *Your Weekly Review*, *Sector Leaders* and others.

If you're busy, I suggest you start by using the tools and stock lists we covered as part of the Simple Weekend Routine and 10-Minute Daily Routine (Chapter 4). You can dig into other features as you get more comfortable with IBD and investing in general.

Look at Me! Look at Me!

Pay special attention to any stocks that keep popping up on multiple *lists.* There's a reason that happens: These stocks are the true market leaders with the potential to double or triple in price.

They say "the squeaky wheel gets the grease." Here's just one example of how the "squeaky stocks" get the profits:

☑ **Lululemon Athletica:** *196% gain in just 10 months*

The yoga apparel retailer launched that explosive price move when it broke out of a double bottom on September 14, 2010. Here are just a few of the places Lululemon was screaming "Look at me!" to anyone using IBD and the **Simple Weekend Routine** (Chapter 4).

- For well over a month *before* its breakout, Lululemon was continually featured in the *IBD 50* (*IBD 100* at the time) and highlighted as a **Sector Leader**.
- **June 7, 2010:** Featured in the *Daily Stock Analysis* video.

- **September 10, 2010:** Four days *before* it launched its 196% run, Lululemon made a massive 13% gap up on volume 612% higher than normal—a clear sign big investors were buying *heavily*.

  That was a Friday, so when you did your Simple Weekend Routine, here are just some of the features that would have alerted you to that move:

  - *The Big Picture*
  - *Stocks on the Move*
  - *Smart Table Review*
  - *IBD 50*

- **September 13, 2010:** Doing your **10-Minute Daily Routine** (Chapter 4), you would have seen Lululemon highlighted again in *The Big Picture* and *Stocks on the Move*.

- **Key Points:**

  - *All* these mentions of Lululemon came *before* it broke out and shot up 196% in just 10 months.

  - That gave you plenty of time to have the stock on your watch list ("How to Build and Maintain an Actionable Watch List" in this chapter) and set up a trade trigger (Chapter 4) with your broker to make sure you caught Lululemon right when it launched its move.

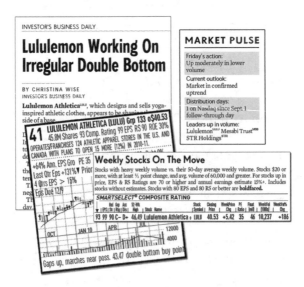

Lululemon Athletica was highlighted in IBD multiple times
before **it surged 196% in 10 months.**

In every strong market uptrend, you'll find similar examples. So while they say good stocks are hard to find, in IBD they're hard to *miss*! You'll see what I mean when you start using the stock lists and features highlighted below.

Never Buy a Stock *Just* because It's Featured in IBD!

 These are *not* recommendations. The purpose is to alert you to stocks showing the most potential. Always make sure a stock passes the Buying Checklist before you invest.

The Big Picture

As we've seen repeatedly in this book, since most stocks simply move in the same direction as the general market, successful investing starts with one basic question: Is the market currently heading up—or down?

You can always find the answer by checking the *Market Pulse* in *The Big Picture* column.

Here's another thing you'll find in the *Market Pulse*: **Leaders up in volume.** As you scan *The Big Picture* during your daily or weekend routine, be sure to check that to see which top-rated stocks made a big move that day. That could be signaling the *start* of a nice run.

THE BIG PICTURE

Stocks Deliver Nice Finish; Distribution Count Drops

BY VICTOR REKLAITIS
INVESTOR'S BUSINESS DAILY

Stocks displayed positive action by rallying into the close Tuesday, starting a holiday-shortened week with moderate gains.

The tally of distribution days, which are sessions with significant selling, also moved in the right direction.

The Nasdaq lost its Dec. 13 distribution day, because enough time has passed that it's no longer relevant. That leaves the Nasdaq and NYSE with four distribution days, while the S&P 500 has just three.

The NYSE fared best Tuesday, climbing 0.5%. The S&P 500 added 0.4%. The Nasdaq tacked on 0.3%, after spending most of the session in negative territory.

In economic news, the National Association of Realtors said existing-home sales slowed to an annualized rate of 4.94 million in December, missing forecasts.

But the report didn't hurt the ly rated railroad, leapt 5% in heavy volume after its quarterly earnings beat estimates. The stock gapped up beyond a buying range established by a recent buy point at 84.08.

On the downside, **SodaStream International**ᴺᴼᴰᴬ tried to break out from a three-weeks-tight pattern.

The Israel-based maker of in-home soda machines popped as much as 6% intraday in fast trade, clearing a 50.08 buy point, then closed below that level with a 2% gain.

After the market's close, several big names delivered upbeat quarterly earnings reports.

MARKET PULSE

Tuesday's action:
Rallies into the close as volume falls

Current outlook:
Confirmed uptrend

© 2013 Investor's Business Daily, Inc.

When & Where

Daily in the *Making Money* section of IBD and on Investors.com

IBD 50

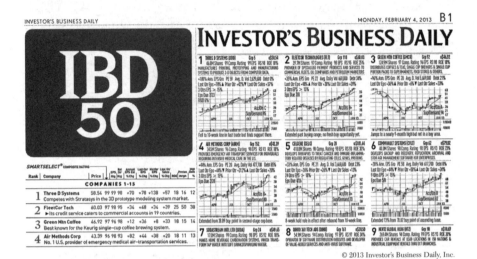

© 2013 Investor's Business Daily, Inc.

IBD 50 highlights the 50 top-rated growth stocks. It features stocks with market-leading earnings growth, a strong return on equity and other key CAN SLIM traits. When checking the *IBD 50*, be sure to read the **Inside the 50** column for more insight into these top performers.

Get a Quick Snapshot of Each Stock's Strength

IBD 50, *Your Weekly Review*, *Sector Leaders*, and *IBD Big Cap 20* also include a chart for each stock that features:

- Current ratings and other vital data
  - IBD *SmartSelect®* Ratings
  - Current and annual earnings growth
  - Return on equity
  - Industry group ranking
- Alerts to any potential buy points
  - See Chapter 6, "Don't Invest *Blindly*"

When & Where

Mondays and Wednesdays in the *Making Money* section of IBD
In the *Screen Center* on Investors.com

Sector Leaders

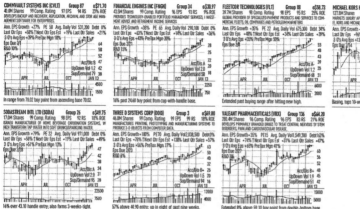

Sector Leaders Charts

© 2013 Investor's Business Daily, Inc.

As the name suggests, this list features the top-rated stocks within their respective industry sectors. To be counted as a sector leader, a stock has to pass a tight screen that looks for exceptional earnings growth, return on equity and other vital factors. Because it's such a demanding screen, only a few of IBD's 33 sectors will have a company that qualifies as a leader.

To get more insight into the current sector leaders—what they do, industry trends, potential buy points—see the *Smart Table Review* column, found daily in the *Making Money* section of IBD and on Investors.com.

Like in the *IBD 50*, a chart with alerts to any potential buy points is included for each stock.

When & Where

Daily in the *Making Money* section of IBD

The related *Smart Table Review* column is also available on Investors.com

Your Weekly Review

© 2013 Investor's Business Daily, Inc.

Your Weekly Review highlights stocks that have 2 of the most important factors to look for:

- **85 or higher score for *both* EPS and RS Ratings**

  We saw earlier (Big Rock #2, Chapter 3) that you want to look for stocks with a strong EPS Rating *and* a solid Relative Strength (RS) Rating. Stocks must have both to make this list.

- **A top-rated stock in a top-ranked industry group**

  Stocks on *Your Weekly Review* are *sorted by industry group ranking,* so you'll find the leading stocks in the higher-ranked groups at the top of the list.

  Like in the *IBD 50* and *Sector Leaders*, a chart with alerts to any potential buy points is included for each stock.

  You'll also find a related column that provides more insight into the stocks on this list.

When & Where

Fridays in the A section of IBD

The *Your Weekly Review* column is also available on Investors.com

Stock Spotlight

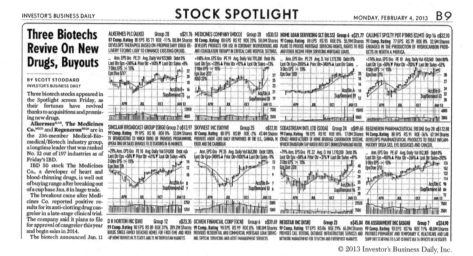

Stock Spotlight highlights 16 leading stocks *forming a base or just breaking out*, making it a powerful way to build a timely watch list.

Be sure to also read the article that accompanies the list. It typically features 1 or 2 stocks from that day's list, noting any potential buy points or other key news.

When & Where

Daily in the *Making Money* section of IBD
The *Stock Spotlight* article is also available on Investors.com

IBD Big Cap 20

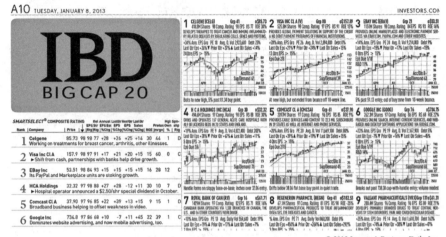

© 2013 Investor's Business Daily, Inc.

IBD Big Cap 20 highlights the top growth stocks with a market capitalization of at least $15 billion.

While all stocks can be volatile, the larger, more established companies that make this list tend to be more conservative and less susceptible to big price swings than smaller cap growth stocks.

For each *IBD Big Cap 20* stock, you'll find the same type of chart found in *IBD 50* and *Your Weekly Review*, with alerts to any potential buy points.

Also look at the *Inside Big Cap 20* column for additional insight into selected stocks and the latest trends affecting the list.

IBD Big Cap 20 can help you reduce volatility in your portfolio but still offer the potential for substantial gains.

When & Where

Tuesdays in the A section of IBD
The *Inside Big Cap 20* column is also available on Investors.com

Stocks On The Move

NYSE Stocks On The Move | Nasdaq Stocks On The Move

Stocks with high volume vs. 50-day avg.,show heavy institutional action. 80 EPS & RS or better + closing price up are **boldfaced.**

CompEPS Rel Acc 52-Wk Rtg|Rnk|Str|Dis| High	Nyse Stock	Stock Symbol	Closing Price	Chg	Vol (1000s)	Vol% Chg	CompEPS Rel Acc 52-Wk Rtg|Rnk|Str|Dis| High	Nasdaq Stock	Stock Symbol	Closing Price	Chg	Vol (1000s)	Vol% Chg
99 93 93A– 20.93 OnAssign o	ASGN	22.00	+1.72	1,153	+296	86 70 92B– 34.86 EchoStar n	SATS	35.01	+0.79	386	+216
86 73 76A– 42.79 Circor	CIR	40.21	+0.62	207	+209	79 86 73C– 40.58 Abaxis o	ABAX	37.82	+0.72	269	+145
96 80 85B– 70.86 Cyteclnd o	CYT	70.92	+2.09	1,141	+179	99 97 96A 35.42 Dorman o	DORM	36.57	+1.23	287	+135
94 84 94B 32.59 PiperJaff o	PJC	33.02	+0.89	253	+168	93 90 92A 22.33 MnPwSy o	MPWR	22.83	+0.55	633	+133
90 89 84C– 102.4 Fomento o	FMX	101.3	+0.60	1,265	+148	97 73 96A– 20.49 AvisBudget o	CAR	20.77	+0.95	2,977	+127
90 77 93B– 136.8 PPGIndust o	PPG	138.6	+3.20	3,186	+148	77 89 73C+ 49.75 ElizArden o	RDEN	45.88	+0.87	390	+115
98 93 97B 21.00 Polyone o	POL	22.20	+1.78	1,885	+138	91 83 70B– 48.50 SilcnLab o	SLAB	43.52	+1.72	628	+114
96 85 81B+ 39.35 Honda Mtr o	HMC	38.36	+1.42	1,223	+138	90 81 80B 30.18 FrghtCar o	RAIL	23.74	+1.32	129	+109
98 87 92A– 65.16 Maxims	MMS	64.71	+1.49	358	+130	82 73 73A 25.25 OtterTail	OTTR	25.74	+0.74	180	+109
99 99 77B– 31.66 NeenahPaper o	NP	30.60	+2.13	160	+128	94 89 85B+ 56.48 FEI o	FEIC	57.77	+2.30	500	+99
80 88 71C+ 26.93 AquaAmerica o	WTR	26.40	+0.98	1,140	+109	99 98 91A– 48.13 Sodastrm o	SODA	46.84	+1.95	1,884	+95
98 97 97A+ 25.61 SoufunHldgs	SFUN	25.99	+0.99	553	+100	89 86 91C 40.66 UrbnOtfit o	URBN	40.98	+1.62	4,555	+94
99 97 82B– 43.85 NeuStar o	NSR	43.68	+1.75	770	+91	89 77 72A– 50.76 RBCBear o	ROLL	51.22	+1.15	138	+91
94 86 87A 55.90 Stepan	SCL	56.08	+0.54	121	+84	98 88 98A– 89.13 GeospaceTech	GEOS	89.84	+0.97	206	+86
96 91 87B+ 66.66 Ingredion o	INGR	67.00	+2.57	970	+81	89 78 78D+ 22.30 Microsemi o	MSCC	21.88	+0.84	855	+78
99 99 95B– 37.80 LithiaMt o	LAD	39.00	+1.58	507	+81	67 81 71C+ 34.70 ArgoGplnt n	AGII	34.49	+0.90	127	+75

Daily print version of *Stocks on the Move*

© 2013 Investor's Business Daily, Inc.

Weekly Stocks On The Move

Stocks with heavy weekly volume vs. their 10-week average volume. Stocks $20 or more, with at least ½ point change, and avg. volume of 60,000 and greater. For stocks up in price, EPS & RS Ratings are 70 or higher and annual earnings estimate 15%+. Includes stocks without estimates. Stocks with 80 EPS and 80 RS or better are **boldfaced.**

SMARTSELECT® COMPOSITE RATING

Rel Grp Acc 52-Wk EPS|Str|Rtg|Dis| High	Stock Name	Stock Symbol	Closing Price	Week Price Chg	PE Ratio	Float (mil)	Week Vol (1000s)	Week Vol% Chg
81 71 77 B B 59.03 Transocean Inc o	RIG	51.82	+7.62	16	356	28,570	+165
69 85 77 D+ B+ 37.25 Sears Hometwn & Outlet o	SHOS	35.06	+1.87	14	5.1	811	+151
95 64 95 A A– 33.80 Piper Jaffray Cos o	PJC	33.62	+1.55	19	16	1,018	+148
99 93 94 A+ A 22.59 On Assignment o	ASGN	22.63	+3.07	23	49	2,846	+118
94 85 77 A B+ 39.35 Honda Motor Co Ltd o	HMC	37.75	+1.33	17	1.8b	4,507	+109
69 78 70 C+ B– 20.60 Pinnacle Fin Ptnr	PNFP	20.12	+1.42	20	32	1,179	+98
98 93 97 A+ A– 22.97 Polyone o	POL	23.22	+3.27	20	86	5,603	+90
97 73 96 B A+ 21.38 Avis Budget Group o	CAR	21.75	+2.37	9	102	10,606	+90
83 91 74 D+ B– 51.45 Gartner Inc o	IT	48.70	+3.35	30	89	3,729	+87
91 77 93 B+ B 140.4 P P G Industries o	PPG	139.47	+6.77	18	150	10,013	+81
99 97 96 A+ A– 37.19 Dorman Products Inc o	DORM	35.88	+1.73	20	29	973	+81
71 88 72 D– C 73.72 Hain Celestial o	HAIN	56.52	+3.84	29	43	4,819	+78
94 89 72 A– A– 56.95 Signet Jewlers Ltd o	SIG	53.87	+0.94	13	80	4,943	+70
99 99 93 B A 21.99 Viewpoint Financial	VPFG	21.72	+0.88	20	38	1,199	+68

Weekly print version of *Stocks on the Move*

© 2013 Investor's Business Daily, Inc.

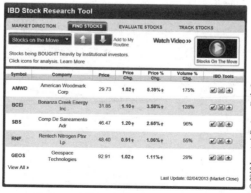

Online version of *Stocks on the Move*

© 2013 Investor's Business Daily, Inc.

Want an easy way to find stocks being heavily bought by institutional investors *right now*? Check *Stocks on the Move*. It highlights stocks making a big price move on *unusually* heavy volume—a sign of professional trading.

There are 3 different versions of this list:

- Daily print edition
- Weekly print edition
- Online version—updated every minute throughout the trading day

Be sure to check the print or digital edition of IBD at night or on the weekends to see which stocks made a big move that day or week. And if you have time, take a look at *Stocks on the Move* on Investors.com while the market is still open. Both are great ways to get new stock ideas for your watch list.

Since winning stocks tend to start a major new price move by jumping higher on a big spike in volume, *virtually all big winners appear on Stocks on the Move in the early stages of their runs.*

How to Get in Early on Winning Stocks

 Learn to spot *future* winners by seeing how you could have found Chipotle Mexican Grill *before* it broke out using *Stocks on the Move*. Take a look at www.investors.com/GettingStartedBook.

When & Where

Stocks on the Move: Daily in the *Making Money* section of IBD

Weekly Stocks on the Move: Mondays in the *Making Money* section of IBD

Online version of *Stocks on the Move*: Home page of Investors.com; updated every minute throughout the trading day

New High List, Stocks Just Out of Bases, Stocks Pulling Back to 10-Week Line

"You Can Find Winners in IBD's New High List"

(stock list tables — New Highs, Finance, Medical, Software, Real Est, Insurance, Building, Business Svc, Banks, Food/Bev, Energy, Retail, Telecom, Consumer, Utility, Agriculture, Chips, Chemical, Leisure, Auto, Transport, Media, Internet, Misc, New Lows, etc.)

NYSE (n) – 202 New Highs, 3 Lows
NASDAQ – 129 New Highs, 5 Lows
AMEX (a) – 11 New Highs, 3 Lows

Boldfaced stocks show high EPS Rating 90 or more. On Investors.com, see an IBD chart, archived story and Stock Checkup before buying. Stocks in each sector listed by % volume increase. Stocks under 10 a share or 60 EPS are omitted. †See chart in Stock Spotlight.

New High List Analysis

BY PAUL WHITFIELD
INVESTOR'S BUSINESS DAILY

A handful of top-rated stocks pushed to new highs Monday despite signs of hesitation in the major indexes.

China Lodging Groupᴴᵀᴴᴸ added 0.88 to 18.80 in volume that was 626% above average. The stock is now 6.5% past a 17.65 buy point in an untidy consolidation. A stock should not be bought once it is 5% past the ideal buy point.

The small-cap stock is thinly traded, turning only 123,000 shares daily.

China's economy has suffered seven quarters in a row of decelerating growth. In Q3, China's GDP rose 7.4%, the least in more than three years.

However, some economists expect China's GDP to pick up the pace in 2013. Deutsche Bank, for example, estimates China's growth will reach 8.5% in the second half of this year.

China Lodging has seen some earnings acceleration in recent quarters — rising from a loss of 2 cents a share in Q1 to profits of 19 cents and 27 cents a share in Q2 and Q3. The Street expects EPS of only 8 cents a share in Q4, which would represent a 10% drop from the year-ago period.

The company is a 2010 initial public offering.

Grupo Financiero Santander Mexicoᴮˢᴹˣ, a September 2012 IPO, tacked on 0.75 to 17.79, as it notched a new high.

Volume, though, was only 3% above average. The stock is extended from a December breakout.

Milwaukee-based water-heater maker A.O. Smith ᴬᴼˢ popped 1.47 to 66.05 in 58% faster action as it scored a new high. The company will announce Q4 and full-year results before the market's open on Jan. 24. The Street expects 19% earnings growth on a revenue increase of 6%. The 6% sales growth would be the slowest in two years.

Other stocks posting 52-week highs included biotech Celgene ᴄᴱᴸᴳ, which advanced for a 10th consecutive day, fiber laser company IPG Photonics ᴵᴾᴳᴾ, and RV and manufactured homes components maker Drew Industries ᴰᵂ.

Drew Industries is in a strong industry group. The RV and manufactured home group was No. 13 of 197 groups in Monday's IBD.

Stocks Just Out Of Bases					Stocks Pulling Back to 10-Wk Line				
Comp Rtg	Stock Name	Symbol	Closing Price	Chg	Vol% Chg	Comp Rtg	Stock Name	Symbol	Closing Price	Chg	Vol% Chg
93	Polaris Inds	PII	88.68	-0.22	-14%		98	Strategs Ltd	SSYS	79.34	-1.42	-47%
96	Valeant Pharmaceuticals	VRX	63.58	-0.05	-56%						

Supply/Demand				
Comp Rtg	Stock Name	Symbol	Closing Price	Chg	Vol% Chg
94	Three D Systems	DDD	60.71	+0.36	+12%

Each day in IBD, you'll find these 3 powerful lists all on the same page—giving you a quick snapshot of stocks to keep an eye on.

- **New High List**

  Remember what we learned earlier: *Stocks hitting new price highs tend to go higher.* This list shows you which stocks just hit a new 52-week price high that day. Be sure to also read the *New High List Analysis* article right below the list. That gives you more insight into the action of specific stocks.

- **Stocks Just Out of Bases**

  Stocks tend to launch a big move by breaking out of a cup-with-handle, double bottom or other type of pattern (Chapter 6). This list highlights stocks that *just* did that. Still, you want to make sure the stock passes the Buying Checklist and is not "extended" beyond the 5% buying range.

If the stock *is* extended, keep an eye on it. It may go on to offer an alternative buying opportunity, like a pullback to the 10-week moving average line, which brings us to . . .

- *Stocks Pulling Back to 10-Week Line*

As we saw earlier ("Alternative Buy Points," Chapter 6), after a stock breaks out, it may take a breather and pull back to that benchmark line. If it finds support and bounces higher on *heavy* volume, it could offer a buying opportunity.

When & Where

Daily in the *Making Money* section of IBD
You can also read *New High List Analysis* column on Investors.com

IBD TimeSaver Tables

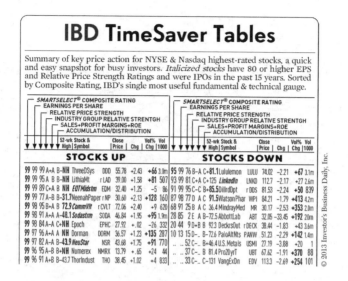

As the name implies, this list makes it quick and easy to see which top-rated stocks showed bullish action that day. The *TimeSaver Tables* are sorted by Composite Rating (Big Rock #2, Chapter 3) to help you zero in on the true market leaders.

When & Where

Daily in the *Making Money* section of IBD

The New America

THE NEW AMERICA

3D SYSTEMS *Rock Hill, South Carolina*

A 3D Printer In Your House Might Be The Next Big Thing

BY BRIAN DEAGON
INVESTOR'S BUSINESS DAILY

Twenty-six years ago, Chuck Hull received a patent for a system he called stereolithography.

The patent described a procedure of creating three-dimensional objects with a computer-controlled system that shoots ultraviolet light into a pool of liquid polymer or some other "fluid medium."

The fluid at the surface turns solid when hit by UV light. The object is then lowered as layer upon layer of light beams hit the liquid surface and stitch together, sliver by sliver, the object the computer has been programmed to produce.

As the Hull patent described, "stereolithography is a method and apparatus for making solid objects by successively 'printing' thin layers of a curable material, one on top of another."

That same year, in 1986, Hull co-founded 3D Systems™, now based in Rock Hill, S.C., where he is currently the chief technology officer. It began making and selling expensive 3D printers used in aerospace and automotive manufacturing to develop prototype parts, plodding along in a niche market.

3D Systems
3dsystems.com

Ticker	DDD
Share price	Near 44
12-month sales	$322 mil
5-year profit growth rate	180%

IBD SmartSelect Corporate Ratings

Composite Rating	99
Earnings Per Share	98
Relative Price Strength	98
Industry Group Rank	5
Sales+Profit Margins+ROE	A
Accumulation-Distribution	B

See Investors.com for more details

Today, 3D Systems makes a long line of 3D printers ranging in price from $1,300 desktop printers for the home hobbyist to large $1 million printers able to make parts for supersonic jets. One of its biggest markets is the health care field, where 3D printers make custom parts for hearing aids, prosthetics and orthodontics, among other items.

Wide Applications

Its 3D printers also make parts for aerospace, military and transportation industries. They can print most anything that can be designed on a computer, from con-

photos and videos into printable 3D objects. And it acquired Rapidform, a provider of 3D scanning and computer aided design and inspection software tools, for $35 million. Its products are used by engineers and manufacturers.

Asian Presence

Rapidform, based in Seoul, will expand 3D Systems' presence in Korea and Japan. It also has offices in Australia, Italy and the Netherlands. The company has acquired about 30 firms in the last three years, many of them acquired Rapidform, widening its platform of capabilities and widening its patent portfolio to more than 1,200.

Since its introduction of stereolithography 26 years ago, 3D Systems has developed other 3D printing technologies for an array of applications. Its printers also use a wide variety of print materials, about 100 of them, that replicate the performance of plastics, metals, waxes, rubbers and other composites.

3D parts can be made in as little as 20 minutes or take more than 40 hours, depending on the complexity. About half its printers currently sold are for manufacturing applica-

© 2013 Investor's Business Daily, Inc.

The "N" in CAN SLIM stands for "new"—a new innovative product, new management or new industry trend.

It's a key driver of a stock's climb, as we saw in *Big Rock #2: Focus on companies with big earnings growth and a new, innovative product or service*.

Each day, *The New America* page profiles companies that have that all-important "N."

Be sure to also check out our *New America Analysis* videos, which highlight the latest chart action, ratings and trends of companies recently profiled in *The New America* column.

When & Where

Daily in the A section of IBD and on Investors.com
New America Analysis videos updated weekly under the "IBD TV" tab on Investors.com

IBD Smart NYSE + NASDAQ Tables

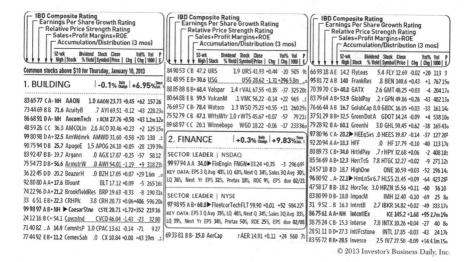

© 2013 Investor's Business Daily, Inc.

Not all stock tables are created equal.

Most publications either no longer even print stock tables—or just include bare bones data like how much a stock was up or down that day. Most don't even include "volume" —and without volume, you can't tell if institutional investors are heavily buying, heavily selling or just sitting tight.

We call our stock tables "smart tables" because they include a remarkable amount of vital data in one easy-to-use location. Here's a quick look at what you'll find:

- **IBD** *SmartSelect*® **Ratings** for every stock to easily separate leaders from laggards
- **Volume % Change** for that day: Was it *unusually* heavy or light?
- **Sector Rankings:** The tables are sorted by sector strength so you can see where institutional investors are moving their money and identify the top stocks in the top industries.

When & Where

Daily in the *Making Money* section of IBD and on Investors.com

IBD Screen Center

IBD Screen Center

| | SCREEN OF THE DAY ▼ | TOP SECTOR PERFORMERS | CAN SLIM® SELECT | TECH LEADERS ▼ | INTERNATIONAL LEADERS | IBD 50 |

Expand Details ±

Estimate Beaters

Companies that beat earnings estimates by a wide margin are worthy of further research since its earnings growth that drives a stocks price performance. More

View by: Fundamentals ▼   ☐Export | ☐Print

Symbol	Company Name	EPS Surprise % Chg (Last Qtr) ▼	EPS % Chg (Last Qtr)	EPS % Chg (Prior Qtr)	Sales % Chg (Last Qtr)	EPS Est % Chg (Current Qtr)	EPS Est % Chg (Current Yr)	Tools
CYMI	Cymer Inc	342.9	-14	-66	2	-98	-52	✔ ✉ +
NFLX	Netflix Inc	200	-80	-89	8	300	293	✔ ✉ +
AZPN	Aspen Technology Inc	160	117	N/A	16	400	N/A	✔ ✉ +
BC	Brunswick Corp	125	N/A	28	9	-9	15	✔ ✉ +
LNKD	Linkedin Corp Class A	100	267	45	81	58	106	✔ ✉ +
FNF	Fidelity Natl Finl Inc	90.7	94	49	70	45	78	✔ ✉ +

© 2013 Investor's Business Daily, Inc.

Here are just a few of the lists you'll find on the *IBD Screen Center*:

- **Screen of the Day:** A rotating list of screens that looks for "Small-Cap Leaders," "Young Guns," "Estimate Beaters" and more.
- **CAN SLIM® Select:** A list of today's top CAN SLIM stocks.
- **IBD 50:** The online, sortable and printable version of the *IBD 50* list found in the paper.

When & Where

Updated daily and found under the "Research" tab on Investors.com

IBD TV

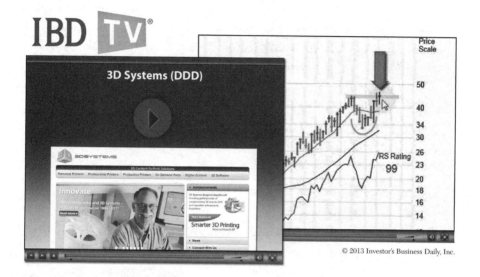

© 2013 Investor's Business Daily, Inc.

If you've been doing the Action Steps throughout this book (and I hope you have!), you're already familiar with these *IBD TV* videos.

- **Market Wrap**

    Think of *Market Wrap* as the video version of *The Big Picture* column.

    It walks you through the latest market action, highlighting important moves and potential buy points of selected leading stocks. Since it's in video format, you get a detailed look at chart patterns and other key price and volume movements. It's a great way to **stay on top of the latest market trends, improve your chart-reading skills and get new stock ideas all at the same time.**

- **Daily Stock Analysis**

    Like the *Market Wrap* video, **the *Daily Stock Analysis* (DSA) helps you build a quality watch list as you also improve your chart-reading and stock-picking skills.**

    Each *DSA* video walks you through the latest action of a leading stock. It highlights chart patterns and potential buy points and takes a look at the story behind the stock, as well as the company earnings growth, analyst estimates and other factors that could affect its performance.

- *IBD 2-Minute Tips*

These short "how to" videos are a great way to see key investing strategies in action and get to know IBD's tools and features. You'll find videos on everything from *How to Handle a Market Correction* to *IBD 50 Charts— A Profitable Tool for Your Portfolio*.

When & Where

All videos are found under the "IBD TV" tab on Investors.com
Market Wrap: Monday–Friday
Daily Stock Analysis: Thursdays and Fridays
IBD 2-Minute Tips: Occasional

Radio Show: *How to Make Money in Stocks with Investor's Business Daily*

© 2013 Investor's Business Daily, Inc.

I hope you'll join Amy Smith and me each week for the latest episode of the IBD radio show. It's an easy way to stay on top of the market and learn to use key investing rules and strategies.

Tune in to hear about:

- Current market conditions
- Stocks to watch

- How to apply key investing rules to today's market
- Insights from members of the IBD Markets Team and other special guests

You'll also find show notes for each episode featuring chart markups, related videos and other resources that will help jump start your investing skills.

When & Where

For details on how and when to tune in, and to check out the show notes, visit www.investors.com/radioshow
You can also download current and past episodes for free on iTunes

---

Investor's Corner

Reading this column regularly is like having your own personal investing course—which you can take on your own time, at your own pace. It's a great way to enhance and expand on what we cover in this book.

When & Where:

Daily in the *Making Money* section of IBD and on Investors.com

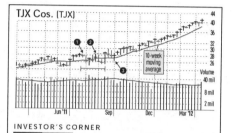

INVESTOR'S CORNER

A Flat Base: Making 'Flat' A High-Performance Term

BY ALAN R. ELLIOTT
INVESTOR'S BUSINESS DAILY

"Flat" is not a high-currency term in the investment trade.

Flat earnings, flat sales and falling flat — none stirs joy in investors' hearts.

But the flat base lives in another category. This base often shows a stock impatient to move on to new highs.

It says a stock is not in need of a deeper shakeout, correcting 15%

reach of its TJ Maxx, Marshall's and Home Goods chains.

The stock broke below its 10-week moving average in heavy trade, but found support several times at its 40-week moving average during the base. Normally, a flat-base buy point comes from the base's high point generally near the left side of the base. But in this case, TJX set up an early option, at 56.66 — a dime above the Aug. 25 high — for aggressive investors ❷.

© 2013 Investor's Business Daily, Inc.

How to Find & Own America's Greatest Opportunities

A *must-read* weekly column by IBD founder William J. O'Neil

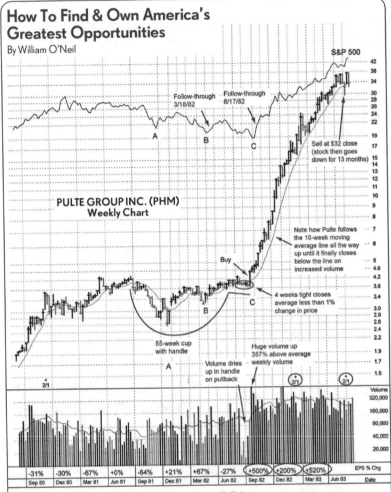

How To Find & Own America's Greatest Opportunities
By William O'Neil

S&P 500

PULTE GROUP INC. (PHM)
Weekly Chart

Follow-through 3/18/82

Follow-through 8/17/82

Sell at $32 close (stock then goes down for 13 months)

Note how Pulte follows the 10-week moving average line all the way up until it finally closes below the line on increased volume

Buy

4 weeks tight closes average less than 1% change in price

55-week cup with handle

Huge volume up 357% above average weekly volume

Volume dries up in handle on pullback

Before Pulte broke out of its 55-week cup-with-handle base on July 23, 1982, it had increased in price more than 10 times since January 1976. So, Pulte was an outstanding growth stock in the notoriously cyclical homebuilding industry.

It tried to break out after the S&P 500 follow-through on March 18, 1982. However, the S&P rolled over and made a new low that temporarily stopped Pulte's progress. It's very important that you learn to spot and understand that during a declining general market where the S&P 500 at points A, B, and C makes new lows, Pulte's price at A, B and C does not make new lows, but holds 20% higher each time. This is a tremendous sign of counterpower, and as soon as the general market finally turns up for real, the stock should be a big leader.

This example also tells you: No. 1 you need to develop your skill at chart reading, No. 2 don't ever get discouraged and stop doing your market homework, and No. 3 once you learn to buy real leaders at the right time, you must have and execute proven sell rules to keep you in for most of the big move up but get you out on the way up to nail down your big gain while you still have it. You don't want to wind up giving it all back.

One rule that works well with many new big leaders is, once you buy right and are ahead, hold until your winner closes for a week clearly below its 10-week-moving-average line in greater than average volume.

By now I think this point is clear: To find *tomorrow's* big winners, you need to know what *past* winners looked like just *before* they made their big price moves. So as part of your search for the next "great story" stocks, be sure to also study past successes.

One of the best ways to do that is to always read Bill's weekly column, where he walks you through the complete "life cycle" of a huge market winner. You'll see:

- The explosive earnings growth and other CAN SLIM traits the stock had before it surged
- What innovative product or service was driving that growth
- The type of chart pattern that launched the stock's big move
- Buy, sell and hold signals that showed you the right time to get in—and out

It'll help you spot future winners—and handle them properly and profitably when you do.

When & Where

Wednesdays in the *Making Money* section of IBD

Leaderboard™

Leaderboard—IBD's premium online service—is another way to find winning stocks before they launch a major price move.

Here's how it works:

- **Leaders List:** The IBD markets team searches for the best-of-the-best stocks and adds them to this small, manageable list.

- **Leaders near a buy point:** Here you'll find alerts to *Leaders List* stocks that are in or near a potential buying range.

- **Intraday chart analysis with buy—and sell—signals:** Typically *before* the breakout, the markets team annotates the charts so you can see the pattern, the exact buy point and any positive or negative signs to keep an eye on. *After* a stock breaks out, the team continues to track the stock, alerting you to any signs that it might be time to lock in your profits.

Because you get ongoing markups and analysis of the charts, I *highly* recommend Leaderboard as a way to learn chart-reading, while also getting alerts to both buy and sell signals in the top-rated stocks.

The Results Are In

Here's just one example of the kind of gains you can tap into using Leaderboard.

Leaderboard Q1 2012 Leaders List Performance

−10%−0	0−10%	11%−20%	Over 20%
Google (−9.3%)	Coinstar (0.2%)	GNC (11.3%)	Tractor Supply (29.1%)
Caterpillar (−7.1%)	Dollar General (1.2%)	VMware (11.4%)	Buffalo Wild Wings (34.3%)
Concho Resources (−2.8%)	Michael Kors (2.0%)	MercadoLibre (11.8%)	Rackspace Hosting (34.4%)
Tangoe (−2.1%)	Autozone (3.7%)	Mastercard (12.8%)	Priceline.com (35.6%)
Transdigm (−1.5%)	Sourcefire (3.7%)	Texas Capital Bancshares (13.1%)	SolarWinds (38.3%)
	UnderArmour (9.8%)	Panera Bread (13.8%)	Invensense (48.5%)
		Celgene (14.7%)	
		Lululemon Athletica (15.0%)	
		Intuitive Surgical (17.0%)	
		Continental Resources (17.2%)	

See How Leaderboard Works—and Take a Free Trial

To watch a video my radio show co-host Amy Smith and I did that shows Leaderboard in action—and to try Leaderboard free for 2 weeks—visit www.investors.com/GettingStartedBook.

• ACKNOWLEDGMENTS •

I want to thank Bill O'Neil for his generous support, insight, and mentoring, and Kathy Sherman for the countless hours and invaluable feedback she put into this project. This book wouldn't have happened without her. Thanks also to Kofi Anan, John Becker, Sharon Brooks, Chris Gessel, Jonathan Hahn, Justin Nielsen, Amy Smith, and Christina Wise for their assistance along the way, as well as to Mary Glenn, Patricia Wallenburg and the excellent staff at McGraw-Hill Education.

Finally, special thanks to my family for their patience and support from start to finish.

• ABOUT THE AUTHOR •

Matthew Galgani is co-host of the *How to Make Money in Stocks with Investor's Business Daily* radio show, editor of the *IBDextra Newsletter*, and IBD TV® market commentator. Together with IBD chairman and founder, William J. O'Neil, he developed the *IBD Meetup Investor Education Series* used by investing clubs across the country.

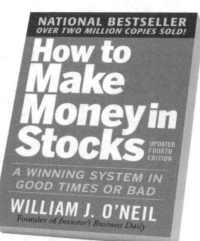
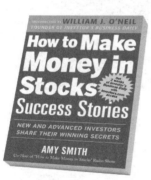
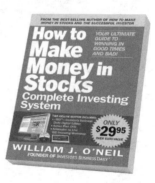

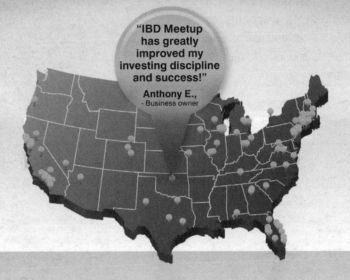

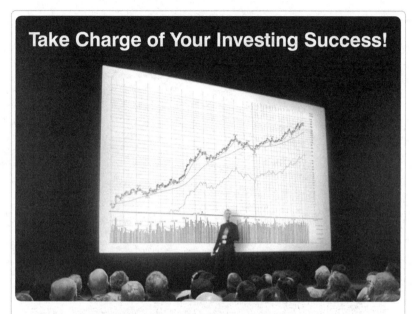

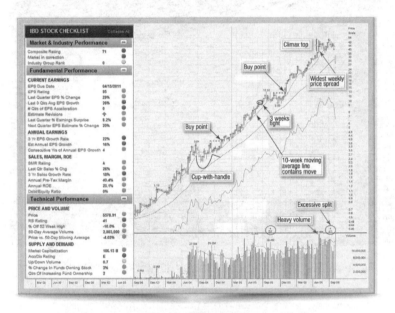

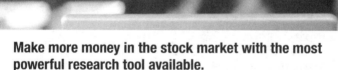

3119202041 3488